BEING INDIAN IN HUEYAPAN

A STUDY OF FORCED IDENTITY IN CONTEMPORARY MEXICO

BEING INDIAN IN HUEYAPAN

A STUDY OF FORCED IDENTITY IN CONTEMPORARY MEXICO

JUDITH FRIEDLANDER

ST. MARTIN'S PRESS NEW YORK

To the Memory of My Father,
Martin Friedlander

ACKNOWLEDGMENTS

To thank only those who were with me during the last few months of this book's preparation would be a great injustice. Actually I would never have been able to write it had I not received considerable help earlier. Consequently I want to thank all those people who have, in one way or another, contributed to my work. To begin with, I am forever grateful to Junius Bird and Milica D. Skinner for having adopted me into the American Museum of Natural History "family" when I was seventeen, giving me reason to believe that I too could be an anthropologist. Over the years a number of friends have also been extremely important in helping to develop and clarify many of the ideas included in this book. In particular I would like to thank Sally Haimo, Catherine and Paul Lawton, Paula Webster, Esther Newton, Nancy Foner, Joel Beck, Larissa Lomnitz, Sara and Ilya Adler, Andrés Medina, Jorge Serrano, Edith Turner, Julie Skurski, Fernando Coronil, Marianne Lorenzelli, Gabriel Moedano, Ellen and Michael Schwartz and my many sisters in the Women's Movement, some of whose names I have already mentioned.

I am also indebted to my professors at the University of Chicago who encouraged me during my undergraduate and graduate school days. I would like to thank Ruth Webber, George Playe, Julian Pitt-Rivers, Eva Hunt and Raymond Firth. To the members of my dissertation committee, for which the original description of my research was written, I am sincerely grateful for the assistance they gave me at various stages of my work. In particular I thank Robert Adams for having helped me to reassess my treatment of history. I thank Stanley Freed for having given of his time so generously to discuss my work with me at the American Museum of Natural History. To Victor Turner I am extremely indebted for the assistance he gave me in the field, helping me to get settled in Hueyapan and talking over aspects of my research at great length in Mexico City and in Chicago. Finally I would like to express my deepest gratitude to Paul Friedrich, who has both encouraged and influenced my work since my undergraduate days at the University of Chicago. I cannot thank him enough for having helped me to view my ideas more critically.

In addition to these people, I would like to thank a number of other friends and colleagues who specifically helped me with the manuscript for this book. I am particularly grateful to Bell Chevigny, John Attinasi, Barbara Price, Susan Rollins and Mary Elmendorf for their careful reading and many helpful suggestions. I appreciate as well the hospitality and encouragement of Françoise Basch, Suzanne Dodin, Robert Peccoud and Aline and Pierre Vellay, who generously offered me their homes and their ears while I was rewriting the manuscript in Paris. I also thank Alexandra Soutar for typing the entire manuscript for me. To Peter Schwab I am grateful for having recommended my work to St. Martin's Press, and I am very appreciative of the enthusiasm and assistance of my editor Barry Rossinoff and the rest of the editorial staff.

I want especially to thank my parents, Silvia and Martin Friedlander. The intellectual and emotional support they had always given me continued while I was in the field and while I was writing up my material. My father spent the last two months of his life reading, re-reading and carefully correcting the manuscript of this book. Too ill to leave the house by that time, he forced himself to stay alive long enough to see the manuscript through. I submitted the final draft to St. Martin's Press on Wednesday, March 13, 1974; and on the following Sunday, Martin died.

Let me express my warmest thanks to the people of Hueyapan, who generously accepted me into their community and encouraged me to write about them. I want to point out that the villagers know of the publication of this book; in fact, in a town meeting held on August 4, 1973, those in attendance unanimously voted in favor of using the real name of the pueblo and of identifying correctly those individuals referred to in the text. I have followed the request of the villagers and have been careful to represent Hueyapan and the Hueyapeños as honestly and respectfully as I could. I hope my friends in the pueblo will not be disappointed.

Of all the villagers I am particularly grateful to Doña Zeferina Barreto and her son Maestro Rafael Vargas. Without really knowing who I was, they generously opened their home, feeding and lodging me during the year I lived in Hueyapan (1969-70) and during all the visits I have made there since (1971, 1973, 1974). With the help of Doña Zeferina I have had the opportunity to experience the more traditional aspects of life in the village. More importantly, Doña Zeferina and I grew very close to one another; she even came to refer to me affectionately as her North American daughter. I only hope that I can live up to the very high standards she has set for me and I thank her from the bottom of my heart for having broken down many of the cultural and class barriers between us, making it possible for us to get to know each other as well as we did. I am also extremely grateful to Maestro Rafael for his friendship and his willingness to find me a position in the school, thereby providing me with a respected and useful role in the pueblo.

My major field trip was funded by the University of Chicago. Then in 1971 the Wenner-Gren Foundation for Anthropological Research sponsored a short return visit to Hueyapan. Furthermore, the American Museum of Natural History granted me an Ogden Mills Fellowship in 1971-72, during which time I wrote the final draft of my doctoral dissertation. Finally, The State University of New York, College at Purchase, freed me from my responsibilities in January 1974, so that I could work without interruption in rewriting my material into the manuscript for this book. I am grateful to all of these institutions for their assistance.

Although I could never have written this book without the considerable help of my family, friends, and professors/colleagues, I would like to make clear that I am entirely responsible for any errors that might appear on the following pages.

CONTENTS

Introduction   xiii

1
Doña Zeferina Barreto
and Her Family during 1969-1970   1
The House   1
Members of the Household   3
A Day with the Family   7

2
The History of
Doña Zeferina and Her Family   27

3
The History of Hueyapan   53
The Village before 1900   53
The Early 1900s and the Mexican Revolution   56
Hueyapan since the Mexican Revolution   61

4

What It Means to be Indian in Hueyapan   71

Indian-ness and Political Factions in Hueyapan   79
Customs Identified as Indian   83

5

Religion in Hueyapan   101

The Virgin of Guadalupe Fiesta   104
The Moors and the Christians: San Juan Amecac Version   109
The Guadalupe Fiesta at the Home
of the Virgin's Sponsor in 1969   114
Protestants in Hueyapan   122

6

**Post-Revolutionary Government Agencies:
A New Period of Evangelization in Hueyapan   128**

Cultural Missions   131
The School   144
Primary-School Textbooks   147
National Holidays and School-Run Assemblies   152

7

Cultural Extremists   165

The Movimiento in Mexico City   171
Cultural Extremists and Hueyapeños   182

8

Conclusion: The Anthropologist and the Indians   189

Bibliography   195

Index   199

INTRODUCTION

Since Mexico's Revolution of 1910-1920 the government of that country has been working to give the Mexican people a proud sense of their national heritage and culture. Politicians, historians, philosophers, writers, painters, architects, educators, anthropologists and others have been employed by the government at various times to help create the image of and the explanation for what it means to be "Mexican." We are told that Mexicans today are the descendants of Indians and Spaniards, the offspring of a union that mixed both blood and tradition. Neither wholly Indian nor wholly Spanish, the Mexicans are said to belong to a distinct culture—they are a single people with a double heritage.

Throughout the nation monuments have been erected to honor Mexico's hybrid or Mestizo man. In Mexico City, for example, there is a square known as the Plaza of the Three Cultures, or Tlatelolco. Aztec, colonial Spanish and modern Mexican traditions are represented there by three imposing structures: an Aztec pyramid, a sixteenth-century Catholic church and a recently constructed government building. In one

rejected+resented by utopians

corner of the Plaza there is a simple bronze plaque that explains the significance of the place: "On August 13, 1521, heroically defended by Cuauhtémoc [the last Aztec emperor], Tlatelolco fell into the hands of Hernán Cortés. This event was neither a victory nor a defeat. It was the painful birth of the Mestizo people, the people of Mexico today."

Despite the eloquent sentiments expressed on the plaque, the monuments in the Plaza suggest a different interpretation. They tell the story of Spanish victory and Indian defeat, of how the Spaniards destroyed Aztec culture and substituted their own. The Catholic church, built over 400 years ago, was constructed out of the very stones of the Aztec pyramid. This church is in excellent repair today and serves a large congregation, carrying on traditions that were introduced during colonial times. The Aztec pyramid, on the other hand, is in ruins. It functions only as a reminder of a once great, but now demolished, Indian culture. In the Plaza of the Three Cultures, as well as throughout Mexico, colonial Spanish and modern Mexican traditions are represented by buildings and institutions in which the religious and secular customs of the country are practiced. Indian culture, however, is typified by prehispanic ruins, statues of long-dead martyrs and museums that collect artifacts of a "primitive" way of life.

To find evidence of Spanish culture in modern Mexico has been relatively easy; to identify the Indian has proved more of a challenge. With great enthusiasm post-Revolutionary scholars and amateurs alike have organized archeological expeditions and conducted archival research. Furthermore, impressive numbers of cultural anthropologists have descended upon that segment of Mexico's rural population still considered to be Indian. Many of the projects have been aimed at preserving what was left or still known of prehispanic Mexico for the edification of the "more complex" modern Mestizo. More often than not, however, the efforts have ended in the reconstruction rather than the preservation of Indian traditions.

This book examines the contradictions that exist between the reality of being Indian in contemporary Mexico and the idealized image of the Indian as a representative of Mexico's prehispanic heritage. Specifically, I discuss what it means to be

Indian to the inhabitants of the rural community Hueyapan, a village of 4000 people situated in the highlands of the state of Morelos. Using historical and ethnographic material, I argue that like the Aztec pyramid in the Plaza of the Three Cultures, the Hueyapeños' indigenous culture is in ruins and has been for centuries. Nevertheless, the villagers are acutely aware of still being Indians, for they are continuously so designated by outsiders.

Few pre-Spanish customs actually survive in Hueyapan today. What is more, most of those that do lost their prehispanic significance long ago and display only the merest traces of the past. In colonial times a number of indigenous traditions were allowed to continue, but only after they had been transformed to conform to the cultural system of the dominant elite. Thus, from the perspective of "culture," the villagers are virtually indistinguishable from non-Indian Mexicans.[1] Where they do differ is in their social status within the larger society.

I suggest that the Hueyapeños' so-called Indian identity relates more precisely to their low socioeconomic position in the national stratification system than it does to their culture. Since early colonial times the villagers have served as a source of cheap labor for the upper classes. As they worked the colonizers' lands, their Indian blood was diluted and their culture dramatically altered. By analyzing the villagers' so-called Indian identity, I hope to demonstrate that their Indian-ness is not a distinct cultural entity but, rather, a reflection of the culture of a highly stratified contemporary society.

It was actually quite by accident that I came to study the problem of being Indian in Hueyapan. When I first went to Mexico in July 1969 I had no intention of living in an Indian pueblo. Instead I had wanted to work with a group of individuals in Mexico City who were trying to revive Aztec culture in Mexico. I had assumed that this group, which I will refer to as the Movimiento, had much in common with the Black Power and Native Amer-

---

1. When I say "culture" or "cultural system," I am using the terms in the tradition of T. Parsons, C. Geertz and D. Schneider—to mean a "system of symbols." See D. Schneider, *American Kinship* (Princeton, N.J., 1968), p.1.

ican Red Power movements in the United States. Therefore, I
was particularly interested in comparing the ideology and activities of the Movimiento with those of the other political
groups. I also wished to see whether the Movimiento's interpretation of Aztec culture differed very much from that of the
academic establishment.

After a few months I became disillusioned. Although I had
been told that the Movimiento was well organized and had
between 400 and 800 members in Mexico City alone, I soon
learned that there were at most thirty people. Furthermore,
although I had been led to believe that the Movimiento had a
large Indian constituency, I found that in reality almost all the
members were Mestizos, middle-class urban professionals,
primarily school teachers, who simply met among themselves in
one another's homes. In sum, I was disappointed, confused and
angered by the group. As far as I was concerned, they had let me
down—a curious formulation, I agree, but there it was. Not until
much later did I realize that I felt hostile toward the Movimiento
because it was an accurate, albeit embarrassing, caricature of my
own middle-class romantic view of the Indian.

Since I was uncomfortable working with the Movimiento, I
decided to change my field project and live in a rural community
with individuals who would be considered Indians by the
Movimiento, by anthropologists and by the Mexican people in
general. In other words, I would find a community where the inhabitants still spoke a prehispanic indigenous language. After
visiting a number of villages in Central Mexico I chose
Hueyapan, a bilingual Nahuatl- (the language of the Aztecs) and
Spanish-speaking pueblo. I wanted to see how the villagers
defined being Indian and how they felt about this identity. Were
there, for example, any grass-roots Indian Power groups in the
area as I had originally expected to find in Mexico? Also, I was
interested to see whether the villagers had heard about the
Movimiento and/or other urban efforts to revive indigenous
cultures. If so, how did the Indians respond to this city-inspired
enthusiasm?

I stayed in Hueyapan twelve months in 1969-1970 and since
then have returned for brief visits in 1971, 1973 and 1974. During

my association with the Hueyapeños I found answers to many of my questions. Furthermore, I discovered that the work I had initially done with the Movimiento was not a waste of time, but a crucial aid in interpreting the subsequent information I gathered in the pueblo. Living with the Hueyapeños also taught me in very direct and personal terms what it means to be oppressed and how confusing it is for the Indian to be discriminated against for being Indian and at the same time admired for being the "real soul" of Mexico, living proof of Mexico's noble prehispanic heritage. In addition, the Hueyapan experience led me to see parallels between the villagers and other oppressed ethnic and racial groups who have become mascots for a romantic and alienated middle class.

There are so many levels to be analyzed here, so many different ways to approach a study such as this one, that I suggest we begin as I did in Hueyapan, by getting to know some of the villagers. Let us start by looking at a day in the life of Doña Zeferina Barreto and her family. These are the people I stayed with while I was in Hueyapan. As I became closer to Doña Zeferina she told me about her past. What she related to me I will share with you, partially in her words, but mostly in mine. The more abstract ideas that I present later will be more meaningful, I believe, after we have acquired a sense of what life is really like in the pueblo, at least from the perspective of one Hueyapan family.

Next we will jump to a higher level of analysis. From the personal account we will turn and look at the entire village. I will discuss the history of Hueyapan from the time of the Spanish Conquest to the present. Then I will talk about how the Hueyapeños themselves define their Indian identity. While I lived in the village I had the opportunity to discuss the matter formally and informally with several hundred Hueyapeños. Finally I will analyze the specific roles various non-Indian groups —Catholic priests, Protestant missionaries, school teachers, government social workers and members of the Movimiento— have played in transforming the Hueyapeños' indigenous culture while preserving the villagers' Indian identity and low socioeconomic status in Mexican society.

Being Indian in Hueyapan

The section on Doña Zeferina may seem to have very little to do with the question of being Indian. That, however, is just the point. Doña Zeferina, like every other Hueyapeño, is first and foremost a poor peasant who happens to belong to a community where cultural vestiges of the prehispanic past linger on. These reminders of another culture are mere traces of a destroyed cultural heritage. They have virtually nothing to do with the daily life of a peasant woman. What is significant about these prehispanic remnants, as we shall see later, is the importance outsiders place on them. For the time being, then, let us be concerned only with what actually goes on in Doña Zeferina's home and with what aspects of her past this woman felt were important enough to relate to me.

I want you to get to know Doña Zeferina, not because I think of her as typical of most Hueyapan women I knew. On the contrary, I consider Doña Zeferina quite exceptional. Her extraordinary qualities, however, dramatize what I saw in many Hueyapeños, women and men alike. For Doña Zeferina almost every action has been in reaction. Put another way, Doña Zeferina's story is a collection of incidents that illustrates how clever she has tried to be in manipulating a hostile social environment. In a world characterized by fear and poverty, Doña Zeferina takes pride in her generally acknowledged ability to outwit the aggressor who is usually, but not always, a representative of Mexico's non-Indian—hispanic—elite. Her intelligence, which under other circumstances might have been used more productively, has been spent in cultivating defensive tactics that could save her life in the face of danger, allow her to "sneak" more food, protect her reputation as a moral woman and help her make a little extra money. As she herself summed up her philosophy of life, "A person must know how to defend herself."

DOÑA ZEFERINA BARRETO AND HER FAMILY DURING 1969-1970

1

The House

In relation to other villagers, the family of Doña Zeferina Barreto lives reasonably well, but its members are not among the wealthier residents in Hueyapan. Like many other homes located near the plaza, Doña Zeferina's establishment, shown in Figure 1, conforms to traditional Spanish architectural ideas about private space. The house has been constructed to maximize the family's isolation from the outside world. One wall of the home, together with a huge wooden gate, hides an inner courtyard from the street, permitting the family to perform many activities out of doors without being scrutinized by neighbors.

Doña Zeferina has two plots of land 75 by 25 meters each, on which she cultivates corn, beans, calabash squash and chiles. One of these plots is within the walls surrounding the house; the other is about a mile away. She also has some fruit trees. Although Doña Zeferina does not produce enough to feed the family entirely, she is able to provide nearly half the amount of vegetables the family eats and she manages to make a little extra money as well by selling pears, walnuts and other fruit. In addi-

1

FIGURE 1

Schematic Drawing of the Home of Doña Zeferina Barreto's Family

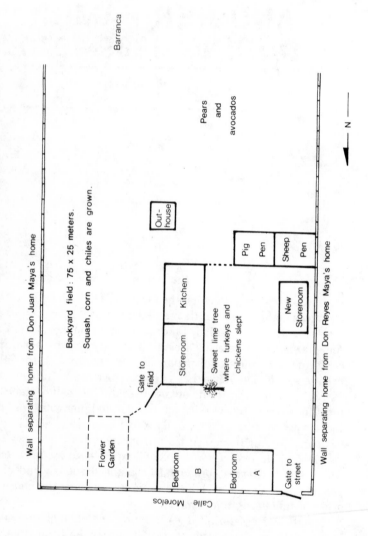

Wall separating home from Don Juan Maya's home

Backyard field: 75 x 25 meters.

Squash, corn and chiles are grown.

Barranca

Pears and avocados

Out-house

Pig Pen

Sheep Pen

Kitchen

Storeroom

Gate to field

Sweet lime tree where turkeys and chickens slept

New Storeroom

Flower Garden

Bedroom B

Bedroom A

Gate to street

Calle Morelos

Wall separating home from Don Reyes Maya's home

N

tion, Doña Zeferina maintains a herd of fifteen sheep, ten chickens, four turkeys, two sows, one horse, three dogs and two cats. The sheep provide wool and the fowl supplement the family diet on very special occasions. The pigs are fattened up and then sold to the village butcher.

Members of the Household

Doña Zeferina—the head of the house. A strong and domineering woman who has been twice widowed, Doña Zeferina learned early how to take care of herself and her family. Although she is sixty-five years old, she still contributes substantially to the family income by selling plastic toys, variety-store plates and utensils, and dried condiments such as chiles and garlic in the weekly market. Furthermore, Doña Zeferina serves as one of the local healers in town.

Don José—Doña Zeferina's third husband. Don José is a quiet man, about the same age as his wife. He spends his time farming his own land and that of Doña Zeferina. In addition, he takes care of his wife's flock of sheep, chops firewood and performs other household chores. One of Don José's problems is his tendency to drink too much.

Maestro Rafael—Doña Zeferina's oldest son.[1] Maestro Rafael is forty-three years old, a school teacher in the local primary school and one of the major political figures in the pueblo. At twenty-eight years of age Maestro Rafael, who had never finished primary school, returned to his studies and managed to get a teaching degree. Presently he is preparing himself for the rank of regional school inspector by studying on the weekends in Cuernavaca at the Instituto Federal de Capacitación Maesterios. Having had a particularly difficult childhood, helping his widowed mother support the family, the Maestro's achievements are considered quite impressive by his friends in Hueyapan. Maestro Rafael was married by the church and state

---

1. There is another son, Ernestino, who left Hueyapan seventeen years before to work in a textile factory in Cuernavaca.

to a Hueyapan woman twenty years ago. They were childless for a number of years and then, almost immediately after the birth of their son Arturo, they separated. Since that time the Maestro has been living with a distant cousin of his first wife.

Doña Juana—Maestro Rafael's second woman. Doña Juana is thirty-two years old and is the mother of six of the children living in the house. At present she is pregnant with a seventh. Juana is always working. Since she has to care for her children, as well as do almost all the cooking for the entire family, she rises earlier than everybody else and goes to sleep after the others have retired. Doña Juana is very quiet, hardly ever initiating a conversation with anybody other than the children.

Arturo—Maestro Rafael's son by his first marriage. Arturo, who is fourteen years old, stayed with his father when his parents separated and was raised by Doña Zeferina. In June 1969 the boy finished secondary school. He had been studying in Yecapistla, a nearby pueblo, and living with school teacher friends of his father's. In the fall of 1969 Arturo took and failed the highly competitive entrance examination for preparatory school. He will have to wait until next year to take the test again. In the meantime, Arturo is living at home, helping Don José work the lands, care for the animals and attend to other such chores.[2]

Rosa—Doña Juana and Maestro Rafael's oldest child. Rosa is twelve years old and is in her last year of primary school. She is a good-natured, quiet girl who has already begun to take on many responsibilities in the house.

Raúl—The second child of Doña Juana and Maestro Rafael. An aloof boy, Raúl is ten years old and is in the fifth grade.

Héctor—The third child of Doña Juana and Maestro Rafael. Héctor is eight years old and is repeating first grade for the second time. Héctor's skin is slightly darker than that of the other

---

2. In the fall of 1970 Arturo did pass the entrance examination for normal school and began his studies in Tenería, Mexico, to prepare himself to be a rural primary school teacher like his father.

children and everybody chides the little boy unfairly because of
his color. ~~(contradicts Iwanska - "the darker the littler~~

Maribel—The fourth child of Doña Juana and Maestro Rafael.
Maribel, who is often called by the nickname Maruca, is six
years old and eager to begin school. Loud, a bit bossy and clearly
very bright, she is said to resemble her grandmother Doña
Zeferina.

Reina—The fifth child of Doña Juana and Maestro Rafael. A
very affectionate and coquettish little girl, Reina, who is four
years old, is her father's favorite. When the Maestro is home, she
always climbs into his lap and cuddles. Wherever the Maestro
goes in the village, little Reina tags along.

Angel—The sixth child of Doña Juana and Maestro Rafael.
Usually called by his nickname Quico, Angel, who is two years
old, is shy and temperamental, demanding a lot of attention. As
the year progressed, Quico grew up remarkably fast. For example, he was weaned without a whimper a couple of months before
his second birthday.

Maestra Angelina—Doña Zeferina's only daughter and youngest
child. Maestra Angelina is twenty-eight and the mother of Lilia,
the eighth child living in the house. About six years ago Maestra
Angelina left home with a man against her mother's wishes. The
couple had a civil marriage and settled down in the lowlands.
After only a few months, however, Maestra Angelina, who in the
meantime had become pregnant, left her husband and returned
home. As Doña Zeferina had warned, the man Angelina had
married treated her badly. Maestra Angelina had her baby at
home and has since returned to school to finish her teaching certification degree. During the week she lives in Hueyapan with her
daughter and family and on weekends she goes to Cuernavaca to
study at the Instituto Federal de Capacitación Maesterios. When
she goes to Cuernavaca she leaves her daughter behind in the
care of Doña Zeferina. In the city Maestra Angelina stays with
her brother Ernestino, his wife and their child.

Lilia (back left), Maribel and Angel in front of the storeroom.

Lilia—Maestra Angelina's daughter. Lilia is five years old and receives more attention from Doña Zeferina than do the other children in the house. Like Arturo, Lilia is really Doña Zeferina's ward. Although she is pampered and indulged, the child is not selfish or spoiled. On the contrary, Lilia is extremely gentle and generous.[3]

A Day with the Family

Doña Juana is the first to rise. It is about 6:30 A.M. Having gone to sleep in her slip and underclothes, she silently puts on a cotton dress, a cotton apron and plastic shoes. Then wrapping herself up in a cotton *rebozo* (shawl), she hurries out into the brisk morning air. Juana is in a rush because she wants to beat the long lines that will soon be forming at Don Reyes Maya's corn mill. Since the corn was prepared yesterday, all Juana has to do now is fill a bucket with the *nixtamal*, as the cooked corn is called, and go to the mill, which, conveniently, is just next door. As far as Juana is concerned, it is well worth the twenty *centavos* (equivalent to two cents in U.S. currency) to have the corn ground at the mill. She vividly remembers, she told me, how every morning her "poor mother" had to spend a couple of hours on her knees grinding corn on the *metate* so that she could serve hot *tortillas* (flat round bread) to the men before they went to the fields. Juana's mother would rise at 4:30 A.M.

After the corn is ground Juana returns to the kitchen to get the fires going. Then she puts two pots of water on to heat, one for

---

3. The sleeping arrangements were the following: in bedroom A (see Figure 1), in one double bed, slept Maestro Rafael, Doña Juana, Reina and Angel; in a single bed slept Rosa and Maribel. In bedroom B, Doña Zeferina, Don José and Arturo shared a double bed; Maestra Angelina and Lilia shared a single bed. Raúl and Héctor slept together in the storeroom off the kitchen in a single bed made of wooden boards. I slept in bedroom A for most of my stay on a torn army cot that the family had purchased several years before for Arturo to use while studying in Yecapistla. At times when there was company, I shared Rosa's bed and Maribel slept with her parents, Reina and Angel. In June 1970 Doña Zeferina bought a new double bed for Maestra Angelina, and I then shared this big bed with the Maestra and Lilia. Arturo inherited the old single bed. With the exception of Raúl and Héctor's homemade bed, all the beds were store-bought with double frames. On the headboards were painted religious scenes.

the coffee and another for Rafael, who insists on having hot water to wash and shave with. Next the beans, prepared the day before, are reheated and the metal *comal* (griddle), used for cooking the *tortillas*, is washed down with water and lime (the mineral product, not the fruit). Once everything is under way in the kitchen, Juana goes to the backyard to cut a few chiles for the hot sauce she will serve with the beans. All that is left to do now is to make the *tortillas*, a time-consuming job for this large family.

Don José rises a little after Juana. He slips on a shirt and a pair of pants over the long underwear he slept in. Next he puts on his well-worn *huaraches* (sandals), a weather-beaten straw hat and his woolen *gabán* (poncho). Silently the old man goes out to begin his early morning chore—fetching drinking water from the stream at the bottom of one of the *barrancas* (gorges) that surround the village. Placing a wooden yoke on his shoulders, Don José is able to balance two large tin cans of water. Two trips of this sort from the *barranca* are usually sufficient to fill the huge earthenware water jugs kept in the storeroom off the kitchen. Almost every morning Doña Zeferina tries to get Arturo out of bed to help Don José carry the water, but the sleepy boy refuses to budge.

Next to make their morning appearances are Raúl and Héctor. They are expected to sweep the front yard with two homemade brooms that are always falling apart. Reina and Quico stay in bed a bit longer and play with the pillows. Maruca slips out of Rosa's bed and joins her younger siblings in their parents' bed. Soon, however, they all want to get up and they call Rosa to come take charge of little Quico.

The twelve-year-old girl drags herself out of bed. She, like her younger sisters, has slept in her dress, a torn sweater and a pair of pants. She takes off the pants, puts on her plastic shoes and straightens out the wrinkles in her dress. Then Rosa picks up Quico, wrapping him and herself in Juana's wool *rebozo*. By this time, the little boy has begun to cry, tearfully demanding his morning piece of bread. Rosa takes Quico to the kitchen, where Juana quiets his insistent plea for "*pan, pan*" by giving the little fellow a twenty-*centavo* piece. Rosa then carries the cranky child down to the corner store to purchase him his bread—a sweet roll.

Next Angelina rises to heat up a bottle of milk for Lilia. Although both Doña Zeferina and Maestra Angelina have tried to discourage this habit, Lilia insists on having her milk in this way and will not get out of bed until she has emptied her bottle. Reina too continues to drink milk from a bottle, but unlike her cousin, she does not receive special attention and has to wait until her mother finds time to prepare one for her.

Except for Lilia and Arturo, Doña Zeferina is the last to rise. She has been awake, however, since Don José got up, but as she told me many times, it was too cold to bother leaving her bed any earlier. Since it is Tuesday, market day in Hueyapan, and she will therefore be selling in the plaza, Doña Zeferina plans to put on a clean dress and apron instead of what she has been wearing for the past few days. She will not change until after breakfast, though, and so for the time being she puts on her soiled clothes over the slip she slept in. As she leaves the bedroom she puts on her agave-fiber sandals, her favorite coral-colored sweater and a cotton *rebozo*.

Crossing the courtyard that separates the bedrooms from the kitchen, Doña Zeferina authoritatively orders the children about: "Raúl! Héctor! Why aren't you sweeping? If you've finished, then go help Don José carry water. . . . Arturo! Get out of bed—that child is lazy as can be when it comes to working, but quick as anything for being sullen. . . . Angelina, Lilia is crying. . . . *Dog*! Get out of the kitchen."

Doña Zeferina finds her little squat chair and sits down by the fire where the coffee is heating. "Juana," she asks, "is there any *aguardiente* [brandy]?" Nothing is left from last night, so Doña Zeferina gives Rosa 1.20 *pesos*[4] and tells her granddaughter to take the family's half-pint bottle over to their *comadre's*[5] house across the street and ask Doña Epifania to fill it up. Doña Epifania and her husband Don Adelaido make their own *aguardiente*.

---

4. One *peso* equals eight cents and there are 100 *centavos* in a *peso*.

5. *Comadres* (female) and *compadres* (male) are individuals who have entered into a formal religious association with one another that has been sponsored by the Catholic Church.

Angelina has given Lilia her bottle and helped the child get dressed. The two of them then come into the kitchen and Lilia goes over to Doña Zeferina to be cuddled by her *mamacita*. Angelina sets about preparing a bit of *nixtamal* for the chickens and turkeys. Kneeling down in front of the *metate*, she rapidly grinds up a bit of corn and then gives the coarse gruel to her mother. Doña Zeferina goes out into the yard and calls her birds in a high-pitched voice: "Ki ki ki ki." In no time she is surrounded by a hungry, peeping flock. How the old woman loves her birds! She never stops commenting on how beautiful they are, particularly her only rooster.

While Doña Zeferina is outside feeding the chickens and turkeys Angelina helps Juana in the kitchen. Angelina usually takes over the preparation of the chile sauce or the frying of some eggs, which the more important members of the family eat occasionally. Juana, thus freed from these chores, starts the endless job of "throwing" *tortillas*; in a single meal this large family eats about forty of them.

Suddenly the 8:00 bus is heard groaning in the distance as it makes its final ascent into the Hueyapan plaza. Héctor bolts out of the house and dashes down to the plaza. He wants to see his father get off the bus. The Maestro had some business to settle in Cuautla[6] the day before and had spent the night away from home. A few minutes later Héctor casually ambles into the front yard and cooly informs everyone that *Papá* has arrived. Rafael, however, has joined a few friends at Don Timoteo's store for a quick drink before coming home.

Eventually Maestro Rafael opens the heavy gate and enters his family's front yard. Raúl, Héctor, Maruca, Reina, Lilia and even little Quico all run over to greet him, several hanging on to Rafael at once. In whining voices the children plead, "*Papi, Papi, give me twenty centavos.*" Rosa and Arturo look on from a distance, in their father's view so that they will not be forgotten, but too self-conscious to carry on like their younger brothers and

---

6. Cuautla is the second most important city in Morelos; Cuernavaca is the first. The bus going to Hueyapan originates in Cuautla.

sisters. In his customary authoritative and slightly irritated tone, Rafael calls to Rosa. He gives her ten *pesos* and tells the girl to go to the store and change the bill. Since today is market day Rafael has decided to treat the younger children to fifty *centavos* each instead of the usual twenty and the older ones to a *peso* each. Everybody is delighted.

Finally the children let their father pass and Rafael goes over to the kitchen. As he enters Rafael asks for his mother: "And the boss lady?" By this time Doña Zeferina has returned to her little seat by the fire and she smiles proudly at her son. They chat briefly and the two of them have a drink together. Once he has caught up a bit on the local news, Rafael turns to his wife, whom he did not bother to greet when he came in, and says, "Give me some water." The woman silently leaves her cooking, fetches her man a pail and mixes boiling water with some cold water until it reaches just the desired temperature. Without another word, Rafael takes the bucket from her and goes outside to shave. Despite the chilly morning air, he takes off his shirt and meticulously washes himself. Rafael then goes to the bedroom to find a clean shirt; every day the Maestro wears a different shirt. Now properly dressed for school, he returns to the kitchen and tells Juana to serve him breakfast: "*¡Dame de comer!*"

While Rafael eats, Juana continues to make hot fresh *tortillas*. Don José and a few of the children join the school teacher at the table. Little Reina insists on sitting right next to her beloved *Papi*. Doña Zeferina, however, remains seated in her favorite chair by the fire and, using a little bench for a table, eats her breakfast there. Most of the conversation is between Rafael and his mother. In Cuautla, Rafael tells her, he heard that a group of *campesinos* (farmers) from Tlacotepec[7] had gotten into a terrible car accident while they were on their way to a political rally in Cuernavaca for the new governor of Morelos. Several people had been severely injured. Rafael muses philosophically on

---

7. Tlacotepec is eleven kilometers from Hueyapan. It is the last village before Hueyapan on the Hueyapan-Cuautla bus route. Tlacotepec is a lowland pueblo and the ascent from the village to Hueyapan is quite arduous.

how strange it is that some people travel about all the time and nothing happens, then others leave the village only once and they immediately fall victims to disaster. ₁₂ₒ₿

Rafael looks at his new 1500-*peso* watch. It is almost 9:00; he must go to the plaza to help get the children lined up for morning announcements. As he leaves Doña Zeferina asks him to give her some money so that she can purchase beef at the market. He ignores the request. The old woman shouts after her son that there will be no meat for lunch then. She shakes her head in frustration and complains that Rafael never helps out with household expenses, an unfair accusation. Later in the morning Doña Zeferina, using her own money, will give in and buy some beef anyway from her *compadre* Don Lauro, the butcher.

Angelina and Juana are the last to eat. They are close in age and enjoy each other's company very much. Despite the fact that Angelina has nearly completed her studies for a school teacher's degree and Juana cannot even read, they are good friends. One of their most affectionate habits is to call one another "Patricia," a name they both think is pretty.

While Doña Zeferina slowly washes herself, combs and braids her hair and changes her clothes, Don José, Arturo, Rosa, Raúl and Héctor carry the innumerable boxes of merchandise to the plaza. Soon the 9:00 bell rings. Rosa, Raúl and Héctor dash off to join the other pupils in front of the school.

Just as the children file into their respective classrooms, Doña Zeferina turns the corner of her street, Calle Morelos, and majestically walks up to her selling post in the market. Over one arm she carries a straw basket in which she keeps some change, and in her hand she holds a small scale used to weigh the chiles. Passing other vendors, Doña Zeferina stops to greet them and to see what there is to buy today.

Finally she arrives at her spot. Arturo and some of the preschool grandchildren are there waiting for her. Doña Zeferina and Arturo set about systematically arranging first the chiles, then the kitchenware and the toys, in a particular order which never varies from week to week. Doña Zeferina also attaches some plastic sheets to the awning that covers her selling area in order to protect herself from the sun. By 9:30 she is settled and the long day formally begins.

In the busy market place Doña Zeferina is entirely in her element. Every Tuesday she has the chance to bargain and gossip with people she does not normally see during the week. *Compadres* who live in the outlying *barrios*[8] of Hueyapan and in neighboring pueblos are sure to come down to the main plaza on Tuesdays. Everybody stops to chat. Some even pick up little toys for their children or grandchildren and perhaps a new plate for the house as well. Others purchase five *pesos'* worth of *pasilla chile* and a bulb of garlic. No matter what the day brings, the old woman sits patiently on a *petate* (straw mat), her feet delicately curled under her. Surrounded by colorful plastic merchandise, the short corpulent woman flashes a warm alert smile to potential customers as they pass by.

Doña Zeferina strikes a hard bargain. Gifted in the art of price haggling, she rarely has to come down on the amount she first cites to a customer. Since the local people know and trust Doña Zeferina, they usually are willing to pay what she asks with little discussion, confident that Doña Zefe is not going to cheat her *paisanos*.

Doña Zeferina is quite a different person, however, in Mexico City and at large fairs in nearby villages. Many years of experience have taught her that most strangers are thieves. Some steal by pickpocketing, others by charging the unaware exorbitant prices for inferior merchandise. Even Doña Zeferina, who seems so sophisticated in Hueyapan, is at times outwitted by the crafty "wheelers and dealers," and she in turn tries to outsmart them.

At the Tepalcingo, Morelos fair in February 1970 Doña Zeferina wanted to purchase a few dozen decorated gourd bowls

8. Hueyapan is divided into five *barrios* or intravillage sections, each one named after a different Catholic saint: San Miguel, San Jacinto, San Andrés, San Bartolo and San Felipe. I frequently refer to San Miguel and San Jacinto as the Centro and to the other three as the outlying *barrios*. The market is located in the Centro as is Doña Zeferina's home.

to sell back in Hueyapan. Although she was clever and even a bit
coy at times, in the end she lost out. Doña Zeferina visited one
stall after another on the fairgrounds, trying to determine where
she could get the best price for the bowls. Each time she went
through the same routine:

Doña Zeferina: What do you sell these for, *marchante*?
Vendor: Three *pesos* apiece, *marchante*.
Doña Zeferina: And why so much?
Vendor: I should charge even more!
Doña Zeferina: And in lots of a hundred?
Vendor: I don't sell by the hundreds.
Doña Zeferina: Well, then, by the dozen?
Vendor: 2.80 *pesos* a bowl if you buy by the dozen.
Doña Zeferina: Did you say 2.60? [Her "poor" hearing always managed
     to lower the price.]
Vendor: No, 2.80!
Doña Zeferina: I am purchasing these in order to sell them. If I pay you
     as much as you are asking, how will I ever make a profit myself,
     marchante?

Then Doña Zeferina would walk away, hoping the vendors
would come down in price. They never did. Finally she found a
spot off the fairgrounds where the bowls were being sold in large
lots for 2.50 *pesos* apiece. She purchased fifty at this bargain
price, only to discover later that the thieves had given her seven
cracked bowls.

Back in the Hueyapan market, a *señora* from the San Felipe
Barrio stops to see Doña Zeferina. She owes the old woman one
peso for an injection the latter gave her son last week. Pleased to
hear that her patient has improved from his cold, Doña Zeferina
takes the money offered to her by the mother. From her basket
she then takes out a small notebook in which she keeps a record
of all those who owe her money. Slowly she goes through the list,
reading each name aloud in a quiet voice, until she comes to the
señora in question. Doña Zeferina boldly scratches out the name
with a pencil and smiles up at the woman. The debt is cleared.
While waiting for Doña Zeferina the woman had the chance to
look over the display of toys. She asks Doña Zeferina the price of

Doña Zeferina making a sale in the market.

a plastic watergun. 1.50 *pesos*. That sounds quite high, but since Doña Zerferina refuses to let her have it for 1.25, the mother buys the toy anyway as a gift for her recently recovered son.

Next a man from Santa Cruz, Puebla passes by and greets Doña Zeferina. He brings sad news from his pueblo. One of Doña Zeferina's Santa Cruz *compadres* died in a brush fire last week. The deceased and two of his sons had seen a blaze in some hills near the pueblo. They went immediately to try to put it out, but they could not control the fire. As they made a last desperate attempt, the *compadre* hurt his foot and could not escape. He yelled to his sons that they should run for their lives. Since they would have died as well if they had stayed behind to help him, the boys sadly obeyed their father, leaving him to burn to death. Doña Zeferina is aghast. How terrible . . . the "poor man" . . . and his wife! She presses the Santa Cruz man for more details. Doña Zeferina shakes her head; this *compadre* used to come regularly to Hueyapan on market days. She is going to miss him.

The 11:30 school recess bell rings. Children come racing out and crowd the market area. First they go to buy some candy and snow cones. Many then wander over to Doña Zeferina to see the toys. Fortunately, Arturo is there to help keep an eye on the children, for some of the more rowdy boys are capable of stealing. The two of them together manage to control the children. During the half-hour recess Doña Zeferina sells several twenty-*centavo* doll purses to young girls and a few larger plastic guns and trucks to the boys. Most of the children who surround Doña Zeferina just look on longingly, not buying anything; they save their *centavos* for a little something extra to eat.

Maestro Rafael and some other school teachers are in the plaza chatting among themselves. The district school inspector will be holding a meeting in Tetela[9] later this week, and the *maestros* are discussing the fact that they will have to cancel classes in order to attend. Then the subject turns to less serious matters, and one native school teacher entertains the others with

---

9. Tetela (whose full name is Tetela del Volcán) is the seat of the municipality to which Hueyapan belongs.

a joke. He tells the following one for my benefit in particular: "In the United States people think that their government is so advanced technologically because, with the help of computers, election results can be tabulated and announced within hours after the polls close. In Mexico, however, things are even more efficient. Here the public knows the results six months before the elections take place!"

By noon Juana and Angelina have finished the morning chores. Beds have been made, bedrooms and kitchen swept clean, all the breakfast dishes washed and the dogs and pigs fed. Angelina goes to the plaza to pick up the kilo of beef that Doña Zeferina purchased for the afternoon meal. Always the one who decides what will be eaten and how it will be prepared, Doña Zeferina gives her daughter the necessary instructions. They are to have beef soup flavored with green tomatoes, chiles, onions, cloves, pepper and fresh peppermint; also the usual boiled beans and *tortillas*.

Juana goes into the kitchen to add fuel to the fires. She wants to start the soup immediately so that the meat will have plenty of time to cook; otherwise it will be too tough. Fortunately, there are still enough beans left over from yesterday and this morning's breakfast so that she will only have to reheat them a half-hour or so before lunchtime.

Quico follows his mother into the kitchen and cries for some bread. Juana gives him the remainder of his early morning piece and tells the boy to go chase the dogs out of the kitchen. Quico scampers off enthusiastically, only to return again a few minutes later, this time without any pants on. Juana admonishes the child gently for walking about in such a fashion and teasingly warns him that if he does not wear his pants, the dogs will bite off his *pajarito* (penis, literally little bird). Quico giggles shyly and permits Juana to dress him once more.

When school lets out at 2:00, lunch is ready. The children drift home one by one and ask to be fed, each brusquely demanding, "*Mamá, dame de comer.*" Juana complies, giving the younger children tiny portions of beans and morsels of meat. Since children have little tolerance for chiles, she does not serve them any soup. Angelina is also among the first to eat, for she has to go to the plaza to relieve Doña Zeferina temporarily for a lunch break.

Don José, who had been grazing the sheep, returns home at about the same time as Doña Zeferina and Rafael. While they eat Doña Zeferina mentions the tragic news about their Santa Cruz *compadre*. Somewhat self-conscious about her great interest in gory details, the old woman comments on how Angelina always criticizes her for having this fascination. Nevertheless, Doña Zeferina goes on, she does have a great tolerance for blood, and that is why she is a good healer. Even the government nurses who came to Hueyapan in 1945 commented on this fact.

Rafael reports that soon the family will have running water. On his way home for lunch he ran into Don Juan Maya, and things are just about organized now. About twenty-five families who live in San Miguel and San Jacinto Barrios (i.e., the center of town) have decided to dig a deep well at the site of an excellent natural pool of water that they have found in the hills surrounding Hueyapan. Each family will have to contribute 350 *pesos* for the effort and provide seven days of labor. In addition to the digging of the well, rubber hoses will have to be laid down to connect the individual homes to the water supply, which is five kilometers away. Everybody is delighted. How nice to know that they will no longer have to carry water up to the house from the *barranca* twice a day.

Doña Zeferina gets up to return to the market. As she leaves she tells Juana to prepare the *temascal* (the adobe, or mud-brick, steam bath) for this evening; the hay must be changed in the bathing chamber and the fire must be set. For a couple of days now her head has been hurting, Doña Zeferina complains. Therefore, she has decided that she better take a steam bath and cure herself. The cause of the headache is no mystery: while she was returning to Hueyapan on the bus this past weekend a melon fell off the rack above and hit her on the head.

When the Maestro finishes eating he joins some men in the plaza to discuss local political matters. Rafael has been concerned recently because the conservative *ayudante* (village mayor) publicly attacked him and another native Hueyapan school teacher, Maestro Regino. According to the *ayudante*, the two teachers are not doing acceptable jobs in the classroom. Not only are Rafael and Regino furious with the *ayudante* over this, but so are several other members of the progressive faction. It is generally agreed among the progressives that the *ayudante* is in no position to criticize others, for he has been negligent in his own duties. Furthermore, the progressives consider the *ayudante* "uncultured" and therefore incapable of judging the performance of "educated" school teachers. The progressives have resolved, therefore, to take concrete action against the *ayudante*. Several local officials will write a letter to the governor of Morelos to ask him to authorize the removal of the *ayudante* from office and the substitution of the present vice-*ayudante* (*suplente*), a man whose allegiance to the progressive faction is well known. Today is the day chosen to write the letter, and Rafael has volunteered to help the others draft the formal complaint.

Back at the house Rosa helps her mother Juana and aunt Angelina wash the luncheon dishes. Juana then puts up some beans for tonight's supper and tomorrow's meals. She also prepares the *nixtamal* for the following day's *tortillas*. Leaving Rosa to take care of Quico, Juana goes off to do some laundry at a nearby stream. At the washing place she meets several other women. They chat among themselves as they kneel down by the water and scrub their families' soiled clothes on huge rocks that have been placed in the middle of the stream for this purpose.

At 3:30 those people who came to sell in the plaza from villages on the Hueyapan-Cuautla bus route pack up their goods and cram into the blue and red Estrella Roja (Red Star) bus line's second-class vehicle. By this time most visitors from neighboring pueblos within walking distance of Hueyapan have also left for home. Only the local people remain in the market, and in another hour and a half they too return to their houses. Doña Zeferina is one of the last to leave the market, for it takes her and Arturo a long time to repack all the toys and kitchenware. At 5:30 Don José, Arturo and a few younger children drag the cartons home again and tuck them away for another week, under Doña Zeferina's bed and in the corners of the storeroom off the kitchen.

Doña Zeferina's chores for the day are not over, since she still has a sick call to make. Maruca pleads with her grandmother to be taken along. Once she has organized her curing kit,

Juana brings dirty dishes out to Rosa, who is washing.

Doña Zeferina nods to the child to come, and the two of them start to make their way north on Calle Morelos. As they walk, Doña Zeferina exchanges greetings with everybody who passes by. Most often a simple *madiotzin* (good-bye)[10] suffices. Occasionally, however, somebody calls out, "Good afternoon, Doña Zefe, where are you going?" The old woman replies with a vague gesture of the hand and says, "Over there." Actually she is on her way to the home of Maestro Regino's old uncle and aunt who live in the San Andrés Barrio. Both of them have been suffering from severe colds all week. Doña Zeferina visited them yesterday to give the couple injections. The wife, however, would not let the healer give her a shot. Today Doña Zeferina is going to give the man his second injection.

The couple is extremely poor and lives in two small broken-down adobe buildings, one of which is the kitchen and the other the bedroom. The man reports that he is feeling better today than yesterday, but he is still bedridden. He sleeps on a raised wooden platform, cushioned somewhat by a straw mat. Covering him are an old blanket and several burlap bags. He is wearing a pair of soiled *calzones*.[11] The old man explains that he has even been hungry today, but his wife tells him that there is nothing to eat. As for the woman, although her condition is little better than that of her husband, she is up and about, dressed in a ragged *xincueite*.[12]

Doña Zeferina is not very thorough about sterilizing the hypodermic needle. Although she rubs it with some alcohol, she does not submerge the needle into a container of flaming alcohol, as she was taught to do by the government nurses. Once she has filled the needle with *clorhidrato de tetracaina* (tetracaine), the healer tells her patient to roll over and she gives the man a shot

---

10. This is a Nahuatlized version of the traditional Spanish-Mexican greeting *adiós*. The *tzin* suffix is a form of respect. Frequently the villagers, especially the young, use the Spanish greeting instead.

11. White linen pajamas—the traditional dress of rural peasants in the area, Indians and Mestizos alike.

12. A long black wool skirt—the traditional skirt worn by Indian women in the region.

in the buttocks. Then Doña Zeferina gives each of her patients a teaspoon of cough medicine, making use of the same spoon for both of them. Tomorrow she will check in again, Doña Zeferina assures the couple. In the meantime they should drink tea and keep warm.

By the time Doña Zeferina returns from her healing trip it is about 6:30. Juana and Angelina have already made a couple of trips to the bottom of the *barranca* to fetch water. Don José has taken the horse Norteño to the communal lands where he cut some firewood. He then transported the logs back to the house by skillfully tying them on the animal's saddle. The fire in the *temascal* has been set and will be sufficiently hot for a steam bath in about an hour.

While waiting to bathe, Doña Zeferina prepares the medicine that she uses to cure her headache. She calls to several of the children and instructs them to urinate into a chamber pot. Although they complain that they "do not have to go," Doña Zeferina insists. Finally, complying with their grandmother's command, Lilia, Maruca and Raúl take turns using the metal receptacle. Doña Zeferina pours the urine[13] into a smaller pot and adds tobacco leaves. Next she heats this over a small fire in the kitchen until the urine begins to boil. Then she removes the mixture from the hearth and pours in a bit of alcohol, the final ingredient. Using the tobacco as a sponge, Doña Zeferina applies some of the medicine to her aching head; the rest is saved to rub down the bathers' bodies before they steam themselves in the *temascal*. Doña Zeferina ties a scarf tightly around her head to keep out the cold. Throughout the following day she will keep her head covered in this manner.

Every evening one of the young girls in the house waves some copal incense before the family's image of the Virgin of Guadalupe and lights a large candle which is left burning all night long. Tonight Doña Zeferina teaches Maruca and Lilia how

---

13. Only children's urine is used for medicine. According to Doña Zeferina, the urine of adults has too many impurities to be safe.

to pray to the Virgin while performing this nightly ritual. Prayers such as these are informal, she explains: they come from the heart: "My Mother of Guadalupe, Queen of the Heavens, take care of me. Mother of mine, thou who art so powerful, cover us with thine robe and do not forsake us, merciful Mother."

The family goes into the kitchen to have a light supper of beans, reheated *tortillas* and coffee. Although it has been a hectic day, everybody is in lively spirits. The adults all share a half-pint bottle of *aguardiente* that Doña Zeferina had Don José purchase for the family. As Don José takes his serving Rafael jovially says to him, "Come on, Don José, down with it." Don José, who has had quite a bit to drink already, chuckles and toasts, "To combat the cold weather." Even Juana, in her quiet way, enjoys the general hilarity. As she drinks some of the local brandy she remarks in her customary way, "*¡Qué carambas entonces!*" ("I'll be dog-gone!").

The mood is infectious. Maruca, whose strong personality is often compared with that of her grandmother, begins to tease her older brother Héctor. Amused by her granddaughter, Doña Zeferina joins in and sings a song to Maruca, the one that always makes the little girl scream and run out of the room. The song is about a woman named Marietta, but to tease the child, Doña Zeferina substitutes the name Maruca: "Maruca, don't be a coquette, because men are very bad. They promise a lot of gifts, but when the time comes they beat you instead."

Angelina leaves the kitchen after a fast bite in order to put Lilia to bed. The child has to have company until she has fallen asleep or else she will cry. By this time Quico has dozed off in a small wooden cradle that is hanging in the storeroom off the kitchen. Reina has curled up in her father's lap. Once she is asleep Rafael carefully carries her back into the bedroom and lays her down on his bed.

As soon as Lilia is sleeping, Angelina slips out of bed, takes off her clothes, wraps herself up in a blanket and returns to the kitchen. Doña Zeferina has also changed out of her clothes. Kneeling down on the *petate* (straw mat) which has been placed at the door of the *temascal* (diagrammed in Figure 2), the old woman and her daughter crawl into the large chamber and the bathing process begins.[14]

Rafael is the only adult member of the house who does not participate in the *temascal* steam bath. He reminds the others of how once in his youth he got sick and his mother decided to cure him in the *temascal*. No sooner did she begin to beat him with the *cebolleja* leaves than the boy bolted out of the *temascal* and ran into the yard, stark naked. Never again would he subject himself to such treatment. From inside the *temascal* Doña Zeferina laughs at her son's story and teases him about his dread of the traditional bath.

Talking about his childhood bathing experiences reminds Rafael of other times he had been frightened as a young boy.

FIGURE 2
The *Temascal* or Steam Bath in Doña Zeferina's Kitchen
(A) Chamber where fire is built. (B) Bathing chamber.

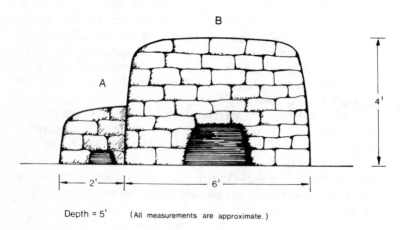

Depth = 5'   (All measurements are approximate.)

14. The *temascal* is an adobe steam bath chamber approximately of the dimensions given in Figure 2. In most houses it is located inside or near the kitchen. A fire is lit in the little chamber (A) about two or three hours before peo-

Calling to his mother to see whether she remembers, he retells the story of the time a man wanted to buy Rafael from his mother. When Rafael was about fourteen he and Doña Zeferina went to the village of Zacualpan one Sunday to sell *pulque,* the alcoholic beverage made from the fermented juice of the century plant. In the market they met a man who had no son of his own. The Zacualpeño suggested to Doña Zeferina that she sell Rafael to him. Doña Zeferina replied that she would think it over and let him know next week at the market. Rafael panicked and told his mother, when they were alone, that he would return home even if she did sell him. On the following Sunday Rafael refused to go to Zacualpan with Doña Zeferina. When he finished the story Doña

---

ple bathe. Fresh hay is placed on the floor of chamber B to provide a comfortable bed for the bathers. In Doña Zeferina's home everybody who bathes in the *temascal* is accompanied by the old woman. She does not leave the *temascal* at all during the two hours it usually takes for those members of the family who so desire to bathe. In addition to Doña Zeferina, the usual participants are Angelina, Juana and Don José. Occasionally Rosa and the other young girls also bathe.

Doña Zeferina and the first bather, usually Angelina, strip and wrap themselves in blankets. Around their heads they tie cotton rags. Once crouched inside the *temascal,* they remove their blankets and lie down. There is just about enough room for a person five feet tall to stretch out completely in a prone position. Before the actual bathing Doña Zeferina rubs herself and the other bather with medicine, a solution of children's urine, alcohol and tobacco. This mixture cuts the oils on the bathers' skins and is supposed to cure aches and pains. Next a bucket of cold water is introduced into the *temascal* by a female member of the family who is in the kitchen waiting her turn to bathe. The same person helps Doña Zeferina close off the chamber opening with a straw mat. Doña Zeferina then splashes cold water on the wall that connects chamber B with chamber A. Since this wall has been heating for several hours, contact with the cold water creates a lot of steam. As the steam fills the chamber, Doña Zeferina and the other bather beat themselves vigorously with *cebolleja* leaves. When the heat gets too great, the door of chamber B is opened; the bathers rest and then repeat the process, throwing more cold water against the heated wall. After about three steamings Doña Zeferina asks for a bucket of warm water that has been seasoned with rosemary leaves. This water is for the other bather to wash with. Using soap and scrubbing herself with small porous stones, the bather rinses off with the pleasant-smelling warm water. When the bather is finished, she asks for her blanket, dries off in the *temascal* and then, wrapped up once again, crawls out. Doña Zeferina does not wash herself off until the last bather has finished.

Large *petates* have been spread out on the dirt floor of the kitchen in front of the *temascal.* The bather usually lies down on the straw mats for a few minutes, then gets dressed and enjoys a cup of herb tea. Almost immediately thereafter the bather goes to bed.

Zeferina called out from the *temascal* that she thought the entire incident was rather funny because she never once seriously considered selling Rafael; after all he was her son, not a donkey.

One by one the older children leave the kitchen to go to sleep. Rosa is the last of the young people to retire, because she must wash the supper dishes before joining her brothers and sisters. Finally by about 10:00 the bathers have finished and they too cross over to the bedrooms and turn in for the night. Juana remains behind a few minutes longer than the rest to turn off the lights,[15] fetch Quico from the cradle and lock the kitchen and storeroom doors with wooden bars.

Before Doña Zeferina turns off the lights in the bedroom she smokes a cigarette and puts on the radio at a high volume, paying little attention to those people who have already fallen asleep. Her favorite soap opera, "Chucho el Roto," is over, but she finds something else to listen to. Rafael, who is not yet asleep, calls to his mother from the next room, again unconcerned about waking the others. He repeats the punch line from a joke they all had enjoyed earlier in the evening. They both laugh. Then the house is silent as everyone drifts off to sleep.

---

15. Electricity was installed in the village in the early 1960s. See Chapter 3 for further discussion.

THE HISTORY
OF DOÑA ZEFERINA
AND HER FAMILY

2

Although the usual residence pattern in Hueyapan is patrilocal —a wife moves in with her husband's family—and although the culture is considered to be male dominated, Doña Zeferina's story is one in which women, not men, figure more prominently. For three generations her family has been held together by women who did not have steady male companionship. Her grandmother, her mother and then Doña Zeferina herself all had to support their families substantially alone, raising children who never really knew their fathers. Of the three women only her grandmother followed Hueyapan tradition and resided in her husband's home. Even in this woman's case, however, circumstances intervened, causing her to spend most of her married years separated from her spouse. In the two succeeding generations, both Doña Zeferina's mother and Doña Zeferina herself remained in their own homes, bringing up their children with the help of their respective mothers.

Doña Zeferina's father, who owned a store in Hueyapan, abandoned wife and business when their only child, Zeferina, was two years old. The man moved to Tlacotepec, where he took up with another woman, and by whom he had several children. Although Doña Zeferina used to visit her father until he died in the mid-1920s, and although she continued occasionally to see her half-brothers, who still live in Tlacotepec, she showed little interest in the history of her father's family. From her mother's side, however, Doña Zeferina had stories to tell that dated back to the mid-1800s, to the days of her great grandparents.

Of all her great grandparents, Doña Zeferina knew only her maternal grandmother's mother, Francisca Perez, and she did not know this woman well. Doña Francisca lived until Doña Zeferina was about eleven, but the old woman did not inhabit the same house as Zeferina and clearly did not make much of an impression on the young girl. What Doña Zeferina did know about life in Hueyapan during her great grandmother's day she learned secondhand from her grandmother and her mother. She was told, for example, that people then were much bigger than they are today. Doña Zeferina's very own great grandfather, Rafael Crisantos, was supposed to have been so enormous that he would eat half a sheep and a dozen eggs at one meal. His daughters used to take turns making *tortillas* for their father, who could eat an entire basketful in one sitting. Nahuatl was spoken almost exclusively in those days. However, the grammar and the vocabulary had already become considerably mixed with Spanish, as they are today. Furthermore, many people did not have last names then; however, Doña Zeferina was quick to add, their first names were always Spanish ones.

In her great grandparents' day Hueyapan had a resident priest and Catholic ritual was more elaborate than it is now. Doña Zeferina's mother told her that on Good Friday, for example, men used to march in processions, carrying prickly pear cacti on their bare backs to share in the agony of Christ. They also wore chains around their feet, causing severe bleeding. Women wore *xincueites* with no slips. Men dressed in *calzones* that had been fashioned out of one piece of fabric. The unfitted cloth was held together by a belt wrapped around the waist. Instead of shirts, they wore wool *serapes*, which were sewn up the sides. Neither men nor women wore shoes or sandals.

mythology

Doña Zeferina also heard some fanciful stories about the old days when her great grandparents were young. First of all, people were very rich. If someone wanted to borrow money he did so by the basketful, not by just a few coins. Her great grandfather Don Manuel Sardinias had a bull's skin that was filled with silver.

It seems that there was a mountain on the outskirts of Hueyapan that in those days had special powers. It was known as *El Encanto* (The Enchantment). At midnight every New Year's Eve one side of the mountain would open, giving passage into a huge cavern. Hueyapeños would enter the mountain to gather up the magical kernels of corn found there. Every corn kernel would turn miraculously into a silver coin, it was said. The mountain would remain open only for a very few hours. Once a man did not leave in time and was closed up in the cavern for an entire year. When the mountain opened again on the following New Year's Eve the villagers found the man still alive and in perfectly good health. He said that it felt as though very little time had actually elapsed between the moment he had been shut in the mountain and the return of his fellow Hueyapeños.

Great grandfather Don Manuel Sardinias bought some land on what is now Calle Morelos.[1] Three generations later Doña Zeferina inherited part of this original purchase. In Don Manuel's time, however, the family had enough land so that he did not have to split this particular plot among his heirs. Instead he passed it down in its entirety to Doña Zeferina's grandfather, Don Dionisio Sardinias, who was his eldest son.

Doña Zeferina's grandparents, Don Dionisio and Doña María, had three children. Soon after their third child was born their life together was unexpectedly interrupted. Don Dionisio was sent to jail in Cuautla for seventeen years. It seems that Don Dionisio had been one of the local *comandantes* (policemen) in

---

1. Originally there were no official street names in Hueyapan. People identified the location of a house by house names alone. The house Don Manuel built was known as Hueyapalcalco (the big house made out of wooden slats). It was so called because the house was constructed out of wood, not adobe. The original plot included land that today belongs to Don Juan Maya, who lives on one side of Doña Zeferina, and to Don Reyes Maya, Don Juan's brother, who lives on the other side.

the pueblo. One day he learned that a Hueyapeño had robbed some livestock from a female cousin of his. He went to see this cousin and she told him who had stolen the animals. The *coman-dante* then ambushed the allegedly guilty man in a gorge and murdered him.

A woman happened to see Don Dionisio kill the man and reported the event to other village authorities. They in turn alerted federal troops, and soldiers came to Hueyapan to take Don Dionisio away. He was sentenced to twenty years in the Cuautla prison. So that they would not forget their father, Doña María would take the children to Cuautla to visit Don Dionisio. Then, when Pablo Escandón became governor of Morelos in 1909,[2] three years before Don Dionisio's term would have been up, the Hueyapeño, together with all the other prisoners in the Cuautla jail, was freed. After being released, however, the poor man lived only another five years.

Since her grandfather left jail when she was four and died by the time she was nine, Doña Zeferina did not know Don Dionisio well. Her grandmother, Doña María, however, who did not die until 1937, when Doña Zeferina herself was a woman of thirty-two, made a great impression on the young girl. Listening to Doña Zeferina reminisce about her childhood, one gets the impression that this grandmother had more influence on Doña Zeferina than even her own mother.

Doña Zeferina had nothing but the greatest admiration for Doña María, whom she described as having been from another "race"—with dark skin and beautiful light hair. Doña María did not wear a *xincueite* because her husband did not want her or his daughters to dress like "Indians." On the other hand, although by this time some of the villagers wore sandals, Doña María preferred to walk about in bare feet. Doña Zeferina remembers that she once gave her grandmother a pair of agave-fiber sandals and the old woman carefully put them away, saying that she would save the sandals to wear when she died and would have to meet her Maker. For everyday purposes she continued to walk barefoot, carrying as many as twenty-five liters of corn on her

2. J. Womack, *Zapata and the Mexican Revolution* (New York, 1970), p. 36.

back for very long distances. Today people cannot even manage ten, Doña Zeferina said.

Once Don Dionisio had been put in jail, Doña Zeferina's grandmother was left with the burden of supporting the family by herself. Therefore, she began to sell *pulque* on market days in nearby villages. Even when she was quite an old woman, Doña María still traveled about, vending this alcoholic beverage. By the time Doña Zeferina was ten she was taken along to accompany her grandmother on these strenuous selling trips. Doña Zeferina remembers that on the days they went to sell *pulque*, Doña María would rise at 3:00 in the morning and go out alone into the fields to collect the juice from the century plant. People would always ask her whether she was afraid to wander about the countryside by herself in the dark. She would reply, "Why should I be scared? I have my dogs and my machete. If somebody attacks me, my dogs will protect me, and if an animal should jump my dogs, I can help them with my machete."

Doña Zeferina's mother, Doña Jacoba, settled down with a local Hueyapan man by the name of José Ocampo. In 1907, two years after Zeferina was born, Don José abandoned his woman. Doña Jacoba, therefore, returned with her daughter to her parents' home and resided there with her mother; her father was still in jail.

About a year later Doña Jacoba accepted another companion, Don Lucio Barreto. This man, who was from the lowland community of Jantetelco, wanted Doña Jacoba to move to his pueblo and set up house there. Doña Jacoba refused to do so, and the two never really lived together for any length of time. Don Lucio would simply come to Hueyapan when he could leave his lands for a few days and visit his woman in her parents' home. Over the years the couple had five children (three of whom died in infancy), and Don Lucio adopted Zeferina, giving the child his patronym so that she would not be different from the other children in the house. Don Lucio died in 1922, just after Doña Zeferina was married.

Like Doña María, Doña Jacoba also had to support her children virtually without the help of a man. She found that she could make a reasonable living as a seamstress and purchased the first pedal-operated Singer sewing machine to be owned by anybody for miles around. As her reputation spread rapidly, people would come from the many villages surrounding Hueyapan to commission her skills. Doña Jacoba tried to encourage her daughter to become a seamstress, but Doña Zeferina preferred the life her grandmother led as a merchant. Thus when the time came to make a decision, Zeferina chose to travel from village to village, selling meat, eggs, fruit and *pulque*.

Since she was growing up during the Mexican Revolution (1910-1920), Doña Zeferina's schooling was extremely poor. Nevertheless, she did have one excellent teacher. This was Maestro Eligio, the son of the man who had founded the Hueyapan school in the 1870s. From the Maestro she learned history, most of which she never forgot. Doña Zeferina claimed that what the children now get in secondary school, she received in the three years of primary-school education she was lucky enough to have. Although a good student in history, Doña Zeferina said she was not very fast in arithmetic. Not until she became a merchant and had a practical use for numbers did she learn how to add, subtract and multiply with ease. As for division, she said she never did master this very well.

As a child Doña Zeferina was not permitted to go out of the house very much. It was too dangerous. Her mother bought Zeferina a prayer book and the young girl spent much of her free time reading and memorizing prayers. She also managed to borrow a book of fairy tales from Maestro Eligio and enthusiastically committed to memory everything she set her eyes on. Today Doña Zeferina is a wonderful storyteller and delights in recalling the adventures of princesses and kings of foreign lands for her grandchildren.

In 1914, when Doña Zeferina was just nine, her mother sent the child away to live with an aunt in Tlacotepec. Zeferina stayed there nearly a year and often wonders now what her life would have been like had she been a little older when she lived in Tlacotepec and, consequently, had met a man and settled down there permanently.

In 1917, when she was twelve years old, Doña Zeferina was again sent elsewhere to live for awhile, this time to Mexico City, where she spent a year and a half in the home of her godmother. Following the tradition of selecting a godparent who would be in the social and economic position to help his or her godchild at a future date, Doña Jacoba had asked a school teacher who was working in the village at the time to officiate at the baptism of little Zeferina. The teacher soon left Hueyapan, married and settled down in her native Mexico City. Then during the Revolution, when the hardships of everyday life made each mouth to feed an enormous burden, Doña Jacoba called on Zeferina's godmother to keep the child for a period of time.

Doña Zeferina said that she enjoyed her stay in Mexico City very much and that she was treated like a member of the family. Most likely, however, her status was more like that of a maid or servant's helper. Although the family was undoubtedly very nice to her, the way Doña Zeferina described her experiences in the house suggests that she was considered to be another domestic. Furthermore, many years later Doña Zeferina did work as a servant in the house of her godmother's sister.

Doña Zeferina also spent a number of the war years in Hueyapan. Like the other villagers, she endured some terrifying experiences during this time. Here, in her own words, is one of the most dramatic incidents she lived through:

Maestra,[3] I am going to tell you about what happened to me during the time of Zapata's war. Well . . . we were children then. I was about thirteen years old. In those days, everybody used to run away. The bells would ring to announce that soldiers were coming and everybody would run away. People used to run because if government troops came, they killed villagers and if the Zapatistas —you know, the rebels—came, they killed the villagers too. So, we would not wait for either of them. It was better to run. Finally, to bring an end to the war, a lot of government troops came to Hueyapan. One general came via Tetela. Another came from the hills we call the Monte. Another came from Tochimilco, Puebla. And still another came from this other place in Puebla called San Marcos. In this way, the five exits of the pueblo were closed off by government troops, so that the villagers couldn't escape.

---

3. Doña Zeferina and almost everybody else in Hueyapan used to call me "Maestra." Although she came to introduce me to others as her American daughter, she would still, out of habit, address me as "Maestra."

Well, here in the house, lived an uncle of mine and he killed a pig. And this pig was big, fat and everything. I had my brothers. We were four, no more, and then my *mamá* . . . the poor thing, since she was pregnant she couldn't run. Also she still had to dismantle the sewing machine. She had to carry the arm of the sewing machine, the one that I still have. Well, I carried my youngest brother. And since it upset me to leave the meat, I grabbed a few pieces of meat, *xales, chicharón*,[4] and a bag of *tortillas*. And in this way I took off, carrying the child on my back. I was carrying my little brother who was Quico's age, about two or three. The government soliders were right behind me. And rebels were in front. Then the rebels took a path like this [she points to the left] and disappeared. And I took one towards the gorge [to the right] and the government troops followed me. They thought that I was the rebels' woman, or who knows what they thought. They used foul language with me, Maestra: "Stop, you daughter of a so-and-so!" And bullets whizzed by and more bullets. And then a bullet passed by my little brother's head and made a hole in his hat. But we weren't hurt. And when I got to the bottom of the gorge, I took this little path in order to hide myself, my brother and the food. In this path I leave everything: meat, *tortillas, xales, chicharones*—I leave everything there. And I wait until that "baldy"[5] who had been following me went by. And then I could hear that all the soldiers had left the gorge and gone over to the other side. Since everything is so quiet, you can hear everything. Over there they were breaking windows and well . . . it was ugly. I stayed hidden, but I heard that now they were gone. So I say to my brother, "You'd better not cry, because if you cry, they'll kill us. Don't cry."

I pick him up again and I travel around the entire gorge. Who knows where we ended up, Maestra. Afterwards, I didn't recognize the area. And I didn't want to go down into the gorge again. I say, "Now, where can I go? There are nothing but gorges and more gorges. I just won't go." So I wait there. I was there awhile and I was crying because I was scared. But then two men I know appear. One was Don Francisco Bautista and the other, who is still alive, was Don Estebán Maya. I see them and since I know them, I speak to them.

"Where are you going?"

---

4. *Xales* and *chicharón* are specially fried pieces of pork skin.
5. "Baldy" or *peletón* is one of the derogatory terms used by the peasants for government soldiers.

"We're going over there now, back to the pueblo. Why are you crying?"

"Because I don't know how to return."

"Let's go. Don't cry now, child. Let's go." So they take me back and as we are walking, they say, "The government troops have gone now. The bastards have gone."

We come to the spot where we were hiding before and I say, "I'll go see if the meat is still there." So I go down the gorge again and take the same little path. And there it is! There is the meat, the *xales* . . . everything. So I pick up the food once again and I return to the pueblo. I go to find my *mamá* who, I am told, is now in Don Miguel's house. There I find her and she is crying because they told her that they had killed us, that who knows what. I say to her,"But who could have seen that they killed us when nobody was there? No, here we are. And you, how did you defend yourself?"

"Well . . . I never even left," she says. "The government troops caught me." They put my *mamá* in the house of a certain man whose name was Don Pedro Escobar. It is said that all the people caught were simply put there. But nothing, absolutely nothing happened to my *mamá*. Well, then we went home.

And that is what happened to me during that period . . . when I was a girl. It was like that, all of it true; I saw it. We suffered many things during that time, Maestra.

Once Doña Jacoba's children had grown up, the mother divided the Calle Morelos plot among her three surviving heirs. Until their mother died in 1947, Doña Zeferina and her maternal half-brothers Don Benjamín and Don Falconériz remained together on the land. Soon after Doña Jacoba's death, however, the two men married, and sold their shares of the land to the Maya Cortés brothers; Don Benjamín moved to Cuautla and Don Falconériz moved to Tetela. Several years later the two half-brothers returned to Hueyapan to try to force Doña Zeferina at gunpoint to give up her part of the inheritance. Doña Zeferina's son Rafael, who by this time was a grown man, defended his mother against her two half-brothers. Since then Doña Zeferina has had virtually nothing to do with Don Benjamín and Don Falconériz.

In 1922, when she was seventeen years old, Doña Zeferina married Don Felipe Vargas. She was the first in her family to have an official wedding with both church and civil ceremonies.

The other relatives had simply lived together in free union, without going to the expense of having a formal ritual. Then, as now, to have a religious wedding was costly and quite prestigious.

Doña Zeferina told me that her mother tried to discourage the marriage, warning her daughter that as a wife she would have to work very hard. Although she refused to listen to Doña Jacoba, once she was married Doña Zeferina was sorry. Every few days she had to rise at 4:00 A.M. to grind corn for her husband's *tortillas*. Don Felipe would then go to work in the fields, staying away two or three days at a time. When he returned, Doña Zeferina would again have to serve her husband and work long hours.

After five years of marriage, Doña Zeferina simply refused to get up early to make her husband's *tortillas*. She had infants by this time, she complained, and she objected to being worked so hard. Defiantly she told her husband to find somebody else to make his *tortillas,* and so Don Felipe asked his sister, promising to give her presents if she accepted the work. Although this sister made Don Felipe's *tortillas* for a number of years, she never received a thing from her brother, Doña Zeferina commented.

Doña Zeferina and Don Felipe had four children: Zeferino, Rosalía, Rafael and Raúl. Their son Zeferino, who died when he was seven years old, was born with three testicles and everybody believed that, had he lived, he would have grown into one and a half men. Little Zeferino, people said, was part of the "race" of Doña Zeferina's great grandfather Rafael Crisantos. (Although I never heard that Don Rafael had had three testicles, he was certainly known, as we have already seen, for having been an enormous man.)

Don Felipe and Doña Zeferina's daughter Rosalía died when she was five. Then, in 1931, a few years after their fourth child was born, Don Felipe passed away. He and Doña Zeferina had been married about nine years.

Almost immediately after her husband's death, Doña Zeferina, who was twenty-six by this time, left her children in the care of her mother and went to Cuernavaca to work as a maid in the house of her godmother's sister. Then she spent another two years working in Mexico City in three different households. She

importance of parentage

finally returned to Hueyapan, however, for she found it distasteful to be in a position in which others had the right to order her about. "After all," Doña Zeferina told me, "I was not an orphan and did not have to endure such treatment."

Although she complained, Doña Zeferina also managed to make the most out of her life as a maid and delighted in her ability to cheat her mistresses. She used to enjoy retelling the experiences she had in the home of one family particularly. Each time she started the story, Doña Zeferina would chuckle in her characteristic way, shake her head and say to me, "*Yo soy bien canija, Maestra*" ("I can be a sneaky bitch, Maestra"). The mistress of this house was notorious for being "mean." No maid lasted longer than a month, but Doña Zeferina stayed six. Of great significance to Doña Zeferina was the fact that this family was supposed to be very rich, a rumor that Doña Zeferina confirmed for herself one day when she saw the man of the house open up a huge box filled to the brim with money.

The mistress used to get up very late in the morning, around 9:00 or 10:00. Doña Zeferina was expected to wait for her to rise and serve the woman her breakfast before she herself had anything to eat. Doña Zeferina, however, would boil a pot of milk, theoretically for her mistress, add sugar and then help herself to a huge glassful before the lady of the house had gotten up. So that her "sneak-serving" would go unnoticed, Doña Zeferina would then add to the remaining milk a glass of water, equal to the amount of milk she had taken out. While the woman slept on, Doña Zeferina would get the morning chores done, set the table for her mistress' breakfast and be ready for any extra tasks that her mistress might find for her to do when she finally made her morning appearance. Since she had already helped herself to a hearty breakfast, Doña Zeferina would no longer be hungry. This used to puzzle her mistress, who would ask Doña Zeferina how it was that she was so nice and fat while she never seemed to eat. Doña Zeferina would smile to herself and reply to her mistress that she ate while out at the market.

This "mean" mistress had an irksome habit. She would wait until it was very late before telling the maid to go to the market to purchase some food for the afternoon meal. The maid would be expected to rush out at the last minute and still be able to have everything prepared at the regular luncheon hour. Therefore, instead of waiting for the mistress to tell her what to do, or for the money to do it with, Doña Zeferina would go to a store where she was well known and buy the food for the meal at a reasonable hour, using her own money for the purchases. Thus, by the time the mistress would just begin to think about lunch, everything would be ready. Doña Zeferina commented that her mistress liked her very much because she was so efficient and, Doña Zeferina added, the lady was also very prompt about reimbursing her.

In 1935, about a year after returning from Mexico City, Doña Zeferina again left her children with her mother and went to join her maternal half-brothers Falconériz and Benjamín in San Juan Ahuehueyo, a ranch in the lowlands, where the two men were working as peons. The *rancho* was located south of Hueyapan, near Tepalcingo. Doña Zeferina went there to keep house for her brothers, who were still bachelors at this time, and to make a bit of money by doing laundry for other peons.

Her stay in San Juan Ahuehueyo was rather adventurous. From the beginning Doña Zeferina knew that she did not want to remain in the lowlands, so far from Hueyapan. While she was there, however, she wanted to make as much money as possible. Thus, almost every day Doña Zeferina, accompanied by a few other women, would take laundry down to a little stream located a good distance from the house.

One morning Doña Zeferina went to do the wash alone, which was a dangerous thing to do. A man stopped her on the road and told her that he wanted her to be his woman. If she would not agree to his proposal peaceably, he would take her by force. Although she had told everybody in San Juan Ahuehueyo that she was no longer a *señorita* and that she had children back in Hueyapan, several men still wanted to court her. Faced with this present threat, Doña Zeferina coyly told the man that she would be happy to marry him, but she insisted on a proper ceremony. First he would have to go to Hueyapan and ask Doña Zeferina's mother for her daughter's hand. The man agreed, although he said he had heard that Doña Zeferina was a "sly wench" and could not be trusted. He warned her that she had better keep her promise. Doña Zeferina reassured him and he left without compromising her.

When Doña Zeferina's brothers heard what had happened they got very upset. They told their sister that she would have to stay in San Juan Ahuehueyo and settle down with this man. Doña Zeferina, however, refused and told her brothers that they would just have to find a way to get her out of there. At first they thought they would dress her up like a man and ride her out on a horse at night to a nearby train station, Estación de Salitre, where trains passed by for Puebla and Mexico City. But since they did not have the money for a train ticket, the brothers decided to accompany their half-sister on foot all the way back to Hueyapan.

Doña Zeferina had caught malaria while in San Juan Ahuehueyo and was suffering from severe fever attacks. With her anxieties about the imminent escape, these attacks worsened. Although she was terribly uncomfortable, she said, at least the malaria served as an excuse for her not to attend a dance that was held a few days before she left. Had she gone, she undoubtedly would have been abducted by her amorous admirer.

Finally the big day arrived. Doña Zeferina remembered that it was a Thursday, August 14. Her brothers told her to sell all the corn they had so that they would have some spending money. She was to tell absolutely nobody that she was leaving. When people asked her why she was selling the corn, Doña Zeferina replied that with her frequent attacks of malaria she was unable to grind the maize, and consequently her brothers had decided to buy their *tortillas*.

Later that evening one of the brothers checked to see whether anybody was still up and about. When things seemed quiet, they stealthily left. At one point they had a scare, as some men on horses passed them on the road. Doña Zeferina was hidden behind some bushes until the coast was again clear. By 1:00 A.M. they had gotten as far as Jalostoc. There lived a Hueyapan woman whom they knew well. They went to her house to freshen up and to ask the woman to keep their secret. If any men come by looking for Doña Zeferina, the woman should tell them that Zeferina had not passed through. By 7:00 A.M. they had reached Tlacotepec. Too exhausted to continue, Doña Zeferina decided to remain in this village for the day and enjoy the fiesta that was in progress in celebration of the Day of the Ascension of Mary. Her brothers, however, continued on to Hueyapan to let their mother know what had happened and to bring back a donkey for their sister. Thus, on the following day (August 16), Don Falconériz and Don Benjamín returned to Tlacotepec and accompanied their sister home.

In San Juan Ahuehueyo some men did come looking for Doña Zeferina on the morning of August 15, but it was too late. Actually, Doña Zeferina and the enamored peon from San Juan Ahuehueyo corresponded for a while after this episode, but nothing ever came of the "romance." As Doña Zeferina put it, if the man had been worth anything, which she had doubted from the start, he would have come for her, all the way up to Hueyapan.

In 1936 Doña Zeferina began living in free union with Don Rosalio Noceda, a local Hueyapeño. They settled down in Doña Zeferina's home and they had one child, a boy named Ernestino. A year later Don Rosalio died, leaving Doña Zeferina twice widowed.

Since her two surviving children by her first marriage were now old enough to accompany her on long trips, the recently widowed Doña Zeferina began to work as a merchant, the trade her grandmother had trained her for. She depended on her oldest son Rafael in particular to help her sell *pulque*, eggs, fruit and meat. From the time Rafael was nine Doña Zeferina took him out of school several days a week so that the boy could keep her company over the lonely and rugged terrain that separated one community from the next in this region. Then when he was about fourteen, Rafael began to help carry loads as well. Doña Zeferina would make the following rounds in those days. On Sundays she would take 60 to 80 liters of *pulque* to Zacualpan, twenty kilometers away, where she would sell a mugful for fifteen *centavos*. Then on Mondays she would go to Atlixco (a small city in Puebla) to sell eggs. She said she carried 300 eggs on her back and Rafael carried 200. They would leave Hueyapan for Atlixco at 5:00 A.M. and arrive there around 2:00 or 3:00 P.M. The eggs were

Doña Zeferina (center) and her children by three unions. Clockwise from top left: Rafael, Angelina, Ernestino and Raúl. Raúl was killed around 1948, and Ernestino moved to Cuernavaca about 1952. This formal portrait, a composite of photographs taken at different times, hangs over Rafael and Juana's bed. (Photo by B. Weiss.)

bought at five *centavos* each and sold at ten. Then they would spend the night in Atlixco and return home on the following day. On Thursdays the two would sell pears, peaches and avocados in Yecapistla. Doña Zeferina bought the fruit at ten *pesos* per hundred and sold them at fifteen to twenty *pesos* per hundred. She and her son would leave Hueyapan on Wednesdays at noon and arrive in Yecapistla by 6:00 in the evening. They would spend the night there and be ready to sell in the market early on Thursday mornings. Then on Saturdays Doña Zeferina and Rafael—or sometimes just Rafael and his younger brother Raúl—would go to Ocuituco, about a four-hour walk each way, to buy meat that would be sold in the village throughout the five *barrios* by Doña Zeferina's mother.

Although Doña Zeferina was forced to keep Rafael out of school a good deal, she always saw to it that he studied. When mother and son returned to Hueyapan after their long and exhausting trips, Rafael would sit down and do the lessons he had missed. Since he was extremely quick, he always did well on his exams, despite his poor attendance record.

Doña Zeferina continued to support herself and her family as a traveling merchant until the Hueyapan market opened up in the early 1960s. Then she began to sell plastic toys, kitchenware, dried chiles and other condiments. Most of her merchandise is presently purchased in Mexico City. Once every three months Doña Zeferina and Maestro Rafael make a trip into the city to replenish her stock.

In addition to selling, Doña Zeferina also makes money by serving as one of the village's local healers. Traditionally it is said that to be gifted in the art of healing, an individual has to have had the experience of returning from the dead. Doña Zeferina has come back to life twice, she told me, and that is why she "knows how to heal."

The first time she returned from the dead occurred when Doña Zeferina was a baby, too young to remember the incident. Nevertheless, she knows it took place because her mother told her about it. Apparently, when Zeferina was about one year old she caught a serious case of whooping cough. Her mother, who was not one to mourn the death of a young child, decided rather unemotionally that her daughter had died and lit a candle for the child. One of Doña Zeferina's aunts happened to visit the house and saw that Doña Jacoba had given her daughter up for dead before she really was dead. The aunt, therefore, took little Zeferina in her arms, rubbed the baby's body and "brought the child back to life."

The second time Doña Zeferina returned from the dead took place soon after she had given birth to one of her children. While taking a steam bath in the *temascal*, she fainted. Doña Zeferina believes that she was out for about an hour. During that time, she dreamed that she was entering a large church. The doors opened wide to receive her. The only concern Doña Zeferina had as she was going in was that she did not have her sandals on. She knew she was about to meet her Maker and she was bothered by the fact that she was barefoot at such an important moment. She then woke up and realized that she must have been at the Gates of Heaven.

For years Doña Zeferina cured people with herbs and eggs, using what was known as the "rustic" technique. Then when the government nurses came to Hueyapan in 1945, Doña Zeferina went to classes to learn how to give injections. Since that time she has changed over almost entirely to "modern" methods of curing.

The government nurses were very impressed with Doña Zeferina because she was not afraid of blood or of other people's diseases. They wanted to send her to Mexico City to be trained properly as a nurse. Although she wished that she could go, this was impossible, for she had to stay home with her children; her mother was old and sick by now and could no longer care for the grandchildren. In Hueyapan Doña Zeferina did learn how to give intermuscular and intravenous injections as well as how to bandage wounds. She already knew how to deliver babies by the rustic technique.

In addition to the everyday difficulties of supporting a family without the help of a husband, Doña Zeferina had to defend herself against pillaging soldiers who were still wandering around the countryside. Although the Mexican Revolution had officially ended in 1920, agrarian fighters were still organizing peasants in the area as late as the 1930s. One latter-day Zapatista who was stirring up the highlands of Morelos was Enrique Rodriguez, nicknamed Tallarín (The Noodle). During the years 1936-1938, Tallarín and his followers descended on a number of small villages and killed local government officials, such as tax collectors, school teachers and others who were paid by the state. Tallarín had many sympathizers in Hueyapan, and as a result the pueblo became embroiled in a new wave of violence, reminiscent of the Mexican Revolution.

Since Doña Zeferina was a grown woman in the 1930s, she remembered more from this period than she did from the "real" Revolution. Furthermore, the experiences she had at this later date were considerably more dramatic. One incident she enjoyed recalling is the following:

> Maestra, I am going to tell you a story that took place during the time of Tallarín. Well, at home, Rafael—the one who is now a school teacher—was a child. He was about fourteen years old. In those days, I used to take *pulque* to Zacualpan to sell. Every week, Maestra, I went to Zacualpan. However, since I didn't know how to use pack animals . . . I didn't know how to load up a burro . . . well, I used to look for somebody who did. So I would go to my neighbor Refugio Barrios' house. He's still alive by the way. One day, I went to see him and I say, "Listen, come pack up the burros and accompany me because I am going to Zacualpan."
>
> He says, "Sure, let's go." Well, he lives just over there, nearby, so he comes over and loads up the animals.
>
> While we were getting ready, they were ringing and ringing the bells in the plaza, calling people together. And I say to my neighbor, "Hey, what's going on? It must be a robbery."
>
> "Who knows," he says. "There are a lot of people in the plaza."
>
> Since we live right off the plaza, you could see the people there. But, Maestra, I didn't get scared, or think things like that. I thought it was just a robbery, that people were chasing animals that had been robbed from them. Around here, that's how it's done. When there's a robbery in a pueblo, people come asking for help from other pueblos. They ring the bells and then people gather and go out after the thieves. Around here we call them "thieves"—you know, people who rob. Elsewhere they call them "crooks" or whatever.

Well, Maestra, I left. And I passed a lot of people, really a lot. However, I didn't pay any attention to them. I was going to sell in Zacualpan.

Well, this fellow Tallarín had gone to Ocuituco. He and his men went there to get none other than the tax collector; because in that time they were pursuing all those who belonged to the government—for example, school teachers and tax collectors. Tallarín used to kill all types of government people. In Hueyapan he did not kill even one school teacher, but elsewhere he killed them. Well, in Ocuituco they surprised the tax collector who was dressed in nothing more than his underwear. They wouldn't even let the poor man put on his pants. Dressed like that, they brought him to Hueyapan. But since I'd gone by then, I didn't see him.

Then when I got to the place in the road that we call Las Mesas, I met some people, including a brother-in-law of mine. He says, "Are you going to Zacualpan?"

I say, "Yes."

He says, "They say Tallarín is up there in Hueyapan."

I say, "Really?"

He says, "Well, it's true. There are a lot of people there and it's Tallarín. They have the tax collector also. What do you think is going to happen?"

I say, "Well, we're going to Zacualpan anyway. We'll wait to see what happens at the pueblo." And we continued on our way. I wanted to go to Zacualpan to get some snacks to give out on Christmas Eve. I wasn't scared.

Then after we were there in Zacualpan, other Hueyapeños arrive. You see, people would arrive every few minutes; for in those days, there was no bus and when we walked, some would leave early, others later. In short, people came and went. Some Hueyapeños came over to tell me that they killed the tax collector up there in the village.

"What, they were going to kill him?"

"Yes," they said.

This was done right near the plaza in a place called Tecaxtila. And that was that. My fellow villagers say, "Now who knows what's going to happen to the pueblo, now that they came and did this, now that they came and implicated us."

Since they were chasing Tallarín, in a little while a lot of government troops arrive in Zacualpan—and I mean a lot of them, Maestra. It was about 2:00 in the afternoon. And there . . . well . . . since I sell *pulque*, they came over to drink with me. One soldier says to me, "Where did you bring this *pulque* from?"

I say, "From Hueyapan."

"Is it true that Tallarín is there?"

"It's true. He's there."

"And are there a lot of men with him?"

"Well, they say there are no fewer than 500."

The government soldier says, "Mother of God, we'd better not go!" And with that they didn't go either, Maestra. Instead, they took the road leading to Ocuituco and Yecapistla. I told them that they should go to Hueyapan.

I said, "Come on. You have a lot of men also. Get it over with once and for all." But no, they didn't go, Maestra.

We decided not to go back either. We said to ourselves, "All right now, and if we leave and meet Tallarín on the road he can hurt us; or if we meet up with the government troops—since they are furious because the tax collector was killed—well, something might happen to us on the road. We'd better not go; we'd better stay here in Zacualpan."

This was a 22nd of December. We didn't get back to Hueyapan until the 23rd. And as we were returning, we met more people. They say, "Well, it's true. It took place. They've carried away the dead man now. People from Ocuituco came and took him away." By the time we got home, nothing more had happened. Neither government troops nor the rebels came.

Not until two weeks later, Maestra, did the government troops arrive. And a lot of them came. The first thing they did was to arrest the village *ayudante*. At the time Vicente Hernandez, who was still a very young man, was the *ayudante*. Now he is no longer alive. Well, the soldiers got him and a few other *señores* and tied them up in the plaza. And they were going to kill them. Well, the villagers gathered around and managed to delay the execution. Then the soldiers took these men to Tetela, Maestra. They took them over there to shoot them.

But God was looking out for them and that Vicente Hernandez was a very clever man, very . . . how shall I say . . . well, he did not get scared. He was not frightened because they said they were going to kill him. He was not like that. If they were going to kill him, well, that's the way it was going to be.

So he said to the general, "I, General, yes, I am going to die.

But let me, if you would, first say good-bye to the governor of the state and also to this other person I know in Mexico City who will inform the president that the *ayudante* of Hueyapan is no longer living . . . that they are going to kill him."

And after that, they didn't kill him, Maestra. He called and everything [communicating by telegraph] and then they didn't do anything to him. So the Hueyapeños returned to the pueblo. The soldiers let them go and the government troops also went away.

About a week later, *again* government troops arrive—a lot of them. They were still angry . . . well . . . because that man, the tax collector, was killed. Word was sent around that in all houses food should be prepared so that there would be something for the government troops to eat. The food was not to be given away, but sold: "Make *tortillas*, make beans, make chile sauce, make rice. Prepare things so that when they come, they can be fed." The soldiers arrived and about fifteen of them came to eat at my house.

Then, the *comandante* came to see me—our *ayudante* sent him—to tell me to prepare food for ten big shots—you know, the most important ones: generals and majors and captains and . . . well . . . people of that sort. But since I was selling to the regular soldiers, my kitchen was filled with people. And . . . well, I didn't pay any attention to the *comandante's* orders. I say to myself, "There are so many women selling. Let some of the others take care of these men. I'm not going to do it." And so I did nothing about it.

Then two others came to speak to me. The last one who came was the assistant to the general himself. He said that the general sent him to tell me to make something for him to eat. I reply, "Tell the general that I can't do it because I have so many here to feed already. I have so many and they are eating."

Then in no time the general arrives. Since the plaza is so close, he did not take even ten minutes. He is a big gray-haired man and he has a big pistol in his hand. He says, "Does Señora So-and-so live here?"

And I go out and I say to him, "Yes, My General, at your service."

"And why, daughter of the fucked one, don't you want to feed me?"

"*Ahi,* My General, it is not that I don't want to. Come in and see for yourself how it is here. I *am* feeding people."

When they see their general enter, all the soldiers get up and he says to them, "You can go elsewhere to find something to eat." And then he looks at his watch. "I am coming back to eat at such and such an hour. And Mother . . . there better be something here!"

And I, Maestra, to be sure, I am not easily frightened. I am . . . well . . . brave or I don't know what you call it. So I follow him. "My General, and if I am to make this meal, where will I get money to do so? You chased out those who were going to pay me. Now the soldiers won't pay me. How will I manage?"

Well, my God, if the general doesn't come back and take out his money and give me about 100 *pesos*. "Let's see what you can do with this!" For ten people, Maestra, can you believe it? And he pointed to his watch: "By such and such time!"

Well, since I'm clever and also I am not afraid, I run to the house of a *señor* who has a lot of chickens—Don Estebán Robles . . . he's still alive. I go there and I say to him, "Give me, if you would, some twenty-five or forty eggs, because I am going to make a meal for those who've come. They are a rough bunch." So he gives me the eggs. Then at Don Timoteo's place I was given more. I brought back everything—lard, chile sauce, a huge pot and in short . . . well, what do you expect? There were so many people to feed.

But no *tortillas*! I go to see the *ayudante*. I say to him, "What about the *tortillas*? I can't prepare the meal and the *tortillas* too." Well, immediately he sent me some women and they helped me. Everything was all right then.

After the meal, because the general was angry with me for not taking account of him or for not wanting to feed him, he says to me, "Now we ate. We'll return for supper later and we want a hen . . . or perhaps two. Let's see what you can do." And, Maestra, what could I say to him? I said nothing. So, I go to see a woman whose name is Luisa, but she was asking a high price for the hens. I say to myself, "No, it makes more sense to return and use my own hens." My *mamá* also says that we should use our own. Then, afterwards, if they pay me, fine. And if they don't, I won't lose anything . . . well, I'll lose the hens, but I won't have laid out any money.

We prepared the supper and they came to eat. And that was that. Then the general says, "Tomorrow we'll come to eat early. Again you're going to make us a meal and you're going to make sweetened *tejocotes* [fruit of the Mexican hawthorn]." Maestra, we worked all night long, I and my mother. And well, with such fear, a person continues like a donkey. That's how it was.

After breakfast, they came again to eat at lunch time. And after the mid-day meal . . . after they ate . . . all the officers were very appreciative. Since they were going to leave, they came to notify me of this. They say, "Well, now we're not going to have supper here. We're leaving now. At least you took care of us. Now, how much do we owe you?"

I say to them, "Well, it's up to you. If you feel that things were good, that I served you nicely, then . . . but perhaps you feel I didn't . . . well, depending on how things seemed to you, give me whatever you wish." Maestra, in spite of the fact that they had been so rough with me, now they weren't. They treated me well . . . all of them. One gave me 100 *pesos*; another 80. Almost all of them gave me large bills. And the general himself left me a ten-kilo bag of cheese, a lot of bread, rolls and five kilos of sausage. Well, just a lot of everything. And this was aside from the money. I collected about 600, or at the very least, 500 *pesos*. At this moment I did all right.

But before this I suffered, because they threatened me. If the general hadn't found those soldiers in my kitchen, he would have killed me. Well, so the officers gave me money. Then they said good-bye to me and left. But I suffered, I did, Maestra . . . during that war.

In 1941 Doña Zeferina had a brief affair with a Hueyapeño by the name of Pedro Hernandez. She became pregnant and Don Pedro asked her to settle down with him at his home, but she refused. Her mother was not well and Doña Zeferina did not want to leave the old woman alone. As she herself put it, "I loved my mother more than this man." Don Pedro soon married another woman, but he and Doña Zeferina have remained friends. Doña Zeferina gave birth to a girl whom she named Angelina. Since this was her only daughter, Doña Zeferina explained, she adored the girl.

Soon after Angelina was born Doña Zeferina, accompanied by her two oldest sons, Rafael and Raúl, began to work in the lowlands. For five years they spent June, July, August and December away from Hueyapan, Doña Zeferina serving as a corn grinder and the boys as peons. At times she and her sons would work for different people, which would force the family to live apart, taking shelter in the caves provided for the peons by their own individual patrons.

In 1948, when Doña Zeferina's daughter was six, a five-year-old girl by the name of Julia appeared at the door of the house. Julia was dressed in rags and complained that she had not had anything to eat all day. Angelina asked her mother if they could please feed Julia, and Doña Zeferina invited the child in.

Julia's mother had abandoned her three children and run off with a man. The children were literally left to fend for themselves, sleeping in hay stacks and begging for food. Realizing the pathetic situation the child was in, Doña Zeferina told Julia that she could stay and live with them if she wanted to and that she would be treated like a daughter. There was only one rule: Julia could no longer run about, but had to stay at home and behave like a good girl. Julia accepted the offer and remained with the family until she was grown, at which time Doña Zeferina took her to Cuernavaca to help her find work.[6]

In 1952, when Angelina was ten years old, Doña Zeferina went to live with Don José Flores, a widower who had a house in the San Andrés Barrio. Angelina and Julia were left behind in the care of Rafael and his first wife in the Calle Morelos home. By this time Raúl was dead, having been murdered in a drunken brawl, and Ernestino was in boarding school, on scholarship, in the state of Puebla. Doña Zeferina would return to the family house daily to make sure that everything was going well. In the following year she and Don José were married by the church and moved down to Doña Zeferina's place permanently. They changed residences, Doña Zeferina explained, because she could not stand living so far away from the plaza, way up in the hills. Her regular patients stopped coming to her and, furthermore, she simply felt out of things. Although he agreed to the arrangement and even sold land and livestock in order to have some capital to

---

6. Julia did not want to work, however, and almost immediately found a man and began to have a family. She and her common-law husband, a migrant worker from Guerrero, have four children and live today in the worst slums of Cuernavaca, just off the railroad tracks.

Doña Zeferina and Don José by the storeroom. Doña Zeferina holds a book of medicinal cures given to her by a school teacher. (Photo by B. Weiss.)

invest in Doña Zeferina's home, Don José was never entirely comfortable there. It still remained his woman's place, he told me, and not his.

In November 1970 Don José fell off the roof of a bus in the plaza as he was trying to lower a basket of fruit from the rack. The poor man was drunk at the time and hit his head on the ground. A few hours later he died. Doña Zeferina, again a widow, was left with her children and by now numerous grandchildren. To this day, as in the past, her entire family continues to depend on the old woman for financial and emotional support.

THE HISTORY OF HUEYAPAN

3

The Village before 1900

According to Fray Diego Durán, one of the earliest Spanish chroniclers of Mexico, Hueyapan was originally settled by the people of Xochimilco in 902 A.D.[1] Then between the years 1522 and 1524 the Spanish conquered the village.[2] Durán writes that a Castilian woman by the name of María de Estrada[3] led the Spanish soldiers against the Indians of Hueyapan. This woman joined Cortés and his men on an expedition into the Morelos highlands. One of the soldiers, it is said, suggested to María de Estrada that she ask Cortés for permission to lead the troops in one of the many battles staged against the Indians of the area. This she did, and Cortés reputedly agreed to let her fight the

---

1. Fray Diego Durán, *Historia de los indios de Nueva España y Islas de Tierra Firme*, Vol. II (Mexico City, 1967), p. 21.
2. Durán, p. 573.
3. María de Estrada is mentioned by Bernal Díaz as being the only Castilian woman to have accompanied the Spanish conquerors. See Bernal Díaz, *The Bernal Diaz Chronicles* (Garden City, N.Y., 1956), p. 270.

Hueyapeños. Thus, the story continues, with a sword in one hand and a shield in the other, María de Estrada kicked her horse and raced into combat, calling out to Santiago as she went. A few soldiers followed after her. When the Indians of Hueyapan saw her coming they panicked and fled, hurling themselves blindly into the gorges that surrounded the village. As a result the Spanish took Hueyapan and the neighboring settlement of Tetela with ease.[4]

The historian Martínez-Marín says that Durán's account is probably more fanciful than true, but he agrees that Hueyapan was conquered between the years 1522 and 1524.[5] It is also generally accepted that by no later than 1526 Hueyapan, together with Tetela, was made into a single *encomienda* (land grant) and awarded to María de Estrada's husband, Pedro Sanchez Farfán. When Sanchez Farfán died in 1536 the land remained with María de Estrada, and after she remarried in 1548 it was turned over to her second husband, Alonso Martín Partidor.[6]

In 1558, after Martín Partidor died, there was some dispute about who had rights to these *encomienda* lands and to the Indians living on them. As a result, the case was brought before the Council of the Indies, where it was decided that the lands would be turned over to the government. Hueyapan therefore became part of a *corregimiento*.[7,8] In 1643, as the ethnohistorian P. Gerhard told me, the *corregimiento* was annexed to Cuautla, but still maintained separate jurisdiction. Then in 1784, again according to Gerhard, it was definitively annexed to Cuautla and lost its individual status.

---

4. Durán, p. 573.

5. C. Martínez-Marín, *Tetela del Volcán* (Mexico City, 1968), p. 28.

6. P. Gerhard, "El señorío de Ocuituco, *Tlalocan*, Vol. 6, No. 2 (1970), p. 112.

7. A *corregimiento* was a government-run operation. Whereas the *encomienda* owner was a private person who had received a land grant from the government and who had to pay taxes to the King of Spain, the *corregimiento* belonged to the government and was supervised by a government-paid official.

8. Gerhard, p. 112.

For the Hueyapeños these various administrative changes meant primarily that they were forced to work for different landlords, to till land that used to be their own for a variety of Spaniards representing a number of colonial institutions. At least in this early period the villagers could remain on the land and continue to cultivate crops for their own subsistence. Later, however, probably during the late 1700s, the villagers lost all rights to this land.

According to several villagers, the owners of the Santa Clara Hacienda[9] tricked the Hueyapeños out of the land they had been farming a few hundred years earlier. This event must have taken place sometime after 1784, after the Hueyapan-Tetela *corregimiento* was definitively annexed to Cuautla. Once the area lost its individual jurisdiction, there were no government officials nearby to protect the villagers against the land-hungry *hacendados*.

It seems that the owners of the Santa Clara Hacienda made an agreement with the Hueyapeños that on a certain day the villagers would start to walk from the pueblo's plaza in the direction of the *hacienda* and the *hacendados* would walk from their homes in the lowlands toward the village. Where the two groups met, they would establish a firm boundary, dividing Hueyapan and Santa Clara lands. Since the *hacendados* were rich, the Hueyapeños assumed that they were late risers. The Hueyapeños also counted on the fact that the *hacendados* lived far away and would take a long time to get near the village. The Hueyapeños, therefore, concluded that they themselves did not have to worry about making a very early start. On the specified day, however, the *hacendados* left their homes extremely early and managed to get within a kilometer of the village before they encountered the poorly organized Hueyapan party. The villagers did not get their

---

9. *Hacienda* land is private land, purchased independently by the owner who is called the *hacendado*. Unlike the *encomienda*, the *hacienda* is not a land grant. Consequently, the owner has a good deal more autonomy from the government.

land back again until after the Mexican Revolution of 1910.

Hueyapan was visited by the Augustinians in 1534.[10] Serious effort to convert the Indians to Catholicism did not begin, however, until Hueyapan was made into a *corregimiento,* at which time the Dominicans secured the rights to settle in the pueblo. According to Martínez-Marín, the Dominicans moved in sometime between 1561 and 1563.[11] Within ten years after their arrival in the village the Dominicans had built a monastery, and they remained there until Hueyapan was "secularized"[12] in 1751.[13]

Information about Hueyapan during the 1800s is scarce. Aside from the rather fanciful stories reported by Doña Zeferina about the days of her great grandparents, we do know that in the 1870s the first school opened in Hueyapan. It was organized by a local villager who had learned how to read and write from the resident parish priest. Not until the Revolution was almost over, however, did the village really have an active school system.[14]

The Early 1900s and the Mexican Revolution

According to one old Hueyapeño farmer, Don Facundo, before the Revolution many Hueyapeños used to go down to the lowlands to work on the sugar *haciendas* there. In 1907, 1908 and 1909 Don Facundo himself joined the others, and he was employed by the Cassasano and Calderón Haciendas that were located near Cuautla. As a peon Don Facundo earned sixty-two *centavos* a day. Many of the workers lived in caves near the lands. For food they purchased *tortillas* twice a week from men

---

10. Martínez-Marín, p. 64.
11. Martínez-Marín, p. 63.
12. A village becomes "secularized" when the Catholic Church removes members of the religious orders (e.g., Dominicans, Franciscans, Jesuits) and substitutes members of the "regular" clergy, priests with no affiliation to a religious order.
13. P. Gerhard, personal communication, 1970.
14. I discuss the history of the school and its role in Hueyapan in greater detail in Chapter 6.

who came into the fields to sell. The *tortillas* were very large, Don Facundo said, and five or six carried a man over from Sunday until the following Wednesday, when once again the *tortilla* vendor passed by. Although Don Facundo's recollection of how much he ate hints at exaggeration, there is little question about the fact that the Hueyapeños had very little to eat while working as field hands.

Don Facundo remembers that once while he was working on the Cassasano Hacienda, a band of Zapatistas attacked Cuautla. He and some other peons went down to the city to see what was going on. While they were standing around, some rebels approached and told them to help carry away the dead and wounded. Don Facundo paid little attention to these orders, however, and fled.

In 1912, when he was eighteen years old, Don Facundo encountered a Zapatista soldier in the village of Tochimilco, Puebla. The rebel fighter jumped Don Facundo and stole his straw bag and other possessions. Don Facundo said to himself that he could do that too and decided to join the army. He claimed that at first he knew nothing about the issues at hand; however, since the Zapatistas looked more like his kind of people than did the *federales*, he joined the former group.[15] Don Facundo had many experiences during the six years he spent in the army, and he was with Zapatista troops when they occupied Mexico City in 1914.[16]

From what I was able to ascertain, few Hueyapeños actually volunteered to fight in the Revolution. Of those that did, even fewer are still alive. I had the opportunity to talk with only one man in addition to Don Facundo who had been a soldier at this

15. The Zapatistas were primarily local peasants, whose uniforms consisted of *calzones* and leather-thong sandals, the traditional dress of the rural poor, Indian and Mestizo alike. The *federales* derrogatorily referred to the Zapatistas as *indios*, and it was believed—incorrectly—that Zapata himself spoke Nahuatl.

16. At that time Don Facundo was fighting under General Augustín Casares, who was from Jumiltepec, Morelos. Although this general is not mentioned in J. Womack's comprehensive book *Zapata and the Mexican Revolution* (New York, 1970), when I spoke to the author in 1971 he said that he remembered hearing about Casares.

time, and this Hueyapeño did not serve voluntarily. The store-keeper Don Timoteo Hernandez was captured by some of Huer-ta's troops and forced to join the federal army.[17] Early in the Revolution, Don Timoteo's family had decided to move south into the state of Guerrero to wait out the war. It was during the family's trip to a "safer" place that young Timoteo, who was six-teen at the time, was caught and sent north, where he fought against Pancho Villa. One of his most vivid memories, Don Timoteo told me, was of the time he saw Villa in Guadalajara.

Since Hueyapan was an extremely isolated village, it did not play a major role in the Mexican Revolution. In his book on the Mexican Revolution John Womack mentions innumerable villages in the state that were involved in the Morelos campaign to one degree or another, but he does not talk about Hueyapan. Nevertheless, the villagers did suffer the misery inflicted on rural peasants throughout Morelos and most of the nation.

Food was so scarce during the Revolution that the corn meal used for making *tortillas* was a mixture of ground corn, corn spikes, acorns and *tejocotes* (the yellow fruit of the Mexican hawthorn). According to Doña Zeferina, the resulting *tortillas* resembled donkey excrement. To this day she cannot bear to eat *tortillas* made with red corn because they remind her of the tasteless ones she was forced to eat during the Revolution. In ad-dition, the villagers often had to substitute the red flower of the scarlet runner for beans.

Several villagers mentioned to me that infant and adult mortality rates were exceedingly high. In particular, a terrible epidemic ravaged Hueyapan in the latter part of the war. I was told that people were turning yellow and dropping dead in the streets. There was no time to bury them correctly. Instead, corpses were just wrapped up and thrown into large holes, several to the same grave. The epidemic lasted about two months, and hundreds of people died.

---

17. Huerta, who was the president of Mexico in 1913 and 1914, had been one of Madero's most important generals before that and had staged one of the most devastating military campaigns against Morelos peasants of any of the federal generals (Womack, Chapter 4).

The Hueyapeños undoubtedly caught the Spanish influenza that hit the Morelos area in the late fall of 1918.[18] Having already endured the physical hardships brought about by eight long years of war, the Morelenses were particularly susceptible to this formidable disease that was devastating populations all over the world. If we compare Womack's description of the epidemic with the version I have summarized briefly above, it can be seen that the Hueyapeño account was hardly an exaggeration:

> As winter came on a new and profoundly anxious tone sounded in Zapata's correspondence. He had local worries galore now. The Spanish influenza, rampant throughout the world in these months, appeared in Mexico City in early October [1918] and spread immediately into the south [i.e., Morelos]. There were the perfect grounds for an epidemic—prolonged fatigue, starvation diets, bad winter, continuing moving. In the mountains where the poorest villages [e.g., Hueyapan] were and where many chiefs had their camps, the biting cold broke the health of thousands. In towns bodies accumulated faster than they could be buried. By December Cuautla sheltered only 150 to 200 civilians. Cuernavaca was a refuge of less than 500. As for the open countryside, a family might as well have tried to inhabit Gehenna. In makeshift huts men, women and children lay in shivering chills for days, without food or care, until one by one they all died. Wise survivors deserted their dead and fled into Guerrero, to safer climes, south of the Balsas River. National patrols discovered whole villages abandoned literally to "the peace of the graveyard."[19]

During the Revolution the Hueyapeños had to keep a constant watch for soldiers. On each of the four high hills that surround the pueblo a guard stayed on duty around the clock. When troops were spotted—whether they were rebels or *federales*—the *vigilante* who saw them would set off a firecracker, thereby alerting a fifth guard, who was stationed in the church tower, to ring the bells, the warning signal for the villagers that it was time to run into the hills. Gathering what little food they had, the

18. Womack, p. 311.
19. Womack, p. 311.

Hueyapeños would scurry off, abandoning their homes and meager possessions to the pillaging soldiers.

Doña Zeferina, who was attending school during the latter years of the Revolution, remembered that classes met infrequently. The children would often no sooner get settled in the school house than the bells would start ringing in the church tower and everybody would flee. They never had more than a couple of days of school a week, and frequently they would go for as long as two months without a class.

Perhaps one of the more memorable events that took place in Hueyapan during the Revolution was the time General Fortina Ayaquica, an important Zapatista leader,[20] sent an official warning to the village. As Doña Zeferina remembers the incident, the general announced that any villager found walking about without a safe-conduct pass would be killed. In other words, an individual who did not carry papers indicating that he was sympathetic to the rebel cause would automatically be considered an ally of the enemy and shot. Outraged as well as frightened, the *ayudante* of the pueblo managed to get this decree rescinded. First he sent word back to Ayaquica asking that no soldiers be sent to Hueyapan for a few days because the village government needed time to prepare safe-conduct passes for all the inhabitants. Then, instead of arranging the papers, the *ayudante*, accompanied by the village secretary, went immediately to see Zapata, who was camped in Tlaltizapan, Morelos at the time.[21] The Hueyapeños took with them the threatening decree from Ayaquica, as well as a petition drawn up in the pueblo that asked Zapata to intervene on the villagers' behalf. Zapata immediately sent word to Ayaquica, Doña Zeferina says, informing the general that he had no authorization to demand safe-conduct passes from the villagers. After that, neither Ayaquica nor his troops ever appeared in Hueyapan.

---

20. See Womack's book for details about Ayaquica's role in the Revolution.
21. Tlaltizapan was Zapata's main headquarters during most of the Revolution.

Hueyapan since the Mexican Revolution

When the Revolution was over the national government slowly distributed confiscated *hacienda* lands to the virtually landless peasant communities. The land reform measures prescribed in the Constitution of 1917 were first proposed in 1911 by Zapata and his Morelos agrarian movement in their Plan de Ayala. According to the farmer Don Adelaido Amarro, two Hueyapeños actually signed the original Plan.

In Hueyapan the villagers received two land grants, one almost immediately after the war ended and another in the 1930s. Everybody in the village did not benefit from the land reforms, however. Don Facundo, for one, told me that although he had risked his life in battle, nobody at home bothered to save him any land. Another old Hueyapeño farmer who had remained in the village during the war bitterly commented that he did not thank the Revolution for even one cigarette, let alone any land.

I can offer one explanation for the uneven distribution of the *ejido* lands, as these government grants were called; perhaps there are others as well. When the grants were made Hueyapan land was not considered valuable, for it was extremely unproductive. The law stipulated that an individual was permitted to take only as much land as he promised to cultivate, and many Hueyapeños did not want to commit themselves to tilling sterile soil. Other Hueyapeños, however, who knew about the success chemical fertilizer was having in the lowlands, petitioned large plots of Hueyapan land anyway, anticipating the day when the chemicals would transform the badly eroded terrain into cultivable land. By the time the more conservative members of the community were willing to put faith in the chemical fertilizer, there were no more *ejido* lands available. Hueyapeños, of course, knew about natural fertilizers, but they did not have the necessary equipment to carry enough manure to the fields to make its use worthwhile.

Until chemical fertilizer became popular in Hueyapan in the late 1940s village land was unable to support the post-Revolutionary population. Consequently, large numbers of

Hueyapeños, including Doña Zeferina and her sons, spent several months a year working in the lowlands. During the 1930s, 1940s and even 1950s, villagers with a little capital rented large fields from lowlanders. Then these Hueyapeño *patrones* hired several villagers to work as peons, housing them in abandoned caves found near the rented lands. Instead of sugar cane or other major cash crops, corn, beans and calabash squash were cultivated.

Since wages were more or less standard, villagers accepted work from native lowlander *patrones* as well, but they preferred to work for Hueyapeños. Instead of being paid in money, peons were given six-liter measures of corn kernels and enough land to plant the seed. In a good year a man could harvest about twelve large sacks or *cargas*[22] of corn from this, which was enough to carry him and a family of six or seven through the year. The peons also received a token weekly allowance of one *peso*. Although they left their wives and young children at home, the men usually took along their older sons and daughters. If all the children were grown, a man might take his wife with him, and a woman who was widowed or abandoned often went down, taking her older children to work. While the young boys joined the men in the fields, the women and girls worked as corn grinders and cooks.

At the beginning of their work terms women were given twenty-five *pesos* so that they might purchase cotton cloth to make themselves some light-weight work clothes. At the end of their stay they received as many liters of unground corn to take back to Hueyapan as they had managed to grind in the lowlands for their *patrones*. Finally, they were given weekly allowances of twenty-five *centavos*.

Villagers would spend June, July and August in the lowlands, planting and caring for their vegetables. Then they would return to Hueyapan until December, at which time they would go down again for another month to harvest the crops.

---

22. There are 100 liter measures of corn to a *carga*.

With the advent of chemical fertilizer, however, this pattern of work migration changed.

Since with the new chemicals men could do better cultivating their own lands than working as peons, they stopped going down to the lowlands. Women, however, could still make more money outside the village. Thus, whereas both men and women used to spend part of the year away from Hueyapan, by the late 1950s almost all those who continued to work elsewhere were women. As mills started to replace their utility as corn grinders, more and more women began to migrate to Mexico City and Cuernavaca to work as maids. Although a few men left the village to work in factories, the number was negligible compared with that of the women. By 1969-1970, when the village had a population of nearly 4000 people, well over 100 women were working in Mexico City alone.

In addition to the change in sex ratio, two other differences have emerged between the new pattern of migration and the annual treks previously made to the lowlands. First, most of the young people who leave to work in the urban centers have settled permanently in the cities. Absorbed into the ever-growing ghettos of the poor, these Hueyapeños return to the village only occasionally to see their families. Unlike the peons and corn grinders, the new migrants no longer consider Hueyapan their home.

Second, the urbanized villagers have influenced the standard of living in Hueyapan in a way that the earlier migrants could not. On their visits to the pueblo the new migrants take home money and many of the material objects associated with the city. In this way they are contributing to the process that is incorporating Hueyapan into the consumer-oriented economy of Mexico. Although the peons and corn grinders who worked near Cuautla were also exposed to, and undoubtedly coveted, the material advantages of city life, they did not have the money to spend to acquire these items, for they were paid in subsistence crops, not in cash.

Even more significant than the help Hueyapeños received from the urbanized members of their families is the help they have been able to give themselves ever since the villagers started to work their own lands. Instead of growing exclusively for their own subsistence, Hueyapeños developed a cash crop industry. Since before the Revolution, perhaps since early colonial times, the villagers cultivated fruit trees, but their harvests had been small. With chemical fertilizer, however, the yield increased and the fruit became an economic boon—of sorts—for the community. The major cash fruits were (and still are) small sickle pears and a small variety of peach. Sold as well were (are) avocados, walnuts, apples, custard apples, pomegranates and *tejocotes*.[23]

In 1953 the villagers obtained dynamite from the government and began to build a road to enable buses and trucks to travel the eleven kilometers that separated Hueyapan from the lowland community of Tlacotepec. Once connected to Tlacotepec in this way, Hueyapeños could transport their produce anywhere, for Tlacotepec was already a link in a network of roads and highways that went to Cuautla, Cuernavaca and Mexico City in one direction, and to the states of Puebla, Oaxaca and Guerrero in the other. The construction of the road took five years because the villagers had to depend primarily on volunteer help. Also, the final result was a very uneven affair that has eroded over the years since it had no surface to protect it from the torrential rains that deluge the area during the rainy season. In the mid-1960s the villagers also built a shorter road to connect the pueblo to its municipal seat Tetela.

By 1963 the Morelos Estrella Roja bus line had extended its second-class Cuautla-Tlacotepec service to include Hueyapan. Then in 1973 it provided Hueyapan with a line running between the pueblo and Tetela. In addition, once the roads were passable, cargo trucks—some originating in Mexico City, others coming from lowland communities in Morelos—began to visit Hueyapan regularly to purchase fruit from the villagers and to carry it away to Mexico City for resale. Finally, since the mid-1960s Hueyapeños themselves have been buying trucks to take the fruit to the

---

23. Only the avocados and *tejocotes* are indigenous to Mexico. All the other fruits mentioned were introduced by the Spanish colonists.

Manzanares Market in Mexico City. By 1971 there were seven locally owned trucks in the village.

Two other changes occurred in the pueblo after the Hueyapan-Tlacotepec road was opened to buses and trucks: the villagers had electricity installed, and they opened a weekly market. Neither could have happened without a good road. The electricians had to be able to drive their trucks and equipment to the village in order to provide the Hueyapeños with service, and the lowland merchants required efficient transportation to the village to sell their goods. Today, although it is not a well-stocked market by lowland standards, the Hueyapan plaza offers villagers and individuals from the even more remote pueblos over the Puebla border the opportunity to purchase many food and nonfood items that are produced primarily in the lowlands of Morelos or in Mexico City. A few products from the local highlands are sold as well.

In the spring, when the weather is warm and the rains have not yet made the roads hazardous, the Hueyapan market is at its best. One market day in June 1970 there were fifty-five different vending displays in the plaza, most of which had vegetables—peanuts, roasted ears of corn, green peas, green tomatoes, red tomatoes, potatoes, kidney beans, onions, garlic, fresh chiles, dried chiles; fruit—mangoes, limes, oranges, watermelons, pineapples, bananas, avocados, pears, peaches, cherries, plums; and insect-derived foods—*chumiles* (small edible insects), honey. In addition, one person was selling candies; another, snow cones; another, bread. Two were selling meat—beef and pork; two were selling cloth; one, shoes; one, men's pants; one, plastic toys and variety store kitchenware; one, *comales* (griddles) of metal and clay for making *tortillas*. Several others were selling earthenware pots, and one was selling ribbons and thread. Finally, one woman was selling cooked beans, *tortillas, tamales* and *mole* (a special chile sauce served over chicken or turkey).

Despite the fact that many villagers now send their produce to Mexico City and even though there is a market day in the village, many Hueyapeños continue to travel around to other villages, mostly in the lowlands, to sell small quantities of fruit, a

The Hueyapan market place.

few bunches of flowers and *pulque*. In particular, widows, women abandoned by their husbands and old couples resort to this kind of small-time commerce. This has become the work of the weak and the poor, of those who do not have the physical strength to work the land, the money to purchase enough land to support themselves or the capital to establish themselves in a permanent store in Hueyapan. Now that there is bus service, at least the traveling merchants do not suffer the way they did before; for they no longer have to walk considerable distances over rugged terrain to get to the lowlands. Furthermore, they do not have to carry heavy loads themselves or depend on stubborn donkeys to do the carrying for them.

Two other major changes have taken place in Hueyapan, easing the workload of women in particular. First, corn mills were introduced into the pueblo in the late 1940s, freeing women from the arduous chore of grinding corn meal by hand. By 1970 there were eleven mills in the village. The other improvement is running water. During my field stay in Hueyapan in 1969-1970, only the villagers in one section of Hueyapan had running water piped directly to their homes. By the time I returned in 1971, however, almost every family in the village was enjoying this convenience. Previously women and children, primarily, had to fetch water from streams located at the bottom of the deep gorges that cut through Hueyapan.

The inspiration for many of the changes that have taken place in the village recently came from government officials who spent time in the pueblo helping the villagers "acculturate" themselves to a non-Indian society. Although Hueyapeños, with their long tradition of moving around, knew how the more affluent lived, and although they were slowly earning enough money to purchase some of the material symbols associated with a non-Indian way of life, still they lacked the "cultural" training necessary to be able to make the transition from Indian to Mestizo. It was in the spirit of so educating Hueyapeño adults that members of the government Cultural Missions visited the pueblo in 1945 and again in the 1960s. Similar instruction, on a more full-time basis, has been conducted by school teachers for both adults and primary-school children.

In their attempt to "acculturate" the villagers, government officials have been performing two separate but related tasks in Hueyapan: (1) helping to improve the standard of living of the villagers and (2) educating Hueyapeños in the new "religion" of the country—post-Revolutionary nationalism. For the first task the officials have been teaching the villagers how to earn money more successfully and then encouraging them to spend this newly acquired capital on the material symbols of Mestizo society. As part of their program to convert the villagers to the new national "religion," government missionaries have been using techniques first introduced by Catholic priests during colonial times. While proselytizing a uniform set of beliefs, these government representatives have also "nationalized" particular indigenous themes and integrated them into the government religion, much in the way the priests "baptized" selected prehispanic traditions and incorporated these into the Mexican version of Catholicism. Moreover, the result has been the same: although certain recognizable indigenous elements can be identified in the Hueyapeño observances of both "religions," these "Indian" rituals have been transformed to express hispanic rather than prehispanic cultural beliefs.[24]

In sum, the history of post-Conquest Hueyapan has come full circle. During the early colonial period Cortés made a gift of the Hueyapeños and their land to secular and religious representatives of the crown. Consequently, Spanish officials settled down in the area and reorganized many aspects of the Indians' lives, integrating the villagers into the hispanic cultural system, particularly into the spheres of economics and religion. Thus while the villagers lived and worked on the *encomienda* lands, they learned to participate in Catholic ritual. Once the *encomenderos* and *corregidores* left the region, a lowland *hacienda* took over Hueyapan lands, leaving the villagers with too little land to support their population. As a result the Hueyapeños were forced to migrate to the lowlands to find work. Then, after the Revolution of 1910, when the land was returned to the

---

24. See Chapter 5 for a lengthy discussion of religion and Chapter 6 for one on the Cultural Missions and the government school.

A street in contemporary Hueyapan.

villagers and they began to use chemical fertilizer, the Hueya-peños again settled down to a more stationary existence. Yet just as the villagers were given the opportunity to be sedentary and the option to isolate themselves—or at least minimize their con-tacts with the outside world—government officials returned to the village. Much in the tradition of the early colonial period, once again government-trained people were assigned to the pueblo, to oversee local affairs. Summarizing Hueyapan history since colonial times, therefore, we might say that when the villagers stayed in their pueblo, representatives of hispanic culture came to them; when Hueyapeños moved about, they were inevitably attracted to centers of Mestizo culture. In either case, the villagers were dependent on and integrated into the culture of non-Indians, although to this day it is still said that the Hueyapeños have a distinct indigenous cultural tradition.[25]

---

25. For more information on the history of Hueyapan, particularly on the agrarian economy, see S. López M., "Hueyapan: Un pueblo de la tierra fría," in L. Helguera R., S. López M. and R. Ramírez M., *Los campesinos de la tierra de Zapata, I: Adaptación, cambio y rebelión* (Mexico City, 1974).

WHAT IT MEANS TO BE INDIAN IN HUEYAPAN

4

To be Indian in Hueyapan is to have a primarily negative identity. Indian-ness is more a measure of what the villagers are not or do not have vis-à-vis the hispanic elite than it is of what they are or have. To complicate matters, the standard by which the Hueyapeños are evaluated is always changing. For over 400 years, while Hueyapeños have been filling in the "void" of their Indian-ness by accumulating symbols identified with the hispanic elite, the Mexican upper classes have been continuously acquiring new symbols and rejecting many of the old ones. As the elite redefines its own identity, it demotes characteristics previously associated with its prestigious high status to the low level of nonculture or Indian-ness. Consequently, despite the fact that the "content" of Hueyapan culture is always changing, the "structural" relationship of Indian to hispanic remains the same. The villagers are still Indians by virtue of the fact that they continue to lack what the elite continues to acquire.

The villagers view their Indian identity in an ahistorical way, which reflects the static nature of their social position in the larger society but does not reflect the culture or the historical process responsible for creating this stasis. Having internalized the hispanic elite's view of their own Indian-ness, Hueyapeños do not make the distinction between their "culture," which has been changing, and their "class," which has remained virtually the same. Hueyapeños see their indigenous identity in terms of a concept of the Indian that was constructed during early colonial times when it was valid to describe the villagers as culturally distinct and when it was decided that the Indians were culturally inferior. Although the Spanish subsequently destroyed the Hueyapeños' culture in the name of saving their Indian souls, the original perception of the villagers as culturally different and inferior beings did not change. As a result there is little left of indigenous culture in Hueyapan today, but there remains a considerable sense of Indian inferiority.

Early in my stay I learned that villagers were embarrassed about their Indian identity. To call a Hueyapeño *indio* was as insulting and humiliating as it was to call an American Black "nigger." Even the official euphemism *indigena* (indigenous person) was not much more flattering. Knowing how the villagers felt, I found it difficult to ask them directly about their Indianness. Thus while I lived in Hueyapan in 1969-1970 I simply waited for villagers to volunteer information and limited myself to asking only oblique questions that touched on the subject. When I returned to the pueblo in December 1971, however, I was more straightforward and asked Hueyapeños specifically about their Indian identity. By this time, I felt, people trusted me enough so that we could discuss such a sensitive matter openly without being too uncomfortable. As I had expected, the answers I received to my direct questions did not change my previous interpretation but reinforced it. What follows, then, is a summary of the contexts in which I observed Hueyapeños expressing their attitudes about what it means to be Indian and the responses I received to direct questioning. I interviewed formally and informally several hundred villagers.

A salient characteristic of the Hueyapeños' definition of Indian-ness is the comparative nature of the concept. A person is more or less Indian in relation to somebody else. Since I was a rich North American, almost everybody felt Indian next to me.

Therefore, when I visited the homes of people in the village, from the wealthier to the more impoverished, I was often greeted with, "Please excuse us, we are only poor (little) Indians here." The apology functioned as both an explanation for their poverty and a warning to me that my hosts might unknowingly commit a social blunder. By admitting beforehand that they were Indians, the villagers believed that they could no longer be held responsible for their indigenous and "uncultured" demeanor. Nobody, they assumed, expected an Indian to have either the economic means or the good manners to treat an honored guest properly.

The image of the Indian is so negative for most Hueyapeños that one peasant woman, Doña Gregoria, felt free to use the word *indio* to mean a "bad" person. Defending the pueblo, Doña Gregoria said that although outsiders believed that Hueyapeños were *indios*, actually the villagers were "very good people." Then she qualified her statement, admitting that the Hueyapeños had been much more Indian several years ago. Now, however, largely thanks to the efforts of the Cultural Missions, the villagers are becoming more "civilized."

When I asked villagers what it meant to be Indian, many said that they did not know. I could only be sure to elicit a more complete answer when I rephrased the question in terms of one of the contexts in which I had observed the villagers themselves using the word. Thus I asked, "What did Hueyapeños mean when they said to me, 'Please excuse us, we are only poor (little) Indians here'?" People then explained that villagers felt inferior next to me. Why? Because they did not speak good Spanish and they were poor. After I had broken the ice in this way, many Hueyapeños were then willing to discuss the matter in greater detail.

According to one farmer, Indians "don't know anything." Doña Zeferina's daughter-in-law, Juana, added that "Indians don't know anything; they are foolish." When I asked Doña Juana to explain what she meant by "foolish," she said that we should take her as an example: she did not know how to read and write. A seventy-three-year-old woman explained that to be Indian meant that you ate ordinary food, nothing delicious. Unlike city people, who enjoyed good-tasting delicacies preserved in tin cans, Indians ate only common things like *tortillas*, beans and chiles, she said. Another old woman claimed that Hueyapeños were Indians because they did not know how to speak Spanish well and this was embarrassing to them.

I discussed the matter of why villagers were shy about the way they spoke Spanish with Elvira Hernandez, a young Hueyapan woman who has done a lot of traveling:

J. F.: You once told me, Elvira, that Hueyapeños who go to Mexico City are afraid to speak Spanish. Why?

E. H.: Because they know that their Spanish is bad, that they do not speak well, that they make a lot of mistakes. Then they also know that the city people speak Spanish perfectly and they will pass judgment on the villagers for speaking badly.

J. F.: What do the city people say? If a Hueyapeño is on a bus in Mexico City and he speaks badly, what will the city people say?

E. H.: Well, nothing more than say, "Here is an Indian who doesn't know how to speak well."

J. F.: And does the Hueyapeño feel badly then?

E. H.: Yes, he feels badly because he himself knows that he doesn't speak well.

J. F.: And does that mean he is an Indian?

E. H.: Yes, because of his speech, because of his lack of culture.

The weaver Doña Epifania added that *indios* do not know any better. Since they do not understand how to act properly, it is not their fault when they do something wrong, and consequently they should not be blamed for their mistakes. Only people with education should be held responsible for what they do. As an illiterate farmer explained, Hueyapeños have "squashes" for heads; how could they be expected to amount to very much? The overwhelming majority of the people I interviewed defined Indian-ness in terms of what the villagers did not have or could not do. Few people actually cited tangible customs or qualities defining Indian-ness. Only one person referred to the fact that the villagers spoke a different language; all the others simply said that Hueyapeños did not speak grammatically acceptable Spanish. Furthermore, only one individual mentioned the villagers' traditional costume. I certainly do not mean to suggest that the villagers were unaware of the fact that their language and dress were Indian. I only propose that for the villagers the significance of their Indian-ness could be expressed better by listing what they lacked than by pointing to what they had. To be Indian, in other words, signified primarily that you were poor.

Where responses varied was not in the general perception of what it meant to be Indian, but in the elaborateness of the answers given. Villagers who were better educated and/or had had more contact with urban people went into greater detail. They were less shy. These more sophisticated villagers usually characterized what was Indian about the Hueyapeños with the following expression: it was the villagers' "lack of culture" that made them Indians. A person with "culture," they explained, had education as well as money. Thus, in contrast to an Indian, an individual who had "culture" possessed specific personal traits such as the ability to read and write, the ability to speak with "respect" (in flowery prose), the ability and confidence to speak before a large group and to use a microphone. Also, non-Indians owned and used beds, tables, radios, televisions, trucks and store-bought clothing, to name just a few of the items mentioned.

Most villagers responded to their Indian-ness in one of three ways, all of them negative. Some people, mostly the old and the illiterate, were fatalistic: such was their unfortunate lot, they said, and nothing could be done about it. Their only defense was to project childlike innocence: who, they felt, could expect anything more of them? Other villagers believed that although they were Indians, they could at least try to hide their impoverished cultural condition. Doña Zeferina, for example, would frequently say that the family should keep its home and yard clean so that things would appear "less sad, less poor, less Indian." A native school teacher, interested in minimizing the Indian status of his pueblo, instructed the villagers to mark down on the 1970 census forms that Hueyapeños had modern bathroom facilities. Actually, nobody, with the exception of this particular *maestro* and his family, had anything but an adobe steam bath.

A third response, common among the more upwardly mobile villagers, was to try to lose their Indian identity. For example, to prove how successful a transition he had made from Indian to Mestizo, Maestro Rafael, who was well known for his ability to speak eloquently—a non-Indian trait—liked to tell me about the reaction he often received from school teachers at statewide functions. When the other *maestros* learned that Rafael was from Hueyapan, they would ask in disbelief, "But aren't they very Indian up there?"

When villagers used the word "Indian" it was almost always to insult another or to make a self-deprecating comment or joke. For example, when I asked one Hueyapeño whether another villager was going to participate in a particular project to modernize the pueblo the former retorted, "That guy? He's too Indian." A fourth-grade teacher asked her pupils to give the name of the original inhabitants of Hueyapan. Although the correct answer was the Xochimilcas, one boy yelled out, to the self-conscious amusement of the others, "¡Los Chichimecas!"—a term used by prehispanic peoples of Central Mexico for the "barbaric" nomadic tribes of the North. As the Nahuatl-speaking children in the classroom knew, Chichimeca meant "son of a dog." To call your own ancestors Chichimecas, therefore, was a degrading thing to do.

A number of villagers had heard about some present-day indigenous people in northern Mexico who were less hispanicized than the Hueyapeños. However, these groups, who were considered to be savages, were not called Indians. Instead they were referred to by their specific tribal names. Of particular interest to Hueyapeños were the Yaquis, who could "smell out men in hiding," and the Apaches, who were reputed to "eat" people. The Yaquis fought with the federal troops against Zapata during the Mexican Revolution, and word about their exceptional tracking skills reached Hueyapan. As for the Apaches, Doña Zeferina claimed that there was an Apache in Cholula, Puebla who had a long beard down to his waist. This creature wore no clothes, she said, and had to be kept in a cage because he ate people. The Cholulans, she explained, fed him raw meat.

I was interested to see that when I asked people to define what it meant to be Indian in Hueyapan, nobody said that the

villagers belonged to a distinct race. Although some, like Doña
Zeferina, noted that their ancestors came from another race, the
villagers did not seem to consider racial variation a prominent
feature in their own Indian identity today. There appear to be at
least two reasons for this lack of interest in race as a fundamental
criterion. First, the villagers knew that they did not look very
different physically from most non-Indian peasants in the area.
Second, Hueyapeños were undoubtedly influenced by the post-
Revolutionary official view that the contemporary Indian is
defined primarily by cultural and not genetic standards.

All the same, the villagers were well aware of the fact that
rich Mexicans as well as Americans were usually fair in contrast
to their own brown complexions. Furthermore, Hueyapeños
believed that "White was beautiful." Villagers openly expressed
their preference for light skin, blue eyes, curly and/or blond hair.
Among themselves, families almost always favored their more
Caucasian-looking children. When a baby was born invariably
one of the first questions asked was about its color. As the
children were growing up mothers were continuously warning
them to protect their skin from the sun so that they would not get
any darker.

In colonial times the villagers were taught that white skin
and other Iberian racial characteristics were more attractive
than Amerindian ones. Probably for centuries Hueyapeños have
been measuring their own comeliness by the number of
recognizable Caucasian traits they might have inherited. Also,
despite the post-Revolutionary government's insistence that the
Mestizo or mixed-blood is the "ideal" Mexican, the contemporary public media have done little more than intensify
traditional beliefs, for they have introduced the Nordic image of
beauty in addition to the Iberian one. The occasional newspapers and magazines that reach the village are filled with adver-
tisements in which blond women figure prominently. Furthermore, pinned up on a wall in almost every home I visited was a
calendar, often several years old, with a large color photograph of
white-skinned, light-haired people. Finally, there are several
television sets in the village now and many Hueyapeños, children
and adults alike, are getting into the habit of visiting the homes
of television owners, paying a twenty-*centavo* admission fee, and

watching their favorite programs, usually soap operas. The actors and actresses are almost always Caucasian, and the plots
center around melodramatic romances that often touch on racist
themes.

While I was in Hueyapan in 1969-1970, Doña Zeferina's
neighbor Doña Ermena Hilda invited me to her brother's house
to see television. She and about ten other people were going to
watch the evening episode of one of the most popular soap operas
in the village, "Angelitos Negros" ("Little Black Angels"). I later
learned that this story has been an all-time favorite for years, not
only in Mexico, but in Puerto Rico as well. It appeared in the
cinema in the late 1950s and then again in the 1960s. In addition,
a television version, different from the movie, has run several
times on Mexican television and on a Puerto Rican channel in
New York City. Finally, the story has also been published in a
comic-book series. The Hueyapeños were seeing the television
version for the second time.

Briefly, "Angelitos Negros" is the story of a Black maid,
Merced, who has a daughter by a White upper-class man, the
master of the house where Merced works. As luck would have it,
the baby is born White, with blond hair and blue eyes. The father
asks Merced to give up her maternal rights to the child and serve
as the baby's nanny instead, so that the girl will have a chance to
"make it" in society. The father then dies while the child, whose
name is María Luisa, is still an infant, and the girl grows up into
a beautiful but terribly racist woman, unaware that Merced is
her mother.

In time María Luisa falls in love and marries the famous
popular-song artist Juan Carlos. They have a child and, needless
to say, the baby is Black. We then witness the total rejection by
María Luisa of her Black daughter and the frustration and
bewilderment of Juan Carlos who, despite his fame, has a heart
of gold and a particular warm spot for Black people. Merced, who
took Juan Carlos into her ·confidence when the little girl was
born, convinces the singer to tell his wife that there was Black
blood on his side of the family, in this way protecting Merced's
secret. Finally, María Luisa, in one of her many fits of anger,
pushes Merced down the stairs and the poor woman, who has not

been well, dies. Just before Merced expires, María Luisa learns from her angry husband that this Black woman is her mother. The previously ungrateful daughter cries for forgiveness.

The part of the story that I saw in Hueyapan contained a dialogue between Merced and a young Black woman, Isabel, who sang in Juan Carlos' company. Juan Carlos and María Luisa are on their honeymoon at this time. Merced tells Isabel to beware of men, for they often take advantage of young women. Isabel sadly replies that she does not have to worry; nobody would want her, she's so ugly and Black. Isabel then asks Merced whether the latter had ever been in love. The background music suddenly becomes heavy and gloomy as Merced stares off into the distance and replies, "No, who would love me? I'm so ugly and Black."

As Merced and Isabel were talking, the Hueyapeños were commenting among themselves, "Look how Black they are! All you can see are their teeth!" The implication was clear. Here on television were people who were even darker and, by Hueyapeño standards, even uglier than the villagers themselves.

Indian-ness and Political Factions in Hueyapan

The Indian identity question has been used by political factions in Hueyapan. Although the villagers I interviewed consistently agreed that the village was a homogeneous community of poor Indians, many explained that some of the inhabitants sought to lose their Indian-ness by changing the image of the pueblo while others did nothing. Those villagers who identified themselves as the Progressives wanted to "acculturate" Hueyapan, they said, and they chose to accomplish this by accepting the leadership of, and programs promoted by, non-Indian Mexicans. The members of the other faction, whom the Progressives called the Conservatives, were supposed to be against modernization.

According to the Progressives, the more Mestizo-oriented villagers belong to their faction and the more Indian-oriented associate with the so-called Conservatives. The criteria used to distinguish the Mestizos from the Indians, however, are not, as an outsider might expect, language, dress and income. Almost everybody in both factions speaks Nahuatl fluently, and many of

Progressives vs. Conservatives

the older women in the families of Progressives and Conservatives alike continue to wear the indigenous costume traditional to the area. Furthermore, the wealthier Hueyapeños do not seem to cluster in one faction and the poorer ones in the other. Where the two groups clearly differ is in the willingness of their members to contribute time and money to villagewide projects ostensibly aimed at changing the image of the pueblo.

Upon closer examination a more significant distinction between the two factions emerges. The majority of the self-named Progressives live in the center of town, while the greatest support for the so-called Conservatives comes from those who inhabit the outlying three *barrios*. Recognition of these geographic factors is fundamental to an understanding of what might motivate a Hueyapeño to join one faction over the other.

For literally hundreds of years the Centro—San Miguel and San Jacinto Barrios—has been the hub of cultural activities in the pueblo. Since the sixteenth century when the Catholic church was first built—and perhaps even before—Hueyapeños have been gathering in the Centro for important ritual occasions. Government buildings and later the best educational facilities in the village were also located in the Centro, as were the market and bus depot. The Centro, in sum, has always played a dominant political, social and cultural role in the village.

When the national post-Revolutionary government encouraged Hueyapeños to modernize the pueblo, residents of the Centro wanted to increase their already established power by trying to dominate the new community projects while continuing to control the old ones. Those living in the outlying *barrios*—San Andrés, San Bartolo and San Felipe—became increasingly wary, however, about how well their own interests were being served by the Centro residents. They began to suspect that programs promoted by their fellow villagers in the name of modernizing Hueyapan did much more, in reality, to improve the Centro than they did to help the entire pueblo.

Since those who live in the Centro consider this area the focus of cultural activity and are proud of the fact, when they meet with political resistance from the residents of the outlying *barrios* they interpret the opposition as "uncultured" or "Indian" behavior coming from the hills. This identification of an

Centro vs Barrio

Indian/non-Indian distinction has been further elaborated on by
the Centro's political leaders—native school teachers and other
villagers whose educational and/or economic experiences in
urban centers have given them a certain familiarity with and a
facility for expressing the beliefs and values espoused by the
nation's elite. Thus, although the followers of the Centro faction
do not differ significantly from those of the Barrio group, there is
little question that the Centro's leaders have more "city polish"
than other Hueyapeños. Furthermore, the Centro leaders have
encouraged their followers to think of themselves as more
sophisticated than the members of the Barrio faction.

The characterization of political conflict in the village in
terms of levels of cultural sophistication not only obscures the
real issues, but also expands the conflict into a statewide
political and social controversy. While the Centro supports the
school teachers and their urban ideas about "culture," the Barrio
faction espouses the position of a regional farmers' party, the CCI
(Central Campesino Independiente), which has been warning
peasants not to trust school teachers and other government
employees. Thus, whereas the Centro group criticizes the uncultured *indios* of the outlying areas because they refuse to
cooperate for the benefit of the pueblo, the Barrio faction insists
that the farmers—*not* the Indians—are being forced to defend
themselves against the political corruption of the school
teachers. The Barrio faction is not against progress per se, its
leaders claim; it is only wary of the political and personal
motives of the leaders of the self-designated Progressive
faction.

As long as the Progressives accept the ideology of Mexico's
urban elite, they will undoubtedly continue to interpret political
controversy in the village as a conflict of interests between the
more Mestizo-oriented and the more Indian-oriented Hueya-
penos. To demonstrate that on the contrary political strife in the
village has little to do with the Indian question, let us look at one
of the most dramatic factional disputes to have occurred in the
village in recent years.

Events leading up to the clash began in 1964 when Maestro
Rafael became director of the Centro primary school. At that
time Rafael and several other members of the Centro faction

succeeded in obtaining electricity for the village. Against strong opposition, they finally convinced the majority that a monthly tax was worth paying in exchange for the benefits gained by having electric lights. Then in early 1969 Maestro Rafael also successfully promoted a bill to fix the roof and drainage system in the local government building located in the Centro. Even though the majority of the villagers apparently voted in favor of this improvement, many Hueyapeños simply refused to pay the mandatory fifty *pesos*. The Progressive faction tried to force the recalcitrant villagers to abide by the community's decision with threats of calling in the Cuautla police.

In this tense atmosphere members of the Barrio faction, who had originally opposed the electricity issue, decided to stop paying their monthly taxes. They insisted that they had been pressured into taking electricity in the first place and that they were sick and tired of being manipulated by a few men. As a result the *ayudante*, who belonged to the Centro faction, decided to put one member of the Barrio group in jail as a warning to other tax evaders. The arrested man was taken to Tetela. There a municipal officer tried to avoid more trouble by offering to give the Hueyapeño the money required to pay his bill. The Hueyapeño, however, insisted that it was not the money but the principle of the matter and refused any financial assistance. From Tetela the man was sent on to jail in Cuautla.

In Cuautla the CCI heard about the case. Using political connections, the farmers' party managed to get the Hueyapeño out of jail. Then a CCI representative from Tepalcingo accompanied the Hueyapeño back to the pueblo and called a town meeting.

The villagers crowded into the plaza to hear what the CCI representative had to say. He proclaimed that the real problem in Hueyapan was the school teachers. Hueyapeños were being forced to pay taxes so that the school teachers might get fat. In this pueblo, the politician went on, there was one particular teacher who was most responsible for exploiting the villagers. "And what is his name?" cried the CCI representative. "Rafael Vargas!" the Hueyapeños called back.

Luckily for him, Maestro Rafael was not in Hueyapan on that day, for had he been there, he might have been killed. The villagers were divided pretty evenly on the guilt of the director, and violence was in the air. One man who supported Rafael began to wave his pistol around and shout that he was ready to shoot it out with anybody who questioned Rafael's honesty. Another member of the Centro faction told me that things deteriorated to such an extent that friends of Rafael went to Cuernavaca to seek police protection for the pueblo.

The Tepalcingo representative said that he would return to Hueyapan in order to prove his case against Rafael with hard facts. The man never came back, however, a circumstance which did not surprise Doña Zeferina, who said that the CCI official had been very drunk on that day and did not know what he was saying or doing. Apparently the representative was so confused that he even signed a petition drawn up in Rafael's defense.

A few days later the district school inspector came to Hueyapan to determine Rafael's fate as school director. Another town meeting was held. The inspector called for a vote: all those who supported Rafael were asked to move to one side of the plaza; all those who opposed him to the other. At first only women demonstrated their faith in Rafael, but they were soon followed by their husbands. All the teachers who were working for Rafael also came to their director's defense. In the end the overwhelming majority of the villagers supported Rafael. However, since he did not get paid any more for being director than he received as a regular teacher and since he knew that many Hueyapeños were still angry with him, Rafael decided to step down from his post. The minimal amount of prestige gained was not worth the political anxiety or the concern for his personal safety that as director he would have to endure.

Customs Identified as Indian

As we have already seen, the villagers define their Indian-ness primarily in terms of what they do not have. Nevertheless, there are a number of customs that Hueyapeños do identify as Indian when asked about them directly. Many traditions considered to be Indian today, however, were recognized as Spanish or hispanic Mexican in colonial and postcolonial times. Furthermore, the few truly indigenous customs that did manage to survive into the present did so largely because of the Spaniards, who found certain prehispanic traditions acceptable to their Iberian culture and consequently integrated them into the hispanic-Mexican cultural system. Regardless of their origins, most customs identified as Indian are associated with low status by the Hueyapeños. The villagers continue to practice such traditions, they believe, because they have not yet acquired the necessary education and/or money to replace them with the current standard of hispanic culture.

Whereas the villagers consider themselves Indian more for what they do not have than for what they have, outsiders generally attribute greater importance to those traditions that are found primarily in Indian communities today. Post-Revolutionary upper-class people emphasize such customs mostly out of interest in the "exotic," while lower-class non-Indians in the area point out these so-called indigenous traditions in order to distinguish their own tenuous status from that of the lowest social position that one might hold in the Mexican stratification system.

Let us now look at those customs that are identified as Indian in Hueyapan. Of the traditions that do have prehispanic antecedents, almost all have been transformed nearly beyond recognition over the years. Nevertheless, it is the discernible trace of a survival that has given these customs such extraordinary publicity and significance, although this aspect bears little relationship to the dynamics of culture change or to the meaning these customs have in the context of the entire cultural system. Furthermore, this emphasis on survivals has led to general historical confusion, for prehispanic vestiges have been combined with a residue of hispanic customs that today are obsolete in hispanic centers but can still be found in Hueyapan. Then these combined practices have been identified as evidence of an ongoing indigenous tradition.

The Nahuatl Language   Of all the customs identified as Indian in the village, the use of the Nahuatl language is the most widely practiced. Also, this is one custom that is unquestionably of prehispanic origin. Although there are very few monolinguals

J.F. assents, its simulante i colonial Spanish only the phonetics are changed left, almost every adult and the vast majority of the children still speak Nahuatl. Hueyapeños believe, however, that this language is an inferior means of communication. They call it a "dialect," not a "language," explaining that, unlike Spanish, Nahuatl is only a regional idiom that has no "grammar" or written literature.

Hueyapeños have been convinced by school teachers that the villagers do not speak good Spanish because they use Nahuatl. Consequently, many parents tend to speak only Spanish with their children, hoping in this way to give the young a better chance to succeed in society than they themselves had. During my stay in Doña Zeferina's house the old woman usually spoke Nahuatl with Don José and Doña Juana, but rarely used the language with her own children Rafael and Angelina or with her grandchildren. Rafael and Angelina spoke Nahuatl all the same, as did a number of the grandchildren, for they grew up hearing it at home and in the streets.

Over the years Hueyapan Nahuatl has become increasingly mixed with Spanish, and to this day it continues to borrow both vocabulary and grammatical constructions from the language of the conquerors. Well aware of the interference from Spanish, Hueyapeños told me often that their language had been this way since long before the Mexican Revolution. Actually, Spanish loan words must have been coming into Hueyapan Nahuatl since early colonial times when they were used to identify hispanic cultural items and concepts that were not found indigenously in the village. In addition to the pueblo's history, which points to early contacts with Spanish-speaking people, the loan words themselves indicate an early association. First, the phonetic distortion of many of the Spanish words suggests that such borrowings date from a time when the villagers were unfamiliar with Spanish phonology and were unable to duplicate the necessary sounds. For example, *sombrero* (hat) became *sonplelotle* in Nahuatl. Second, Hueyapan Nahuatl is a virtual historical reservoir of colonial Spanish. In other words there are a number of Spanish words preserved in Hueyapan Nahuatl that have been dropped from modern Mexican Spanish. A donkey, for instance, is a *burro* in Mexican Spanish today, but it is still an *axnu* in

Hueyapan Nahuatl, coming from the Spanish word *asno*. Furthermore, whereas a fraction of a *peso* is called a *centavo* in contemporary Mexican Spanish, it is referred to as a *tomin* in Hueyapan Nahuatl. *Tomin* is actually Arabic, evidence of the linguistic influence the Moors had over the Spaniards during the former's occupation of the Iberian peninsula.

Most Spanish words found in Hueyapan Nahuatl, however, are currently used in Mexican Spanish as well. Major areas of Hueyapan life were greatly transformed by hispanic culture, and consequently new vocabulary needed to be adopted in the domains of food, clothing, medicine, religion, politics, economics, farming, transportation, weights and measures. Even when the prehispanic language had words for equivalent cultural concepts or material objects, often Spanish words were substituted anyway because the cultural context was no longer indigenous but hispanic. The kinship terminology was changed greatly, as was the numerical system.

As the language of the dominant culture, Spanish has been responsible not only for introducing loan words into Hueyapan Nahuatl, but also for preserving many indigenous terms. The adoption of a Nahuatl word into Mexican Spanish has invariably ensured the continued use of the word in Hueyapan Nahuatl.[1] The control Spanish has had in determining what would or would not be preserved in Nahuatl has been so considerable, in fact, that I was able to find only one area of Hueyapan life where Nahuatl vocabulary and its accompanying prehispanic custom have survived nearly intact without having been adopted into Mexican Spanish and the country's generalized hispanic culture. I am referring to the villagers' custom of weaving on the backstrap loom. But even here, in the rare case in which prehispanic technology has managed to survive without receiving reinforcement from the dominant culture, both the fiber used and the style of the clothing are Spanish, as we will see later.

---

1. It is important to note that Nahuatl was the *lingua franca* during the early colonial period. Since this was the language of the Aztecs and, therefore, the dominant tongue in Mexico at the time of the Spanish Conquest, the Spaniards used this language to communicate with the Indians. As a result, when the colonists needed a term to describe something indigenous and foreign to their Iberian cultural experience, they almost always borrowed a Nahuatl word.

In addition to lexical interference from Spanish, Hueyapan Nahuatl exhibits Spanish grammatical constructions. In particular, Hueyapeños use the Spanish prepositions *de* (of, from) and *para* (for) to the near exclusion of prehispanic postpositional forms. Thus, for example, villagers say *niuitz de escuelah* (*vengo de escuela*) for "I am coming to school" and *para nías* (*para ir*) for "in order to go" (first person). Hueyapeños have even integrated the Spanish pattern of contractions into their Nahuatl and use, for example, *den* for *de* + *in* (equivalent to the Spanish contraction *del* for *de* + *el*), as in the following sentence: *in ichcacle cah tlacpac den sonplelotle*. The Spanish would be *la sandalia está debajo del sombrero,* meaning "the sandal is under the hat."

Even if we grant that the lives of the villagers are intimately integrated into the hispanic cultural system and that what is left of their language exhibits considerable interference from Spanish, the question still remains as to why Nahuatl has survived at all. I suggest that Nahuatl has been used by the villagers as a defensive measure, as a mechanism to maintain social boundaries. As we have already seen, Doña Zeferina is very proud of the ways she has found to protect herself from a world she perceives as hostile. So are most of the Hueyapeños I have met. Although Doña Zeferina and other villagers have had to participate in and be exploited by the hispanic cultural system in order to survive economically and to "ensure" their souls a place in Heaven, they have cultivated a few mechanisms to manipulate and close out their oppressors. One such means is to speak a language that the dominant classes cannot understand. Since their own culture has been destroyed, however, all the Hueyapeños can talk about in Nahuatl are hispanic cultural themes, and in order to discuss such matters they have been forced, in the end, to borrow heavily from the vocabulary of the conquerors.

Spinning and Weaving   The Hueyapan tradition of spinning thread with a spindle shaft and whorl and then weaving cloth on the backstrap loom is indisputably of prehispanic origin. Like the Nahuatl language, however, this indigenous technology has been adapted to the hispanic cultural system. The villagers spin and weave wool, a Spanish imported fiber, and produce clothing that conforms to the dictates of a royal Spanish decree.[2] Since factory-manufactured cotton material has become less expensive than raw wool in recent times, and since the labor necessary to sew cotton clothing is next to nothing compared with that of weaving woolen garments, the traditional technology is dying out. All the same, perhaps as many as one-third of the adult women in the village continue to spin and weave.

In prehispanic times Hueyapeños probably wove on backstrap looms similar to those still in use today. At that time the villagers undoubtedly employed a fiber that has been identified in the literature as *agave* because, as Soustelle points out, lower-class people living in highland areas used this fiber almost exclusively at the time of the Spanish Conquest. Only wealthy highlanders, Soustelle explains, could afford to have clothes woven out of cotton, the greatly valued fiber that was grown in the eastern lowlands and sent to the highlands as tribute payments to Aztec lords.[3] Nevertheless, despite the Hueyapeños' almost certain lower-class origin, the villagers did seem to have some cotton, for I have a spindle whorl from the village that is definitely of pre-Columbian origin[4] and that could only have been used to spin a fine fiber. Before the Spaniards introduced wool the only fine fiber to be found in Mexico was cotton.[5]

In Tables 1 and 2 I give the terms used in Hueyapan to identify spinning and weaving implements. Unlike the vocabulary used for kinship, food, medicine, religion and clothing, where there is considerable Spanish interference, the terms used to identify this technology have remained almost untouched. Frequently Hueyapeños I spoke with on the subject did not even know Spanish equivalents for the loom parts. Although there are other cultural domains in which the vocabulary of Hueyapan Nahuatl exhibits little Spanish interference, these almost always

---

2. G. Foster, *Culture and Conquest: America's Spanish Heritage*, Viking Fund Publication in Anthropology No. 27 (New York, 1960), pp. 101-102.

3. J. Soustelle, *The Daily Life of the Aztecs*, trans. J. O'Brian (New York, 1962), p. 132.

4. G. Eckholm, personal communication, 1972.

5. J. Bird, personal communication, 1972.

Doña Epifania, one of the best weavers in the village, weaving a *gabán* on a backstrap loom. She is dressed in the traditional skirt (*xincueite*) and blouse of Hueyapan women.

TABLE 1

Spinning and Weaving Terms[a]

English	Spanish	Hueyapan Nahuatl	Classical Nahuatl	Reference[b]
Wool	*Lana*	*Tomitl*[c]	*To'mi̱-tl*	Swadesh and Sancho, p.69
Teasel head	*Carda*	*Galon*[d]	*Tlapochin-altiloni*	Siméon, p. 578
Thread	*Hilo*	*Icpatl*	*I̱c-pa-tl*	Swadesh and Sancho, p. 84
Spindle whorl	*Malacate*	*Malagatl*	*Malacatl*	Siméon, p. 222
Spindle shaft	*Palito*	*Cogotzin*		
Backstrap loom	*Telarcito*	*Ihguiti*[e]	*Iqui-ti̱a̱*	Swadesh and Sancho, p. 50
Warp		*Nocpah*		
Weft		*Itlan calagueh*		
Woven piece	*Tejido*	*Se'sotl*[f]	*Zo-tl*	Swadesh and Sancho, p. 77
Side selvage		*Iten*		

[a] I have used Spanish terms only when my informants knew them. Furthermore, I have included Classical Nahuatl words—the terms used at the time of the Spanish Conquest—when I was able to locate them in Classical Nahuatl texts.

[b] References cited are M. Swadesh and M. Sancho, *Los mil elementos del mexicano clásico* (Mexico City, 1966); and R. Siméon, *Dictionnaire de la langue nahuatl* (Graz, Austria, 1963).

[c] This word actually means "hair," which by extension includes wool.

[d] The Hueyapan Nahuatl word for teasel head is clearly Spanish. This implement is used for combing out wool before spinning.

[e] The villagers did not have a noun for loom, only a verb describing the act of weaving. This is true, apparently, wherever the backstrap loom or its equivalent is used in America. The reason for this, according to Bird, "is simply that when the work of weaving is completed and the product removed, what remains are the separated sticks which serve as loom bars, heddles and shed rods" (Bird, personal communication, 1972).

[f] When I asked for the Nahuatl word meaning woven material, I was given that for "one piece of cloth"—*se'* meaning one, *sotl* meaning cloth.

TABLE 2

Terms for Parts of the Backstrap Loom[a]

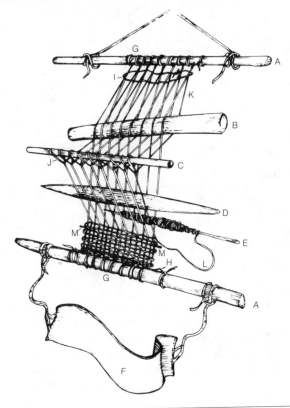

Label in Diagram	English	Hueyapan Nahuatl
A	Loom bars	*Cuahtzomitl*
B	Shed rod	*Ohtlatl*
C	Heddle rod	*Xiotl*
D	Batten or sword	*Tzotzopastle'*[b]

(continued on next page)

TABLE 2 (Continued)

Label in Diagram	English	Hueyapan Nahuatl
E	Bobbin	*Pagüitl*
F	Backstrap	*Tlauixcuaetl*
G	Warp lashing[c]	
H	Heading string[c]	
I	Lease cord	*Cuitlzcole'*
J	Leash cord	*Icpatl bolita*[d]
K	Warp	*Nocpah*
L	Weft	*Itlan calagueh*
M	Tenter	*Octagatl*

[a] The diagram is a modified version of a drawing found in W. Bennett and J. Bird, *Andean Culture History*, American Museum of Natural History Handbook Series No. 15 (New York, 1960), p. 266.

[b] There is a smaller batten used to help change sheds called an *oyastle'*.

[c] I did not get information about the names for either warp lashing (G) or heading string (H).

[d] This is store-bought thread and the *bolita* refers to the fact that the thread comes on a spool.

correspond to Nahuatl terms that have been adopted into Mexican Spanish. In other words, the technology used for spinning and weaving seems to be virtually the only aspect of Hueyapan life in which prehispanic custom and vocabulary have survived without having been integrated into the generalized hispanic culture. Yet even here the clothing produced by this indigenous process conforms primarily to hispanic, not prehispanic, traditions.

Clothing The traditional dress of the villagers is often singled out as evidence of the Hueyapeños' Indian-ness. However, as I have already mentioned, the so-called indigenous clothing styles found in Hueyapan today date to colonial, not prehispanic, times.

According to Soustelle, at the time of the Spanish Conquest men in Central Mexico wore loin cloths (*maxtlatl*) and occasionally cloaks (*tilmatli*). Women wore skirts (*cueitl*) made of one long piece of cloth wrapped around the waist and kept in place by embroidered belts. Lower-class women wore no blouses at all, but the upper classes wore loose-fitting garments called *huipilli*.[6] Wealthier women also wore mantles known as *quex-quemitl*, which the Totonacs of the East introduced to the Nahuas. The clothing of the poor, for both men and women, was usually white, but the wealthier wore colorful and highly decorated garments, especially on festive occasions. Finally, the lower classes went barefoot, while those who were better off wore sandals (*cactli*) with agave-fiber or animal-hide soles and agave-fiber lacings.[7]

During the early part of the colonial period the Spanish ruler sent formal orders to Mexico that Indian clothing had to be modified to conform to Spanish styles and to an Iberian sense of decency.[8] Quite aside from the decree, many indigenous peoples, especially those in the cold highlands, like the Hueyapeños, must have been eager to adopt Spanish clothing, for it was considerably warmer than the prehispanic garments. In present-day Hueyapan many men and women continue to dress in the costumes prescribed by the Spanish colonials, and it is these items of clothing that are identified as Indian.

Almost all woolen garments used in the village are woven locally on backstrap looms. At the present time cotton clothing is sewn by hand or on pedal-operated sewing machines out of store-bought material. Agave-fiber products—small bags that men carry and women's sandals—are manufactured entirely outside the village.

Today men traditionally wear white linen "pajamas," the symbol of the rural peasant all over Mexico. The pants do not have a zipper or button fly, but are closed in front by a flap of material that is held in place by an attached belt that is tied

---

6. The Mayan Indian dress for women is called by this same Nahuatl word in Mexico today.

7. For further discussion of these items of clothing see Soustelle, pp. 132-138.

8. Foster, pp. 101-102.

tightly around the waist. The shirts are white, long-sleeved, pullover garments with Chinese collars. There are buttons on the upper half of the bodice as well as on the cuffs. Previously, even within the lifetime of Doña Zeferina, men wore wool *serapes* that were sewn up the sides instead of linen shirts. Now, brown and blue or white and blue[9] striped *serapes* are used in addition to the shirts on chilly mornings and evenings. Men sometimes wear white and blue striped woolen scarves as well. Finally, men wear straw hats and commercially manufactured leather-thong sandals with rubber soles.

Women traditionally wear long full black wool skirts that are pleated and held in place by elaborately woven red and black wool belts that are wrapped several times around their waists— clearly a modified version of the prehispanic skirt. Their blouses are short-sleeved, and are usually made of white cotton. Sometimes the blouses are decorated with red embroidered designs around the neckline. Women also wear black wool shawls and agave-fiber sandals. Doña Zeferina says she can still remember the time when some of the men and most of the women went about in bare feet.

In Table 3 I give the names used locally for the so-called Indian clothing discussed above. Since the villagers did not have Nahuatl words to identify much of the clothing that they were instructed to wear, they simply borrowed from the Spanish, distorting the words to conform to their own indigenous phonemic system. Even when they were able to use a Nahuatl term, the item of clothing so described had been modified to such an extent by Spanish influences that it only vaguely resembled the indigenous equivalent. The skirt, for example, was now made of wool instead of agave, cotton or bast. Furthermore, this garment was full now instead of straight, and black instead of white. There is perhaps one piece of clothing that did not change very much from the prehispanic original: the agave-fiber sandal presently worn by Hueyapan women. Even this item, however, presents a problem as to its indigenous authenticity for the

---

9. All dyes used in the village are commercial.

TABLE 3

Traditional Clothes in Hueyapan

English	Spanish	Hueyapan Nahuatl	Classical Nahuatl	Reference
Pajamas	*Calzones*	*Gazón*		
Men's sandals	*Huaraches*	*Cuitlaxcactli* [a]	*Cāc-tli*	Swadesh and Sancho, p. 43
Hat	*Sombrero*	*Sonplelotle'*		
Poncho	*Serape*	*Gabán* [b]		
Men's scarf	*Bufanda*	*Bufandah*		
Shawl	*Rebozo*	*Payo'* [c]		
Skirt	*Falda*	*Xincueite* [d]	*Cuē-yi-tl*	Swadesh and Sancho, p. 83
Belt	*Faja*	*Cenidor*	*Max-tli*	Swadesh and Sancho, p. 83
		Ilpigatl	*Ilpicayotl*	Siméon, p. 167
Blouse	*Blusa*	*Saco*	*Uipi-l-li*	Swadesh and Sancho, p. 73
Women's sandals		*Ichcacleh* [e]	*Cāc-tli*	Swadesh and Sancho, p. 43

[a] In this context *cuitlax* means leather, villagers told me, and *cactli* means shoe.

[b] *Gabán* is a Spanish word meaning overcoat.

[c] The Mexican *rebozo* is unquestionably of Spanish origin and in its original Iberian form was often more like a head cloth or *pañuelo*, Foster suggests, than a long shawl (Foster, p. 98). The Nahuatl word *payo'* could very likely be a phonetic distortion of the old Spanish word *paño*, meaning cloth.

[d] According to Swadesh and Sancho, *xi-n(i)* means unsewn or unspun (Swadesh and Sancho, p. 74). *Cuē-yi-tl* means skirt. Perhaps the first woolen skirts seen in the village were on Spaniards, and the villagers decided that this cloth was not spun or sewn.

[e] *Ich(tle)* stands for the agave fiber out of which the sandals were fashioned.

villagers, because, according to Doña Zeferina, the sandal was introduced into the pueblo during her lifetime.

Cooking Technology and Food   The villagers consider their cooking technology to be Indian. Actually, the Hueyapeños have preserved their indigenous methods, as they have many of their indigenous foods, largely because the techniques were adopted by the dominant culture and have become the mark of rural poverty throughout Mexico. As is the case with many indigenous foods, the Nahuatl names for cooking utensils have been adopted into Spanish because there were no equivalent terms for these cultural items in the dominant language. Thus we find in Mexican Spanish today such words as *metate* (*metlatl* in Nahuatl), and *comal* (*comale*), *chiquihuite* (*chiguihuitl*) and *tenate* (*tenatl*).

According to the Hueyapeños, Indian food means "ordinary things," such as *tortillas*, kidney beans, chiles, *tamales*, calabash squash, *pulque* and a few fruits, such as *tejocotes*. Although these foods are indeed indigenous, they are part of the national non-Indian cuisine as well. People who are not from Hueyapan often mention as typically Indian *mole*, a hot chile sauce usually served over turkey and chicken on fiesta days. A look at the ingredients in *mole colorado* (Table 4), the preferred *mole* in Hueyapan, indicates the extent to which Spanish tastes have refined a dish which in prehispanic times was little more than a chile stew.[10] *Mole colorado* actually resembles an East Indian curry, which is understandable when we remember that the Spaniards, together with other Western Europeans, were looking for routes to the Orient in order to obtain Eastern spices at the same time that they were colonizing Mexico. Since *mole* is a fiesta food and since feast days were organized and directed by Catholic priests, it stands to reason that holiday dishes in particular would be dressed up to appeal to new trends in European culinary taste.

10. Soustelle, p. 27.

Hueyapan woman preparing the corn meal for *tamales*.

TABLE 4

Ingredients Used in *Mole Colorado* in Hueyapan

Ingredient	Origin of Ingredient at Time of Conquest
Pasilla chile	Indigenous
Sesame seeds	East India
Turkey or chicken soup	Turkey: indigenous; chicken: Europe
Chocolate (bitter)	Indigenous, but from tropical Mexico
Peanuts	Indigenous
Cloves	Moluccas
Cumin	Hindustan
Garlic	Europe
Pepper	India
Cinnamon	Ceylon and China
Almonds	Morocco and Barbary
Anise	North Africa
Raisins	Mediterranean
Onions	Indigenous, with European equivalents
Salt bread	Europe
Tortillas	Indigenous

Healing   In Hueyapan there are a number of healers who use "rustic" methods to help ailing villagers. Such cures are considered to be Indian and, in general, less effective than the modern techniques, mainly injections, that are used more frequently today. Actually, the ingredients used in these Indian cures derive from a combination of indigenous and European influences. Considering the fact that the Spaniards were extremely impressed by the efficacy of native medicines,[11] it is not surprising that so many indigenous techniques were incorporated into hispanic cures. In Table 5 I give one of the most elaborate rustic cures I found used in Hueyapan.

Although healers today do not usually offer prayers as part of their cures, I was able to collect a few samples of the in-

11. Soustelle, pp. 197ff.

vocations previously employed. In every case the prayers recited addressed Catholic images and involved Catholic symbolism. An example of a prayer used to cure an ailing patient is: "Saint Bartholomew of Castile, you who come on a horse, take this shadow from its place."[12]

TABLE 5

Recipe for Rustic Cure of Bronchitis	
Ingredient	Origin of Ingredient at Time of Conquest
Butter	Europe
White wine	Europe
Green tomato	Indigenous
Cumin	East India
Peppermint	Europe
Balsamon tranquilo	Unknown
Lilimento	Unknown
Fennel	Europe
Oregano	Europe

The herbs are crushed and then heated with the other ingredients in a small pot. The mixture is then applied to the chest and back of the patient once a day for three or four days.

Religion   Aspects of the villagers' religious life are also considered illustrative of the Hueyapeños' Indian-ness by villagers and local people from nearby non-Indian pueblos. As I indicate in some detail in the next chapter, however, the villagers are clearly participating in the Catholic ritual system. What can be identified as indigenous has been "baptized" and integrated into the hispanic version of Catholicism much in the way that the festival tree and other such pagan customs have become part of Northern European Christianity. Praying for rain and crops, for

12. The belief in shadows as a cause of illness was found in Europe and in prehispanic Mexico.

example, is sanctioned by the Church even today, as is the use of copal incense. Furthermore, the tendency to deify saints, hardly unique to Mexican Indians, is being controlled by Mexican Catholicism.

Perhaps the most striking indigenous religious tradition that persists in Hueyapan today is the practice of a few old women rainmakers of eating hallucinogenic mushrooms as they pray for rain. A look at their invocations, which have been published by a Hueyapeño school teacher, Miguel Barrios, in Nahuatl and Spanish translation,[13] illustrates how successful the Spaniards were in "baptizing" indigenous traditions and incorporating them into the local version of Catholicism. The prayers are made to Catholic images, and all the religious objects and symbolism referred to are Catholic.

More often than not, what is identified as Indian is actually of Spanish colonial origin. The elaborate processions, the *mayordomo* system and much of the fiesta food were introduced after the Spanish Conquest. In addition, the special forms of fiesta entertainment—firecrackers, bull riding, pageant plays and special music—date from colonial times. Of particular importance in Hueyapan is the play performed during the Virgin of Guadalupe fiesta which tells the story of the Christians fighting the Moors in Turkey. Another tradition associated with Indian fiesta celebrations is the musicians who play *chirimiyas*, which are actually derivatives of Renaissance double-reed instruments.

13. M. Barrios, "Textos de Hueyapan, Morelos," *Tlalocan*, Vol. 3, No. 1 (1949), pp. 64-66 and 67-69.

RELIGION IN HUEYAPAN

5

With the exception of a few hundred Protestants and a handful of people who belong to an Aztec renaissance culture group, all villagers consider themselves to be practicing Catholics. For Catholics in the pueblo their religion is one of the most important links they have with outsiders. Although Hueyapeños believe that they are inferior to other Mexicans because they are still "Indians with little culture," the Catholics, at least, can claim a common religion with non-Indians. A Catholic identity is so important to many Hueyapeños that they even talk about intrapueblo competition in terms of who the better Catholics are. Those living in the Centro, for example, often describe their superiority over the inhabitants of the outlying *barrios* by pointing to the fact that both the church and the only chapel in town are located in the Centro.

Hueyapeños have been Catholics for a very long time. As we have already seen, by 1534, only thirteen years after the Spanish Conquest, Augustinian missionaries had visited the pueblo.[1]

---

1. C. Martínez-Marín, *Tetela del Volcán* (Mexico City, 1968), p. 64.

Systematic conversion of the villagers, however, probably did not begin until 1561, when a few Dominican friars settled down in the village.[2] Then, according to a pictographic map of Hueyapan, by 1570 there were one church and at least five chapels in the village.[3] Today nobody seems to know what happened to four of the chapels. Finally, by 1581, if not before, the village had been renamed Santo Domingo Hueyapan and the community had been divided into three *estancias*, each one bearing the name of a different saint: San Miguel, Santo Bartólome and Santo Tomás.[4] For nearly 400 years, therefore, the very spatial organization of the pueblo has reflected the villagers' Catholic heritage.

The conversion of Hueyapeños to Catholicism probably followed the procedure common throughout Mexico in early colonial times. Friars went into Indian communities in small groups, barefoot and unarmed. At first the holy men needed interpreters, but soon they were able to preach directly in indigenous languages. In each settlement the friars tried to convert the chief first, confident that the people would follow their leader. Then they performed mass baptisms, destroyed shrines devoted to prehispanic deities and built churches and chapels on sites formerly dedicated to pagan gods.[5]

Perhaps one of the most significant aspects of the "Spiritual Conquest" of Mexico was the way Spanish friars carefully substituted Christian symbols for indigenous ones. While they were destroying temples, breaking images, prohibiting human sacrifices and severely punishing the native priest class,[6] they were also building churches, introducing new saints and a new priest class on the very ruins of the old. It is often noted that the Catholics were so successful in converting the Indians because

---

2. F. del Paso y Troncoso, "Relación de Tetela y Ueyapan," *Papeles de Nueva España* (Madrid, 1905), Vol. VI, p. 289.

3. E. Boban, *Documents pour servir à l'histoire du Mexique*, Vol. I (Paris, 1891), Plate No. 25.

4. Paso y Troncoso, p. 284.

5. C. Gibson, *Spain in America* (New York, 1966), pp. 72-73.

6. C. Gibson, "The Transformation of the Indian Community in New Spain, 1500-1810," *Journal of World History*, Vol. 2 (1954-1955), p. 585.

[handwritten marginalia: "remove gods, leave life — Catholic... N. American Indian"]

they were flexible enough in their interpretation of the dogma to
be able to incorporate into Catholicism many of the customs of
the people they came to convert. This versatility, however, was of
a specific nature: the religious dances and chants of the Indians
were carefully "baptized";[7] that is, they were first stripped of
their original religious significance and then re-dressed with
Christian meaning.[8] Although some of the clergy worried that the
Indians would remain pagans if encouraged to practice their own
ritual, many others realized that those indigenous customs that
did not do violence to Christian ideals could be used construc-
tively. The essential key was to take rites formerly dedicated to
prehispanic deities and transform them into ones for the Virgin,
Jesus Christ and the numerous Catholic saints. The dances and
chants in and of themselves were not dangerous; the beliefs
behind them were. Thus once the ideological foundation was
destroyed, many of the rituals were harmless enough. Today,
however, traditions that were "baptized" at an earlier date to
facilitate conversion are looked upon as evidence of an ongoing
indigenous tradition.

[handwritten marginalia: "manipulation"]

[handwritten marginalia: "evidence to support her point"]

Not only indigenous customs, but even prehispanic gods and
goddesses were transformed at times by Spanish priests. One of
the most important examples of such a "baptism" is the case of
the Virgin of Guadalupe. The story of the Virgin and the traditional ritual performed annually in her honor dramatize the contradiction present in the Hueyapeños' lives. Here we see the
doubly binding position of a people who have followed the
Spanish Catholic campaign of conversion, losing the ideological
content of their indigenous tradition, but not their Indian identity, in the process.

---

7. R. Ricard, *La "conquête spirituelle" du Mexique* (Paris, 1933), p. 221.

8. This pattern was practiced by Christians in Europe as they conquered
and converted most of that continent, long before they came to the New World.
The model was developed, actually, as long ago as 601 A.D., when Roman
missionaries were instructed in how to convert the peoples of Britain. For further
discussion of the early use of this conversion procedure see The Venerable Bede,
History of the English Church and People, trans. Shirley Price (London, 1968),
pp. 86-87.

The Virgin of Guadalupe Fiesta

The Virgin of Guadalupe represents the only apparition of the Virgin Mary to have occurred in the Western Hemisphere. She appeared several times to the converted Indian Juan Diego at Tepeyac, the former site of the Aztec goddess Tonantzin. In 1531, only ten years after the Spanish Conquest, the recently converted Juan Diego was on his way to Mexico City to celebrate the fiesta for the Immaculate Conception on December 8, a day dedicated to the Virgin Mary. On the way he passed by the shrine of his former goddess Tonantzin, and he claimed that at this site he saw the Virgin.

When Juan Diego arrived in Mexico City he went to see the Bishop, a Franciscan by the name of Zumárraga. Since the Bishop wanted tangible proof of the apparition, the Indian returned to the shrine of Tonantzin and asked the Virgin for a sign that he could show the religious leader. The Virgin told Juan Diego to gather up all the flowers on top of Tepeyac. Following instructions, Juan Diego wrapped up the flowers in his cape of woven agave fibers and carried them in this fashion to the Bishop. When he came before Zumárraga and opened his cape, the flowers were gone and in their place was an image of the Virgin, painted on the coarse material of his garment. Zumárraga recognized the importance of this miracle and preserved the cape. In 1533 he had it taken from the cathedral in Mexico City to a little chapel built at Tepeyac for the Virgin's veneration. Then in 1566 Zumárraga's successor, Montúfar, had a silver statue made for the Virgin's sanctuary.[9]

The Virgin of Guadalupe has come to be known as the Dark Virgin, the Indians' Virgin. For non-Indians the story of Juan Diego serves in part as a reminder that Mexico was inhabited by a racially and culturally distinct people, the descendents of whom are still identifiable today. For the Hueyapeños, however, the apparition of the Virgin to a *converted* Indian validates the villagers' rights to claim their historical place in a non-Indian tradition. Thus, whereas the celebration of the Virgin's day

9. Ricard, pp. 227-229.

brings non-Indians closer to Mexico's indigenous past, it reaffirms for the Indians a strong connection to their European heritage.

According to Mexican tradition, on the morning of the Virgin's day, December 12, little children are supposed to attend Mass dressed up to look like "Indians" (*de indito*), in memory of Juan Diego. This occurs to some extent almost everywhere in the country, including Mexico City, Sinaloa and Hueyapan. In spite of the fact that most Hueyapeños know about the custom, on the two occasions I observed the fiesta (1969 and 1971) few children actually came to church in costume. Although quite popular among non-Indians, the tradition has caught on only superficially in the pueblo, because in Hueyapan, for a child to dress *de indito* means to dress like his grandparents or, in some cases, his parents. Today few young children walk around in *xincueites* or *calzones*, but such clothing is still a part of contemporary Hueyapan and cannot be seen as a tradition from a past era.

The seven or eight children who did attend Mass in Hueyapan dressed *de indito* appeared in the following costumes. The girls wore *xincueites* with white embroidered blouses, *rebozos* and agave-fiber sandals. The boys had on *calzones*, *serapes*—to which were pinned little pictures of the Virgin of Guadalupe—straw hats and leather-thong sandals with rubber soles. In their hands the boys carried staffs. On their backs, the girls and boys wore *huacalitos*, small versions of the packs Indians were supposed to have used to carry their meager possessions during the days of Juan Diego.

Much more popular in Hueyapan than the custom of dressing *de indito* is the "folk" religious tradition of performing a play about the Moors and the Christians. Here Hueyapeños find themselves on less vulnerable ground. When villagers dress *de indito* they emphasize their low-status identity that is not yet a thing of the past. However, when they witness or participate in the dramatic presentation of how the Christians defeated the Moors, they enjoy the same sense of cultural superiority as anybody else in Mexico. Originally the friars had introduced a number of versions of this play to the Indians in order to present another case in history of pagan conversion to Christianity.[10] Perhaps the Indians of early colonial times identified their experiences with those of the Moors, as the friars intended. Hueyapeños today, however, no longer do, but proudly associate themselves instead with the victorious Christians; for once the villagers are on the winning side.

According to Doña Zeferina and others, players have been coming to Hueyapan since well before the Mexican Revolution to perform the *Moros y Cristianos*. The story of the Moors, that of Juan Diego and the Passion of Christ make up the conscious religious historical heritage of the villagers. The illiterate Hueyapeño has never heard of Quetzalcoatl, Tlaloc or any other prehispanic god, but there is probably not an adult in the village who does not know the stories about the Moors and the Christians, Guadalupe or the Crucifixion of Christ.

Troops of players also perform in Mexico City at the shrine of the Virgin of Guadalupe during the entire month of December. Each group has a director who teaches the members their parts according to a handwritten script that usually has been in the director's family for generations. Although the details might differ from one version to another, the content is basically the same: a simulated battle mixed with dialogue that is supposed to represent a military conflict between the Christians and the Moors, with two groups of dancers representing the antagonistic factions. Saint James is almost always the head of the Christians and Pilate generally that of the Moors. The show usually ends with the victory of the Christians and the triumph of the Cross.[11]

Although the group I saw perform in Hueyapan came from Icacingo (state of Mexico), the villagers usually invite Don Estanislao Rendón from the nearby pueblo of San Juan Amecac, Puebla. According to Don Estanislao, his family has had a copy of the script of the play since the time of his great grandfather. Unfortunately, Don Estanislao was unable to tell me how his great grandfather first came into possession of the manuscript,

---

10. Ricard, p. 224.
11. Ricard, pp. 224-225.

but he did know that since 1845 one son in every generation had assumed the role of Maestro de los Moros, learning the play and training a small troop of actors in each of the villages where the Maestro had been asked to perform. After some negotiation, Don Estanislao agreed to make and sell me a handwritten copy of the script for eighty dollars.

The San Juan Amecac and Icacingo versions of the play are more or less the same, I am told. It was impossible for even the Hueyapeños to understand much of the dialogue in the Icacingo presentation I saw. Therefore, I had to rely on members of the audience who were familiar with the story to help me follow what was going on. Doña Zeferina's neighbor Don Juan Maya, who knew both the San Juan Amecac and Icacingo versions well, compared the two stories for me. Although the scripts were virtually identical, Don Juan explained that the San Juan Amecac version had parts for only sixteen actors, while the Icacingo one had roles for twenty-four. Furthermore, the costumes used by the San Juan Amecac troop were more picturesque than those of the Icacingo group. In the former, for example, Muhammad was clearly depicted as the devil with horns and a tail.

Throughout Central Mexico the costumes used in the plays are more or less the same, and any variations that exist are minor. In both Mexico City and Hueyapan the Moors dress in long red satinlike robes and the Christians in blue. The robes are cheerfully decorated with designs sewn on in sparkling sequins. On the Moors' costumes are little moons, suns and flowers; on the Christians' robes are crosses, clover leaves and flowers. On their heads the Moors wear crowns decorated with crescent moons—easily mistaken for the devil's horns. The Christians wear crusade-style knights' helmets. A few Moors have sinister-looking beards, and both Moors and Christians brandish straight-bladed machetes.

Accompanying the colorful groups, both in Mexico City and in Hueyapan, are the Maestros de los Moros, dressed in billowing *calzones* and carrying well-worn, handwritten copies of the texts. They frantically run about with the actors, reading the lines first and then instructing the performers to repeat them with the ap-

The Moors and the Christians performing in the Hueyapan plaza during the Virgin of Guadalupe fiesta.

propriate dramatic gestures. At frequent intervals bands play the theme song associated with the play—the same lively tune is performed in Hueyapan and Mexico City—and the Moors and Christians dance, either marching up and down or dueling with one another.

In Hueyapan some local young men dressed in ragged clothes and funny papier-mâché masks interfere regularly with the performance. Known as the *terrones*, these clowns run about the plaza while the actors speak their lines and, during the intermissions, tease both the players and the audience.

During the 1969 Hueyapan celebration of the fiesta the Icacingo troop began on the evening of December 11 and finally finished late on December 13. Except for breaks taken to eat and sleep, the actors performed continuously in the San Miguel Barrio plaza, spending perhaps as many as twelve hours a day acting. Let us now look in some detail at the content of the play and at the reaction Hueyapeños have to it.

The Moors and the Christians: San Juan Amecac Version

The text is entitled *The History of Charlemagne* (Carlos Magno) *and the Admiral* (Almirante) *Balán.* Although the script is not formally divided into acts, different scenes are suggested by changes in action from one locality to another. The play takes place in Turkey, which is thought to be in Africa, and in France, which is also called Rome and Spain. Although the text offers no dates, Padre Diego Sanchez, Hueyapan's native priest, told me the story was supposed to reflect events that occurred during the twelfth century. Actually, incidents and personages come from various historic periods and have been combined in a most imaginative fashion. It is clear that the script has undergone more changes since Don Estanislao's great grandfather acquired it in 1845, among which is the introduction of anachronisms such as telephones and balloons.

Carlos Magno, the King of France, wants to convert the King of the Moors, Almirante Balán, and his empire to Christianity. To accomplish this holy mission the French monarch sends some of his crusaders to Turkey. When the Almirante learns of the Christians' intent he becomes very angry and instructs his soldiers to go to France to capture the image of the Virgin Mary. The Moors believe that if the Christians are separated from their religious icon they will lose their power.

The Almirante's men successfully steal the Virgin Mary and manage to keep the image in their possession until the fall of the Moorish empire at the end of the play. The intervening action centers around the Christians' various attempts to recapture their Virgin and to convince the Almirante to convert to Christianity. The Moorish King, however, continues to refuse and throws one Christian after another into jail. Then, thanks to the Almirante's daughter, Princess Floripes, the crusaders get out of prison almost as quickly as they are sentenced. (Floripes is eager to help because she is in love with one of the Christians and hopes to marry him.) After a series of skirmishes, during which time Floripes renounces her allegiance to the Moorish god Maum and the Christians destroy the Moors' temple, Floripes and almost all the Christians manage to escape to France. The crusader Oliveros, however, is recaptured.

Knowing that the Christians will return for Oliveros, the Almirante is determined that this last crusader will not get away. He therefore orders that Oliveros be well guarded and has the Christian thrown into the most inaccessible prison, where the Filipinos are presently being kept. The Almirante then organizes a border patrol system to prevent the Christians from reentering Moordom. As a final measure he tells his soldiers that if the Christians do find a way in, he must be alerted immediately by telephone.

Despite all the precautions taken by the Moors, Carlos Magno and his men succeed in saving their fellow Christian. After a number of ingenious tactical maneuvers—including the use of disguises and a magic telescope, and a spectacular escape in a large balloon—the prisoner is rescued and all the Christians return happily to France. Once they are back in Christendom, the priest converts Floripes to Christianity and the princess marries her beloved crusader.

Outraged by the serious losses the Moors endured in the last surprise attack, the Almirante sends some soldiers to France to declare war. Since the Christians still want to win back their image of Mary and convert the Moors to Christianity, they willingly accept the challenge, and the two sides decide on the time and place for the battle. On the appointed day, in a battlefield located equidistant from the two kingdoms, the fight begins. Although there are a few tense moments, the Christians easily outduel the Moors. Just before slaying a Moor, each Christian offers his opponent the option of converting to Christianity and thereby living, or of dying by the sword. All the Moors prefer death with the singular exception of the Almirante's son Fierabras, who chooses to convert at the last minute. Thus both the Almirante's children abandon their religious faith and homeland, one for reasons of love and the other for reasons of survival.

The only loyal Moor left alive is the Almirante himself. Although he is sure that he will die, he bravely prepares to take on the entire Christian army by himself. It is decided by the Christians, however, that the Almirante and Carlos Magno should fight this battle alone. After pleading with Maum to help him and after voicing his anxieties about a dream in which he saw that his son would abandon him, the Almirante begins to fight Carlos Magno. The duel progresses quickly, and the Christian King gets the advantage almost immediately. Then, just when Carlos Magno is ready to stab the Almirante, the Moor's converted son arrives on the battlefield and asks the Christian to allow him (Fierabras) to try to convince his father to convert. Carlos Magno agrees.

After much talk, Fierabras finally persuades the Almirante to convert to Christianity by explaining that only Christians go to Heaven. Father and son then go to Rome to find the priest who will baptize the Moor. During the baptismal ceremony, however, all is lost suddenly, for the priest insists that the Almirante renounce the soldiers who have just died for him in battle. This the Moor refuses to do. Although he willingly gives up his religion and even his power, he will not abandon those men who have given their lives for him. Since the Moor does not accept the priest's command, he must be killed and is taken away to be shot. Before the Almirante dies he repeats that he has given up his faith and is presently sacrificing his life for his people. The Almirante then requests that Carlos Magno take good care of his son and that Fierabras be given the Moor's crown, even though the young man had abandoned his own father. The Almirante is shot, a large tomb is erected in his honor and Fierabras and Floripes pray to God to care for their father.

The play closes with a formal good-bye speech to the audience and with special prayers for the Virgin of Guadalupe, the Maestro de los Moros and San Juan Amecac.

The hero of the play, it seems to me, is the Moor Almirante Balán. A symbol of the "noble savage," the Almirante is also a martyr who, like Christ, had to die for the sins of his people. The Almirante's nobility and fineness of character, however, made virtually no impression on the Hueyapeños. Few villagers knew anything more than that the play told the story of how the Christians defeated the pagan Moors. Those who were more familiar with the tale summarized the play as follows: The leading characters are the King of Turkey, Prince Fierabras, Princess Floripes and King Carlos Magno of France. There is a lot of fighting between Moors and Christians, and then finally the Christians win. Although the god of the Moors claims to be all powerful, ultimately he gets killed. The villagers added that one of the highlights of the play is the scene in which Princess Floripes marries a Christian. Not until I returned to the United States and had the opportunity to study the San Juan Amecac text did I discover the Almirante's noble character.

In 1971 I returned to Hueyapan to observe the Virgin of Guadalupe fiesta again. Although I had expected to have the chance to see the play for a second time and discuss the story with members of the cast, there was a slight complication and the Moors and Christians did not perform. Nevertheless, I did interview Don Delfino, a man who had played the part of Carlos Magno in eleven different productions in the past. The Hueyapeño who used to assume the role of the Almirante, on the other hand, was unavailable for questioning. Even though it would have been interesting to compare the interpretation of the actor who played Carlos Magno with that of the man who portrayed the Almirante, I actually doubt that there would have been much of a difference; for Don Delfino's analysis, I discovered, was only a more elaborate version of the explanation given to me by several other villagers who were acquainted enough with the story to answer the questions that I had formulated after reading the text myself. The interpretation that follows, therefore, is not simply the biased opinion of a man personally involved with the role of Carlos Magno; rather it is the view of a Hueyapeño who knows the story better than most villagers, but who shares their perspective.

Don Delfino explained that of all the characters in the play, Carlos Magno is the most noble. We know that this is true, he said, because in the end the Christian King triumphs. The Almirante, on the other hand, is bad, and it is for this reason that the Moor is abandoned. Unlike the Christians, the Almirante and the other Moors do not believe in the Virgin or the Christian saints; instead they worship the devil. Just like the Protestants or the Aztecs who prayed to rocks,[12] the Moors worshipped whatever they wanted to, Don Delfino said. Then the actor again repeated that the Moors took the devil to be their *santo*.

In order to explain the origin of the conflict between Carlos Magno and the Almirante, Don Delfino—independent of the script—told me an abbreviated version of the story of Satan's expulsion from Heaven, substituting the name of Carlos Magno for God and that of the Almirante for the devil: "The two were both born in Rome. However, they could not get along so the Almirante left for Turkey and Carlos Magno stayed in Rome. Carlos Magno was a religious man, and the other one worshipped evil. So he left and in Turkey he found people to follow him."

Neither Don Delfino nor the other Hueyapeños I spoke with felt very much, if any, compassion for the Almirante. The few villagers who were at all aware of the actual story seemed unimpressed by the fact that the Moorish King was willing to give up

12. The fact that Don Delfino put the Protestants and the Aztecs in the same pagan category is not, I suggest, a coincidence. It reflects the degree of disdain Hueyapeño Catholics feel for the "Brothers," as they call the Protestants. What is more insulting than to associate the Protestants with the barbarian Aztecs and Moors! Although the Hueyapeños know that they are Indians, the Catholic villagers are confident that they are no longer seen as Aztecs.

his "pagan" religion, his worldly riches and his land for
Christianity, but would not renounce his valiant soldiers who
had died for him in battle. As far as these Hueyapeños were concerned, the subsequent shooting of the Almirante was simply a
matter of "law"; it was not to be questioned or pitied.

As I have already suggested, the play about the Moors and
Christians, together with other elements of Catholic ritual, were
introduced into Indian villages in order to facilitate the religious
and general cultural conversion of the peoples of Mexico. Today,
however, many of these very same customs are considered
markers of Indian tradition. Often it is maintained that although
many practices were introduced after the Spanish Conquest,
they have been interpreted in such a way that they reflect an indigenous world view, one that is quite different from the imported Iberian culture imposed on the Indians. As far as the
Hueyapeños are concerned, however, not only have they adopted
hispanic symbols and values, but they frequently assume an
even less tolerant stance on the question of cultural variation
than does the dominant culture. Thus in the play about the
Moors and Christians, the villagers identify with the crusaders
and are less willing to show compassion for the pagan, but noble,
Almirante Balán, than does the original script.

Today Hueyapeño children play Moors and Christians the
way American youngsters play cowboys and Indians. What is
more, just as most White Americans believe that their side is
represented by the cowboys—who are, of course, the good
guys—the Hueyapeño children assume that they share the same
cultural tradition as the crusaders and consider the Christians
the rightful victors.

The Guadalupe Fiesta at the Home
of the Virgin's Sponsor in 1969

All fiestas in Hueyapan conform more or less to the same pattern.
They follow traditions that were established during colonial
times in Mexico. Although some aspects of the celebration might
appear exotic or "Indian" to an outsider, again we see that these
so-called indigenous customs have been carefully "baptized"

and serve to dramatize European, not prehispanic, religious themes.

Don Zenaido Ansures was the *mayordomo* (sponsor) for the Virgin of Guadalupe fiesta in 1969. Maestro Rafael was going to have the same honor in two years, and therefore he and Doña Juana, following Hueyapan custom, also had major responsibilities this year. Since they were even required to sleep at Don Zenaido's home for several days, Doña Zeferina and Angelina had to stay behind at home to take care of the children during the fiesta period.

Don Zenaido and his wife Doña Nasia are among the wealthiest people in Hueyapan. Unlike the majority of the residents of the pueblo, they do not live in a plain brown adobe brick house with dirt floors. Don Zenaido went to the extra expense of having both the walls and floors of his house covered with cement and painted bright colors. He, his wife and their grandson David live in three spacious rooms: a large living room that contains a double bed, a smaller bedroom with another double bed, and a kitchen equipped with a gas stove. In addition, the family owns a television set.[13] For purposes of the fiesta, Don Zenaido constructed a temporary kitchen outside with seven fireplaces to accommodate the great cooking demands of the holiday week.

In the early evening of December 8, the fiesta formally begins. This is the day of the Immaculate Conception, and many young children have been whispering excitedly in the plaza all afternoon that soon they are going to accompany the Virgin to the home of the *mayordomo*. By 5:00 P.M., the procession begins.

Three people organize the religious procession: Don Zenaido; Don Abogón, who will sponsor the fiesta next year; and Maestro Rafael, who, as we have seen, will serve two years from now. The large images of the Virgin of Guadalupe and the Virgin Mary (La Imaculada Concepción) are attached to special litters and carried from the church, where they usually reside, to the *mayordomo*'s home. Then, on December 12, Guadalupe's actual

---

13. Approximately five families owned television sets in 1969 and even fewer had gas stoves.

saint's day, there is another procession to return the two images
to the church. The Virgins are kept in individual glass boxes
which have been gayly decorated with white and pink paper
flowers for the occasion. Unlike all other *santos* the Virgin of
Guadalupe is represented not by a statue, but by a painting,
such as the one Juan Diego was supposed to have shown Bishop
Zumárraga.

When the procession reaches the *mayordomo*'s home,
everybody solemnly enters the house through one of the doors
into the living room and walks into the adjoining bedroom. Copal
incense is burning in the smaller room, flowers—mostly
white—are everywhere and *petates* (straw mats) have been laid
on the floor so that people can kneel and pray comfortably. On a
table at the back of the bedroom is a small image of the Virgin of
Guadalupe. This *misterio*, which is in a small glass case, has
been in the *mayordomo*'s care now for almost a year. The large
images are removed from the litters and placed on the table with
the smaller one. As this is done, everybody kneels. Then some of
the guests leave the bedroom, while others remain behind to say
rosary with Don Paco, the village deacon.

After they have paid their respects to the Virgin, the visitors
return to the living room, where Doña Nasia welcomes them formally. First she offers them a drink of *aguardiente* and then she
invites her guests, in groups of seven or eight, to have something
to eat in the kitchen. Although only twenty people participated
in the procession, perhaps as many as fifty visitors have gathered
in the *mayordomo*'s home by the time night has fallen. They all
chat amicably among themselves as they wait patiently to be
served coffee, bread, beans and *tortillas*.

On December 9 there is no organized ritual. Preparations for
the coming festivities continue, however, in the *mayordomo*'s
home. Then on the following evening, December 10, those most
obligated to help with the fiesta—the men who will be *mayor-
domos* in the next two years, their wives and other close *compadres*—go to Don Zenaido's to spend the night. From now until
December 14, when fiesta activities finally subside, these individuals will live in the *mayordomo*'s home and the women will
work almost continuously preparing food for the innumerable

guests. During this first long night the men congregate in the living room, where they drink and make plans for the following day; their wives go outside to the temporary kitchen to cook.

Before the women settle down to the arduous task of grinding the chiles for tomorrow's *mole*, they, their husbands and a few of their children who have tagged along go into the bedroom to pray to the Virgin. The visitors then return to the living room to socialize for awhile. Some sit on the bed and others sit on chairs that have been arranged in a semicircle. In all there are about fifteen people. Doña Nasia comes in from the kitchen to offer the adults *aguardiente* mixed with hot coffee. She serves each guest from the same jigger-sized glass in a slow, methodical way. Both men and women accept drinks from Doña Nasia and they all joke that the strong brandy only serves to combat the cold, not to make a person drunk. As soon as each person finishes his drink, Doña Nasia offers him a cigarette which he carefully puts away to smoke later in private.

Following the drinks everybody is invited into the kitchen for a light supper. The guests are served coffee, bread, beans, *tortillas* and a bit of roasted rabbit—an extra treat, compliments of Don Zenaido, who had gone hunting earlier that day. Finally, by about 9:00, the women retire to the outside kitchen.

December 11 is the first big day of the fiesta. A Mass is performed in the morning, and the Moor and Christian players arrive later in the day. By 7:00 in the morning more women have come to the *mayordomo*'s home to join the regular helpers. As many as twenty women, most of whom are *comadres* of Doña Nasia, spend the day cooking plain and bean *tamales*, *mole colorado*, beef and turkey chile soups, boiled beans and mounds of *tortillas*. There are mothers with nursing babies, old women with no family responsibilities and a few unreliable teenage girls, who are more interested in dancing inside with the men than in helping their mothers and *comadres*.

Despite the enormous amount of work, the women do enjoy themselves. The fiesta gives them the opportunity to visit with one another, to eat a lot of good food and to drink. All the same, they are sorry that their cooking obligations keep them from seeing the processions and the *Moros y Cristianos* in the plaza.

Women serving *mole colorado* at a fiesta.

Furthermore, except for the young girls who do run in and out, the women do not even share in the dancing and hilarity that is going on inside Don Zenaido's house; either they are too busy or they feel embarrassed about how they look after having spent long arduous hours in the kitchen. Of the adult women, only Doña Nasia can be seen bustling about, catching glimpses of the party progressing inside as she goes on one errand or another.

Two music groups have been hired to accompany the various fiesta activities. First there is a brass band which performs with the Moors and the Christians and plays during the major religious procession that takes place on December 12. Next there is a combo which provides dance music in the *mayordomo*'s home. Neither the band nor the combo is a local group. Both were hired from neighboring villages especially for the occasion.

Perhaps as many as one hundred people visit Don Zenaido's home during the evening of December 11. Then fifty guests spend the night there in order to be able to participate in the early-morning procession on the following day. The overnight guests have brought their own blankets. When the time comes, they simply curl up on whatever bit of free floor space they can find in the living room or bedroom and go to sleep. Mats have been spread out everywhere, making the cold floor somewhat more inviting. Those who want to turn in early do so in spite of the blaring television set in one room and the dancing in the other. By midnight nearly all the guests have gone to sleep and by 1:00 A.M. even most of the women who have been working outside have come in to get a little rest, leaving behind only a couple of helpers to tend the fires for the duration of the night.

There is not much room in the bedroom for sleeping guests, for in the center of the floor there is a colorful mountain of freshly cut flowers. At 2:00 A.M. a few women get up and begin decorating special crosses with these flowers. The work takes them a couple of hours, and while they slowly and skillfully recreate traditional floral arrangements, one old woman sings religious hymns in a beautiful, haunting voice.

By 4:00 A.M. the flower crosses are ready and Don Zenaido awakens everybody. He wants the December 12 procession to be on its way early. Despite his best intentions, however, Don

Zenaido is unable to get people organized before 5:30. The large images of the Virgin of Guadalupe and the Virgin Mary, as well as the *misterio* of Guadalupe, are all attached to litters and carried to the church by women. A young girl walks in front of the Virgins, sprinkling flower petals in their path, while her mother waves copal incense before the images. Accompanying the Virgins are the fifty overnight guests who march in two lines on either side of the litters. Each person carries a bouquet of white flowers and a candle. Behind the Virgins two men carry the special flower crosses, while two other men march with Mexican flags on which are attached emblems of the Virgin of Guadalupe.

Behind the procession comes the band. As Don Paco takes a break from leading the group in the singing of appropriate hymns, the band fills in with marching songs. Following the band come several *compadres* who have been selected to light firecrackers, and throughout the solemn procession the staccato sound of exploding rockets announces to the entire village that the Virgins are slowly making their way to the church. The procession takes two and a half hours to go from Don Zenaido's house to the plaza, a walk that could be done in five minutes at a normal pace. By the time the procession reaches the plaza a large crowd has gathered; some people simply watch, but many others join in and accompany the procession to the church, where rosary is said.

Later in the morning Mass is celebrated. Then around 5:00 in the afternoon a small procession leaves the church to return the *misterio* of the Virgin of Guadalupe to the *mayordomo*'s home. The two large images remain in the church now until next year. Finally, throughout December 12 and 13 the Moors and the Christians continue to perform in the plaza and to eat their meals and sleep at Don Zenaido's home.

Don Zenaido's is the center of a continuous party from December 11 through December 14, with crowds of people drinking, eating, dancing and talking. During the four days of festivities the main women helpers do not get more than a couple hours of sleep a night. Then when the fiesta finally is over and they return to their respective homes, the women start right in all over again with their normal series of demanding chores, never really having the chance to catch up on lost sleep.

Rosa and another woman carrying the *misterio* of the Virgin of Guadalupe in a procession to the church. This photograph was taken in 1971.

Protestants in Hueyapan

Since the beginning of the twentieth century several Protestant missionary groups have visited Hueyapan and have been successful in converting a considerable number of villagers. According to Elvira Hernandez, when her grandparents were young people—just before the Mexican Revolution—missionary groups began to make converts in Hueyapan. The Spiritualists were the first to arrive. Next came the Methodists. Although these two sects are no longer represented in the pueblo, there are several hundred Hueyapan Protestants who belong to the Pentecostals, Universalists, Seventh-Day Adventists and Jehovah's Witnesses. Of the four sects, the Universalists have the largest congregation in the village. The Protestants do not participate in villagewide or *barrio* religious activities, nor do they involve themselves in the *compadre* network.[14]

All four of the Protestant sects have built their churches in the outlying *barrios* of Hueyapan: San Andrés, San Bartolo and San Felipe. This, I suggest, is no accident. In the first place it is difficult for the *barrio* people to attend the Catholic church regularly, for the walk to the center of town is long and often arduous. Since the Protestants, with their more portable storefront churches, could provide houses of prayer in the outlying *barrios*, they had a certain appeal from the point of view of convenience alone.

Second, as already mentioned, those living in the center of town traditionally pointed to the Catholic church and the San Miguel chapel as evidence of the cultural superiority of the Centro residents over the *barrio* people. These old colonial structures demonstrated, the Centro people believed, that they shared a long religious tradition with other Mexicans. In other words, the Centro people implied that they had more in common with non-Indian Mexicans than did their neighbors up in the hills. Many individuals living in the outlying *barrios*, however, also wanted to prove that they had strong cultural ties with the outside world. Yet instead of competing with the Catholics in the Centro by

---

14. The only exception to this is the Protestants' willingness to serve as godfathers in the secular school graduation ceremonies.

building Catholic chapels and churches, many turned to the Protestant missionaries.

Although there is prejudice among Catholic Hueyapeños against the Protestants, there has never been a serious conflict between the two religious groups. As I pointed out in Chapter 4, disputes in the village center around secular matters, and political alliances seem to reflect *barrio*, not religious, affiliation. All the same, since most Protestants live in the outlying *barrios*, they are frequently associated with the more "Indian" elements of Hueyapan by the self-named Centro Progressives; hence Don Delfino's deprecating comment about Protestants, Aztecs and Moors. Actually, the Protestants represent some of the most "progressive" Hueyapeños in the community, a fact which helps substantiate the claim that the Centro faction's distinction between themselves and the *barrio* people is little more than an attempt to slur their adversaries.

In addition to being generally interested in modernizing their own *barrios*, the Hueyapeño Protestants have embraced the national culture's interest in preserving Mexico's indigenous heritage. In this spirit Protestant progressives offer as their contribution to Indian tradition religious hymns sung in Nahuatl which they learned from Protestant missionaries. Thus songs taught to the villagers by outsiders are now offered by Hueyapeños as evidence of the pueblo's ongoing indigenous culture. Since there are no traditional Nahuatl songs in Hueyapan, and since the only other Nahuatl songs known were introduced by school teachers and members of a Nahuatl renaissance culture movement, the Hueyapeño Protestants see no contradiction in promoting these hymns as evidence of indigenous music.

One of the Nahuatl-Spanish hymns sung in the village is given on pages 125·127. Hueyapeños learned it from Pentecostal missionaries. It is particularly interesting to note that the Nahuatl used in this and other Protestant hymns exhibits far less interference from Spanish than do the older Catholic texts published by Miguel Barrios.[15] Whereas colonial Catholic priests

---

15. M. Barrios, "Textos de Hueyapan, Morelos," *Tlalocan*, Vol. 3, No. 1 (1949), pp. 53-75.

seemed to have encouraged villagers to borrow freely from Spanish to identify saints and religious items associated with Catholic ritual, the Protestants have tried to preserve, even reconstruct, the indigenous tongue. Yet, despite the nearly pure Nahuatl in the songs I collected, the lyrics as well as the music resemble the kinds of Protestant hymns heard throughout the United States. We might say, then, that the Nahuatl language has been purified by individuals who learned Nahuatl as a second language, to convert native Nahuatl speakers from one European religion to another.

The villagers usually sing this song in both Nahuatl and Spanish, beginning with one language and switching to the other. The musical phrasing shown here varies somewhat when the notes are sung with the Nahuatl words, because the missionaries' translation from the original Spanish does not really fit the music. Though linguistically pure, the Nahuatl lyrics sound forced when applied to the tune. In order not to distort the melody, therefore, I have reproduced the song as it sounds with the Spanish words. The musical clumsiness of the missionaries' translation adds another dimension to the irony of the hymn's being called indigenous.

Canto Bienvenido
(Canto Cualle Micaqueh, or The Welcome Song)

U - nen los san - tos to - dos los san - tos con dul - ce voz

Con re - ver - en - cia porque en pre - sen - cia es - tán de Dios

Bien - ve - ni - dos se hallan her - ma - nos en el nom - bre

ben - di - to de Di - os Hoy re - uni - dos nos

go - za - mos al sa - ber que nos u - ne su a - mor

De - mos gra - cias por ser sal - vos y en nue - stras

al - mas sien - ta gra - ti - tud Por - que so - lo Je - sús nos da

vida y sa - lud Y a la glo - ria al que lle - ve su cruz

Nahuatl Version

Sance cuicame nochintlapacme ince pancinco in Teotl,
Mauesotiga nican ticate itepancinco in Teotl.
Cualle micaqueh nognitzitzin (g)uan itocatzin tlasoh den Teotl.
Axan cecan titaquisqueh ticmahtic tecmololcuia.
Timotlasocamatisqueh cantaquisqueh antualmatzin quimachilia
    tlasotlalistleh,
Ican ce yen Teotl techmomaquilia iuitatzin paquilichle,
Anicuiga quimiquilia cuanepanolti.

Ansacuiliui monechegoxe xlapepenalme xpantzin con Teotl.
Anompa alcuiga quipiasqueh tlaxtlaualistleh tioteguitzqueh.
Cualle micaqueh nognitzitzin (g)uan itocatzin tlasoh den Teotl.
Axan cecan titaquisqueh ticmahtic tecmololcuia.
Timotlasocamatisqueh cantaquisqueh antualmatzin quimachilia
    tlasotlalistleh,
Ican ce yen Teotl techmomaquilia iuitatzin paquilichle,
Anicuiga quimiquilia cuanepanolti.

Spanish Version

Unen los santos todos los santos con dulce voz,
Con reverencia porque en presencia están de Dios.
Bienvenidos se hallan hermanos en el nombre bendito de Dios.
Hoy reunidos nos gozamos al saber que nos une su amor.
Demos gracias por ser salvos y en nuestras almas sienta gratitud,
Porque solo Jesús nos da vida y salud,
Y a la gloria al que lleve su cruz.

Muy pronto unidos los escogidos irán a Dios.
Ya en el cielo tendrán el premio de su labor.
Bienvenidos se hallan hermanos en el nombre bendito de Dios.
Hoy reunidos nos gozamos al saber que nos une su amor.
Demos gracias por ser salvos y en nuestras almas sienta gratitud,
Porque solo Jesús nos da vida y salud,
Y a la gloria al que lleve su cruz.

English Translation

All the saints (sing) together in a sweet and reverential voice,
Because they are in the presence of God.
You are all welcome, brothers, in the blessed name of God.
Today reunited, we enjoy the knowledge that His love unites us.
Let us give thanks for being saved and in our souls feel gratitude,
Because Jesus alone gives us life and health,
And glory be to Him who carries the cross.

Very soon the chosen ones will go united to God.
In heaven they will finally enjoy the fruits of their labor.
You are all welcome, brothers, in the blessed name of God.
Today reunited, we enjoy the knowledge that His love unites us.
Let us give thanks for being saved and in our souls feel gratitude,
Because Jesus alone gives us life and health,
And glory be to Him who carries the cross.

POST-REVOLUTIONARY GOVERNMENT AGENCIES: A NEW PERIOD OF EVANGELIZATION IN HUEYAPAN

6

Following in the tradition of the *encomenderos*, *corregidores* and Catholic missionaries before them, government representatives have been coming to the pueblo regularly since the early 1920s to educate Hueyapeños in Mexico's national ideology and to give the villagers the technology they need to participate effectively, at a specified level, in the post-Revolutionary national cultural system. The new "acculturation" program resembles old colonial policies in three fundamental ways. First, the post-Revolutionary government has directed its efforts toward making changes in the same areas of Hueyapan life that the colonialists were concerned with. Second, the government has reinforced many Catholic symbolic and ritualistic themes introduced by the Spanish by incorporating them into the new secular religion of the country—nationalism. Third, the government, like the Spanish, has provided the necessary conditions to ensure that the distinction between Indian and hispanic will be preserved, while at the same time attempting to integrate the so-called Indians into the rapidly changing social and economic spheres of Mexican society.

Where the post-Revolutionary program seems to differ from earlier efforts is in its interest in glorifying certain elements of indigenous culture. Actually, it is this new attitude that has permitted the government to incorporate the Indians ideologically, socially and economically into post-Revolutionary Mexico and still to maintain both their so-called Indian identity and their accompanying low socioeconomic position in the dominant society. In essence, government agencies have been keeping the Indians Indian by commercializing the concept of Mexico's indigenous heritage, manufacturing an image of the Indian that could be produced cheaply and that would have wide selling appeal. Thus, by using the colonial Catholic technique of incorporating indigenous traditions into a different cultural context, the government has been constructing and reconstructing the image of the Indian. Unlike the Catholic missionaries, however, who were able to pick and choose from a variety of customs, the post-Revolutionary workers have had little "autochthonous" material to work with and have therefore had to devote most of their energies to the restoration of archeological and ethnological ruins as well as to the creation of modern hispanic variations on long-dead indigenous themes.

Aside from the economic advantages derived from commercializing indigenous cultures, there are ideological reasons for the government's interest in promoting the Indian. As part of a nationwide attempt to instill a sense of racial and cultural unity in the country, the Mexican government has actively been supporting the idea that the true Mexican is the descendant of two great strains—the Spanish and the Indian—and that patriotic citizens should take pride in this double ancestry. Yet before convincing the Mexican people to pay tribute to either the Spaniards or the Indians, the post-Revolutionary government has had to break down prejudices held about both groups. Particularly difficult has been the job of changing the traditional image of the Indian, who since colonial times has been considered an inferior being.

The government has been interested primarily in venerating the nation's indigenous and Spanish past, not its present. As far as modern Mexico is concerned, citizens are encouraged to iden-

tify with the Mestizo—a racial and cultural hybrid—and not
with the Indian or the Spaniard separately. Yet in an effort to
glorify the country's indigenous heritage, the government has
found it economically and ideologically useful to keep present-
day Indians Indian, living relics of a previous era. As a result contemporary Indians have been placed in a contradictory position:
while being preserved as living tribute to Mexico's noble indigenous past, they are also being discriminated against for
being Indians in a Mestizo-oriented society.

Two government agencies—the Cultural Missions and the
School—have come to Hueyapan and both have played influential roles in determining the nature of the Hueyapeños' post-
Revolutionary indigenous identity. By reviewing aspects of the
programs of these two groups, we can see how they have involved
the villagers in the contradictory situation described above. On
the one hand, government workers have promoted the
Hueyapeños' Indian-ness to outsiders. They have accomplished
this by publishing articles about various so-called indigenous
customs found in Hueyapan and by organizing official
ceremonies for important hispanic visitors that feature elements
of local traditions in combination with indigenous customs
collected from elsewhere and/or fabricated in national centers.
On the other hand, the same government agents have been
weeding out and denigrating the villagers' so-called indigenous
ways, giving Hueyapeños the desire and a few of the tools
necessary to begin to acquire the most recent set of values that
distinguish the lifestyle of the more prestigious hispanic Mexicans—now identified as Mestizos—from that of the lowly Indians.

Thus, following the colonial pattern, government agents
have settled down in the village with the express purpose of
providing Hueyapeños with the "culture" that they supposedly
lack. Once again Hueyapeños have been taught to denigrate
their own customs and to emulate those of the hispanic elite, that
is to measure their own worth in terms of how closely they
succeed in duplicating the ways of non-Indians. In the context of
modern Mexico this has meant that Hueyapeños have come to
believe that the more material symbols of hispanic culture they

obtain, the less Indian they will seem. Furthermore, they have accepted the idea that by performing nationalistic ceremonies, they will give evidence of their devotion to and participation in a non-Indian Mexico. Yet it is through these secular rituals, as it was previously through the Catholic ones, that the villagers' Indian-ness is in part being preserved.

In sum, we are now faced with the most recent stage in an old hispanic process. The Cultural Missions and the School have managed to incorporate the villagers into the new post-Revolutionary socioeconomic spheres of society and yet, for still another period of Mexican history, to maintain the Hueyapeños' negative Indian identity.

Cultural Missions

The Department of Cultural Missions was organized in 1926 and today falls under the jurisdiction of the Secretary of Public Education. During the years 1926 to 1938 regional centers were set up to instruct teachers working in rural communities in how to conduct effective literacy campaigns for adults as well as how to help the peasants raise their material standard of living. Before a school teacher received federal certification he had to undergo a four-week training session at the Cultural Missions center located in the part of Mexico in which he planned to do his teaching.

In 1942 the Department expanded its program and began to send specially trained people to the pueblos. Cultural missionaries began establishing temporary stations in villages, staying a few months to help the peasants help themselves, and then moving on to offer similar aid to other villages. By 1970 there were 108 such Missions working throughout rural Mexico in so-called Indian and poor Mestizo communities.

The Secretary of Public Education puts out a small pamphlet that explains the philosophy behind and the various services provided by the Cultural Missions. According to the publication, Cultural Missions workers are supposed to organize a series of economic, social and cultural reform programs that touch on almost every aspect of life in a rural community. In addition, the missionaries are encouraged to coordinate their efforts with those of local or regional welfare agencies. They are also directed to establish committees of Economic and Cultural Action in the pueblos, so that after the government workers leave, there will be formal bodies in the communities to carry on the projects they initiated.

The government agents work in teams comprised of the following specialists: director, social worker, nurse/midwife, agriculture instructor, livestock-raising instructor, music instructor, masonry instructor and instructor of industry. Each of these team members has a comprehensive series of obligations to fulfill individually and collectively with other members of the group, working in a way reminiscent of the colonial period of evangelization. First, like the Catholic missionaries, these government workers are trained to believe that they are bringing salvation to the deprived. Second, continuing in the old tradition, the new evangelists come to resettle, where necessary, rural peoples, to give them medicine, to improve their living conditions, to improve their food, to teach them social amenities, to instruct them in how to make good use of leisure time, to give them a "religion" —Mexican nationalism—to incorporate local traditions into nationalized ritual and to compile and publish information on indigenous customs for the edification and use of the dominant elite. Then, like colonial landlords, albeit with more compassion, government agents have been reorganizing the economic system of rural Mexicans, improving their farming technology and introducing new crops. Finally, not only has the post-Revolutionary government repeated colonial acculturation techniques, but the social and material improvements that the modern Missions have been introducing are actually replacing the work of the earlier representatives of hispanic culture. The so-called indigenous traditions presently being described in publications represent European practices or native customs that have been preserved in a transformed state by previous missionary efforts.

There were no Cultural Missions workers in Hueyapan during my stay. Furthermore, my attempt to find some official record of the Missions' visits to the village at the Department's Mexico City headquarters failed, for the material could not be located in the archives. As a result, I have had to depend on the Hueyapeños' impressions alone for my information about what occurred in the pueblo. According to the villagers, Cultural Missions teams visited Hueyapan twice, once in 1945 and then again in the early 1960s. I am told that at first many villagers were hostile both to the government workers and to those Hueyapeños who participated in Missions-sponsored activities. In part, many villagers refused to cooperate because they thought the government program was a Protestant missionary project. The name Cultural Missions confused them, and the reputed evangelical fervor with which the government agents executed their campaign confounded them. Yet by the time I came to the village most Hueyapeños had been converted, and those who discussed the Missions with me spoke of how grateful the villagers were for the improvements introduced by the government workers. They were also quick to explain that the Missions were not of a religious nature.[1]

Doña Gregoria's analysis of the effect the Missions have had in Hueyapan was very much to the point: government workers had brought "civilization" to the village, she said. Before, she suggested, Hueyapan had been much more "Indian." In order to train the villagers, the agents had to be very strict, Doña Gregoria continued; they did such things as insist that Hueyapeños eat only when they were properly seated at tables. Doña Zeferina told me that Missions workers used to visit individual homes to instruct the villagers, and they would frequently ask her to accompany them because she was well respected in the pueblo and was therefore very helpful in convincing the villagers to trust the government representatives.

Missions workers, I am told, were responsible for building a bridge, strong enough to hold vehicles, over one of the deepest gorges in Hueyapan. In addition, they helped to encourage the wider use of chemical fertilizer and other agricultural aids.

1. The problem of confusing the Cultural Missions with religious missionary programs seems to have been widespread. When I visited the Mexico City office of the Cultural Missions, one of the first things I was told was that this was not a religious project.

Thanks to the Missions, more villagers began to build adobe homes and to cement-face the outer walls of their houses that looked out onto the street. Previously many Hueyapeños had lived in wood plank homes that were draughty and posed fire hazards.

The teams' carpenters encouraged villagers to build latrines, tables, chairs and beds. Today, although some villagers continue to use homemade furniture, an ever-increasing number of them prefer to own the more prestigious store-bought pieces. Particularly popular are the colorfully decorated straight-back chairs with straw seats, metal-frame beds with religious scenes at the head and small compartments at the foot, as well as *roperos* (cupboards) used for hanging and storing clothes.

Social workers encouraged the women to use hibachi-like stoves in addition to their stone and adobe hearths for cooking. They also taught Hueyapeño women how to jar fruit so that this kind of food could be preserved, and instructed women in embroidery and other decorative sewing techniques.

With the hope of transforming local weaving skills into a profitable industry for the villagers, members of the Missions teams introduced mechanical looms to the pueblo. However, although there are a few mechanical looms in Hueyapan today, most women who still weave have not bothered to make the investment in the modern looms and continue to work in the traditional way. This seeming lack of enthusiasm about adopting the new technology was motivated by a variety of factors. First, the villagers saw more opportunity for advancing themselves through the fruit industry than through weaving, and have therefore devoted most of their money and energies to improving the productivity of their orchards. Second, Hueyapeños prefer the backstrap loom because the finished product is thicker and warmer. Third, the villagers have learned that their indigenous technology commands a much higher price than the more modern product would from the few tourists who come into the area in search of Indian weaving.

The Cultural Missions were particularly influential in the area of medicine. In 1945 several traditional healers like Doña Zeferina enrolled in the nursing program and subsequently began using modern methods of healing, almost to the exclusion of rustic techniques. Also, about twenty women who had had no healing experience before were trained in the rudiments of modern medicine and now serve as part-time healers in the village. The Missions nursing program consisted of lessons in how to give intermuscular and intravenous injections as well as how to bandage.

Given the method of healing used, it is not surprising that Hueyapeños call their modern healers "healers who inject." In essence, the art of modern healing does involve little more than giving a patient an injection, usually of penicillin, and prescribing an antibiotic, usually in the form of a pill. Since medicine can be purchased throughout Mexico without prescriptions, Hueyapeño healers simply go to Cuautla and buy whatever the Missions nurses recommend or the doctor in Tetela suggests. Then, according to Doña Zeferina, after a period of trial and error, each healer develops her own list of favorite cures.

The Cultural Missions also helped to organize a reasonably well-equipped infirmary in Hueyapan. This is located in the home of Doña Modesta Lavana, one of the healers who lives right off the main plaza in the village.

In addition to providing medical training, the 1945 Missions nurses appointed three Hueyapeño women to serve as cleanliness inspectors for the school. Doña Zeferina, who was one of the women chosen, said that every Monday and Wednesday the inspectors would attend early-morning flag exercises and inspect each and every child individually, looking to see whether the pupils were wearing clean clothing and whether they were well scrubbed. If a child was dirty, he was publicly bathed before his fellow students. Many mothers were infuriated by this new regulation because it gave them more work. Yet they knew that if they refused to send their children to school clean, they were admitting that they were "lazy Indians."

In conjunction with the intensive program to integrate Hueyapeños into post-Revolutionary Mexican society at a certain level, Missions workers joined school teachers in promoting the villagers' indigenous identity. First, these government agents organized performances featuring young Hueyapeño girls dressed in *xincueites*. Also, together with a few school teachers, Missions workers introduced several Nahuatl songs to the Hueyapeños. Then, although I never saw the official report, I am quite sure that the cultural missionaries who worked in the village collected information about the Hueyapeños' so-called indigenous customs. I am confident of this because they were instructed to do so in the published list of duties put out by the Secretary of Public Education and, furthermore, I have seen two examples of such material compiled by school teachers who were similarly advised.

Let us now look at some of the Nahuatl songs taught to the villagers by government agents and at the ethnographic data collected by them for the edification of outsiders. Although the villagers did not have any traditional songs with Nahuatl verses, I did manage to compile seven Nahuatl songs during my stay. Two of the pieces were introduced by Protestant missionaries, four by school teachers working with cultural missionaries, and one was composed recently by Lino Balderas, a Hueyapeño who used to sing in the Bellas Artes in Mexico City and had been a member of a Nahuatl cultural renaissance movement. Of the four songs that Hueyapeños learned from government agents, two are in a Nahuatl that exhibits very little Spanish interference—despite the fact that their themes are indisputably European—and they seem to be the careful handiwork of school teachers interested in refining Indian Nahuatl. The lyrics of the first piece, "Güilotl Istac" ("White Dove"), are about a person in love who would like to hear the gentle songs of the white dove that he heard when last in the company of his sweetheart. The second song, "Xipatlani Ompa" ("Fly Over There"), entreats the aid of a bird—this time a swallow—to serve as a messenger between the person singing the song and his beloved.

More interesting than the above pieces are "Xochipitzauac" ("Slender Flower") and "In Tamalera" ("The Tamale Maker"). Actually, although these two are supposed to be separate songs, the music and versification are virtually the same. Unlike "Güilotl Istac" and "Xipatlani Ompa," these two songs use a Nahuatl considerably mixed with Spanish. Furthermore, the verse structure is casual and the lyrics a bit off-color. All this informality leads me to believe that the school teacher responsible for introducing these songs to Hueyapeños learned them in other so-called indigenous communities and passed them on in the form in which he found them.

Doña Zeferina told me that in the poor Mestizo lowland community Huazulco, "Xochipitzauac," in a Spanish rendition and combined with a little dance, is traditionally performed as part of the informal ritual that accompanies a religious marriage celebration. In fact, the song and dance are known throughout Nahuatl-speaking Mexico and, consequently, it has been suggested that they might be pre-Columbian survivals.[2] Some scholars have proposed that the song and dance were originally part of a rite dedicated to Xochipilli (Goddess of the Flowers) and subsequently transformed by Catholic priests into one dedicated to the Virgin Mary. Yet when the musicologist Castellanos tries to demonstrate the traces of prehispanic culture preserved in this ritual, all he can say is that the "simplicity" of the stanzas and the "chaste" manner with which the dance is performed suggest that such is the case.[3] In my opinion the lyrics, the melody and the Catholic context in which the song is traditionally sung overshadow the significance of whatever vague remnants of pre-Columbian times might have survived.

The version of "Xochipitzauac" that the Hueyapeños learned tells about several stages in a man's life. First we see him courting his beloved. Then we see him as an older man reminiscing about how much better life treated him when he was younger: clothes (all Spanish in style) were cheaper, and when he was with the priest he even had clothes with buttons. Now he has nothing but a pair of colored *calzones*, not even the more acceptable white *calzones* that most poor peasants wear. Finally, the man is ready to die, but before he takes leave of the world he manages to make an off-color joke about kissing a young girl's breast.

The song "In Tamalera," which I consider to be another version of "Xochipitzauac," deals with cooks having fun at a fiesta. Once again European features are emphasized. The only person

---

2. The oldest known version of the song dates to the eighteenth century. For discussion of this theory see P. Castellanos, *Horizontes de la música precortesiana* (Mexico City, 1970), p. 83.

3. Castellanos, p. 83.

identified is Doña Dominga, the *tamale*-maker.[4] While this woman, who has a Spanish Catholic name, and another cook are dancing, a silk shawl is dragging on the ground. Furthermore, there is a playful lamb (a European import). Finally the song ends with a scatological joke that is tacked on somewhat inelegantly. The music in this and all other songs conforms nicely to the kind of hispanic-Iberian music popular throughout Central Mexico.

Below I give "Güilotl Istac" and "Xochipitzauac" to illustrate the contrast between the two styles of songs introduced to Hueyapan by school teachers and cultural missionaries.

Güilotl Istac
(Paloma Blanca, or White Dove)

4. Although *tamales* are indigenous, they are prepared mainly on fiesta days and all fiestas are Catholic or modern patriotic holidays.

Nahuatl Version

Gŭilotl istac itegŭitz costic,
Igan ihyo nicnegui tlahtos.
Nicnegui caguis mosel igŭigas
Nigan tlatenco aguatitlan.
Nega yoale cuactimonosqueh
Nan onic piaya mocualtu tlahtol.
Nicnegui caguis mosel igŭigas
Nigan tolhuisque tiutzin tiutzin.

Spanish Version

Paloma blanca piquito de oro,
Con el aliento quisiera hablar.
Quisiera oír tus tiernos cantos
Por las orillas del ensinal.
Aquella noche que platicamos
Tenía presente tu linda voz.
Quisiera oír tus tiernos cantos
Para decirnos adiós adiós.

English Translation

White dove with your beak of gold,
I want to speak with your breath.
I want to hear your gentle songs
By the edge of the stream.
That night when we (my true love and I) spoke,
Your beautiful voice was there.
I want to hear your gentle songs,
So that (she and I) might say adieu, adieu.

Xochipitzauac
(Flor Delgada, or Slender Flower)

Nahuatl Version

Xochipitzauac del alma mía,
Cualani in monana por acmo nía.
Manin mostla, manin uipla,
Tinemisque en companía.

Cuac onia nipiltontlia,
Tlen sombrero, tlen tortilla.
Axan yi niueuetzin,
Sa sombrero de a cuartía.

Cuac onia tetlan cura,
Tlen botones, tlen botones.
Axan yi niueuetzin,
Sa nogazon de colores.

Tech in copa, tech in chile,
Nictlahcali in nodespedida.
Manin mostla, manin uipla,
Ticpitzosque in cone chichile.

Doña Zeferina's Spanish Translation

Flor delgada del alma mía,
Se enoja tu mamá porque no voy más.
Sea mañana, sea pasaoo,
Andaremos en companía.

Cuando fuí muchacho,
Cuánto sombrero, cuánto tortilla.
Ahora que soy viejo,
Solo sombrero de a 25 centavos.

Cuando estaba con el cura,
Cuánto botones, cuánto botones.
Ahora que soy viejo,
Solo mi calzón de colores.

En el copa, en el chile,
Tiro mi despedida.
Sea mañana, sea pasado,
Besaremos la chichi de nene.

English Translation

Slender flower of my soul,
Your mother is angry because I no longer come by to see you.
(Don't worry) be it tomorrow or the next day,
We will be together.

When I was a boy,
I had so many hats and a lot to eat.
Now that I am old,
Just to buy one hat is expensive.

When I lived with the priest,
I had so many buttons, so many buttons.
Now that I am old,
I have only my pair of colored calzones.

With a drink and with a hot chile pepper,
I'll take my leave of the world.
(But before I do) be it tomorrow or the next day,
We will kiss the breast of some young girl.

Although there was no traditional Nahuatl music to be found in the village, school teachers and Missions workers did find a certain amount of ethnographic information that could be presented to outsiders as evidence of the Hueyapeños' so-called Indian-ness. Several types of data were collected and made available to both the public at large and government agencies privately. As noted earlier, the native Hueyapeño school teacher Miguel Barrios published several texts concerning religious practices in the pueblo.[5] In addition, the school teacher presented several short stories and one game that men are still playing in the fields today. Although Miguel Barrios did not include fairy tales about kings and princesses, like the ones I collected in the village, the dominant themes in the stories he presents are European. In one tale, "The Rich Man and the Poor Man," the wealthy landlord forces a lazy worker to separate wheat grain (a European import) that has been mixed with a pile of sand. Then there are a couple of stories in which the evil witches are burned to death. In one tale the women are vampires. In two stories the dominant theme is a spoof on Latin machismo, in which women literally castrate men who are unfaithful to their legitimate wives. Finally there is one tale that describes how Saint Anthony was responsible for giving a village near Hueyapan the name it bears today.

The game reproduced in Barrios' publication is called the "Deer Game," and it could very well be a survival from prehispanic times. Nevertheless, it demonstrates nothing about the villagers other than that they have a rather scatological sense of humor—a characteristic hardly unique to Nahuatl-speaking Mexicans. The game consists of tricking one member of the group into trying to grab a piece of cloth smeared with human feces; the cloth is supposed to be the tail of a deer. I might add that another game that used to be popular in Hueyapan many years ago is called "Jesus Christ." However, this game, like the fairy tales about kings and princesses, was not published by the school teacher. One plays "Jesus Christ," Doña Zeferina told me.

---

5. M. Barrios, "Textos de Hueyapan, Morelos," *Tlalocan*, Vol. 3, No. 1 (1949), pp. 53-75.

by tricking a person into accepting to be Jesus Christ. The victim is then tied up and his hair and clothes are burned.

Rural primary-school teachers are required to write theses about the communities in which they do their practice teaching before they receive their master's degrees. In these presentations they are asked to discuss local customs and traditions. I had the opportunity to read one such thesis about Hueyapan, written by a native school teacher. Unlike the school teacher Miguel Barrios who published in *Tlalocan*, this Hueyapeño was interested not in glorifying indigenous customs, but in singling them out in explanation for the difficulties he, as a school teacher, was having in educating the villagers. Of particular concern to Maestro Cecilio were the Nahuatl language and severe alcoholism. The only local traditions recorded by the Maestro about which he did not make derogatory comments were the custom of dressing up in "funny" clothes during Lent[6] and the villagers' elaborate Good Friday processions. As is usually the case with Hueyapeños and outsiders alike, Maestro Cecilio makes no distinction between truly indigenous traditions, patterns of behavior found among most lower-class Mexicans that are attributed to Indians, and hispanic customs that have disappeared from hispanic cultural centers but are still found in a number of so-called Indian communities.

The difference in the attitudes of the two native school teachers toward the value of the village's Indian-ness point directly to the dilemma of being Indian in Mexico today. Maestro Miguel left Hueyapan for Mexico City in the early 1940s. In the city he found work teaching Nahuatl, in this way capitalizing on his Indian-ness. The other Hueyapeño teacher, however, remained in the village, dedicating himself to the job of ridding Hueyapan of those attributes associated with being Indian. In other words, by staying home and living the impoverished life of the Indian, Maestro Cecilio could not liberate himself from his traditionally negative understanding of what it

---

6. Although Maestro Cecilio did not explain this in detail, every Sunday during Lent a few Hueyapeños dress in red costumes to represent the Jews and wander about the village making nuisances of themselves.

meant to be Indian. All the same, Maestro Cecilio was still a school teacher, and as such he believed enough in the idea of glamorizing the villagers' Indian-ness occasionally for outsiders that he did join the other teachers in Hueyapan in organizing ethnic programs for hispanic dignitaries who came to the village on official visits. As the Maestro himself used to say, it was his "duty" to honor these important visitors in this way.

The School

The Hueyapan school was organized in the early 1870s, just a few years after Benito Juarez promoted his bill for free and compulsory education throughout Mexico. The man who opened the school was Maestro Cecilio's grandfather, a native Hueyapeño who had learned how to read and write from the village's parish priest. In those days, I am told, classes were informal and were held in private homes. Then by the early 1900s teachers who were not from the village started to come regularly to the pueblo and hold classes in schoolrooms that had been constructed in the main plaza out of part of the old municipal palace. Perhaps some of these visiting *maestros* had been trained under Justo Sierra's program.[7] All that I was able to learn about these teachers was that none of them ever stayed very long in the village and that they were drunks and poor instructors. In sum, by the time the Mexican Revolution broke out in 1910, the school was definitely a fixed institution in the village, albeit a somewhat corrupt and inefficient one.

During the war classes met only sporadically. Then in 1919 a group of Hueyapeños became so discouraged with the situation that they decided to stop depending on outsiders to teach their children and to assume the responsibility themselves. Since they all had farming to do, these villagers agreed to share the job of teaching; first one person would be *maestro* for a few months,

---

7. Justo Sierra was one of the most important educators in Mexico's history. For an excellent account of this man's role in the organization of a free education system under Porfirio Díaz, see J. Vázquez de Knauth, *Nacionalismo y educación en México* (Mexico City, 1970), pp. 81ff.

then another, and so on. Maestro Cecilio's father Eligio, who was still a single man at that time, was elected to begin the program. When it came time to replace him, however, everybody felt that Maestro Eligio was doing so well that he should continue as the permanent instructor for the village. To make this financially feasible, it was also agreed that the villagers would pay him fifty *centavos* a day.

In 1921 a man representing Alvaro Obregón's government came to the pueblo.[8] This individual, whose name was Rómulo F. Hernandez, announced that he had the authority to affiliate the Hueyapan school with the national school system. He also told the Hueyapeños that anyone who wanted to obtain federal teaching certification should go to Mexico City on a certain day. As a recognized government teacher, a *maestro* would receive a salary of two *pesos* a day, Maestro Rómulo explained. Although most Hueyapeños were afraid that if they went to the city they would be captured and drafted to serve in the army, Maestro Eligio decided to take a chance and go.

In Mexico City each of the teachers who dared come to the meeting was given 300 *pesos* in "pure silver," I am told. Having nothing large enough to hold so much money other than their hats, the men poured the coins into their *sombreros* and returned to their respective villages. When Maestro Eligio triumphantly arrived in Hueyapan others in the pueblo decided to go to Mexico City and try their luck, but it was too late.

By the 1930s the school was well organized and there were instructors teaching all six grades of primary school. Furthermore, Maestro Eligio, who was the director of the school at this time, turned the Hueyapan plaza into a beautiful square *(un zócalo)* with a kiosk and flowers. Then in the mid-1930s, when the socialist Cárdenas was president, Maestro Eligio and the other teachers marched the children around the village and at every corner they all shouted *"Viva el Socialismo."* This, together with an apparently unfounded rumor that a boy and girl

---

8. According to Vázquez, in 1921 Obregón established a new ministry of education that had as its goal the creation of a nationally uniform school system (Vázquez, p. 133).

had been forced to undress themselves in school, so angered the villagers that they closed down the school. In addition, the Hueyapeños destroyed the beautiful square. The school did not open again for another two years, and when it did it only offered instruction up to the fourth grade. As for the square, it was never fixed up again, for the villagers preferred to use the plaza for bull riding instead—a fact often pointed to by the so-called more sophisticated villagers as evidence of the Hueyapeños' Indianness. Although Maestro Eligio was permitted to teach again, he was not reinstated as the director.

This period of intense conflict between school teachers and Hueyapeños reflected the general mood of the state and nation during Cárdenas' presidency. In fact, the Hueyapeños themselves identified their local disputes with the larger political factions that were gaining power during these years. Most of the anti-school teacher element in the village, for example, supported the Morelos rebel leader Tallarín, who was rampaging the countryside in the late 1930s, killing teachers and other government employees.

By the early 1940s things began to quiet down in the village. Nevertheless, as we have already seen, bitter disputes still continue to erupt periodically between school teachers—many of whom are native Hueyapeños—and some of the villagers. Also, despite the fact that the school never closed down again after the Cárdenas period, it was not until 1960 that the Hueyapeños managed to have all six grades of primary school taught once more. Children who go on to secondary school still must pursue their studies in Tetela, Tlacotepec or elsewhere.

In Hueyapan today control of the village school system remains in the hands of Maestro Eligio's family. Although Maestro Eligio himself retired about twenty years ago, his children are carrying on the tradition. Maestro Demetrio is presently the director of the main school in the San Miguel Plaza; Maestro Cecilio is the director of the two-grade San Felipe school; and a third son, Maestro Octavio, is the director of the three-grade San Bartolo school. Thus only the three-grade San Andrés school is independent of the family's influence, and its director is not a local villager.

Primary-School Textbooks

The village children study geography, national language (grammar), history, civics, arithmetic and natural sciences. All these subjects are covered in the textbook and workbook series that since 1959 the National Commission of Free Textbooks has been publishing and distributing to every community where there exists a primary school affiliated with the federal government. The material that I discuss here is from the history-civics and national language texts and the accompanying workbooks. These books have been written primarily from the perspective of the Mestizo working-class child, who is usually, but not always, pictured in an urban environment. When an Indian appears, he (she) is represented as an outsider, either as the former ruler of Mexico who practiced noble but strange customs, or as the poor humble Indian of the present who should be treated kindly by the Mestizo youngster and helped to assimilate.[9]

As the Hueyapeño pupils read these books, they find the story of the prehispanic Indian as alien from their own experience as do the Mestizo children, but they do see themselves in the portrayal of the contemporary Indian, the one who still does not belong. Since these texts emphasize how wonderful it is to be a working-class Mestizo, the village students are strongly encouraged to want to conform to this idealized image of the Mexican and to forfeit their own Indian identity. In other words, the Hueyapeño children learn that they should try to overcome their Indian-ness, for if they do not, they will remain marginal, just like most of the Indian people who appear on the pages of these books: smiling, gentle observers who rarely get to participate in the fun.

Beginning in the first grade, the children are introduced to the ideal Mestizo home. The houses illustrated are all colorfully painted, two-story, cement-faced or brick establishments, not one-story adobe structures. Furthermore, the rooms are nicely

---

9. It should be pointed out that in 1973 a new set of books was issued throughout Mexico correcting many of the objectionable features of the series in use during 1969-1970. In particular, a considerable effort was made to modify the urban bias of the previous books.

furnished with the popular wood-frame chairs with straw seats, beds, chests of drawers, cupboards, tables, curtains and rugs. In the kitchens there are gas ranges, refrigerators and electric blenders.

Students also read about the idealized Mestizo family: the affectionate mother, the hard-working father and the dutiful children who love school. Even the dullest children in Hueyapan cannot help but see the unfavorable contrast between their own daily routines and that of the lucky little boy in the reader who starts his day with a good-morning kiss from his mother, a warm bath and a well-balanced breakfast served by his gentle, smiling *mamá*. As we have already seen, when Doña Zeferina's grandchildren get up they straighten out the wrinkles in the clothing they have slept in, and they perform a series of household chores before they eat a breakfast served by their silent over-worked mother.

In the first-grade reader the most direct reference to Indians appears in a poem entitled "Indian Boy." A Mestizo child calls to an Indian boy to come and play, explaining that all American[10] children should love one another. The Mestizo then tells the Indian that he will teach the latter to read because all children of America want to learn. Accompanying the poem are two illustrations. In the first we see one young boy dressed in pants, a shirt and shoes. He is leading by the hand another young boy who is wearing white *calzones*, a hat and sandals. The former, who clearly represents the Mestizo child, is noticeably lighter complexioned than the Indian, but definitely not white. In the second picture, the Mestizo and the Indian are seated on the grass; the Mestizo has his arm around the Indian and is helping him read.

At the end of the first-grade reader the children receive their first history lesson. It is about Hidalgo, who is referred to as the Father of the Country. Hidalgo loved the Indians, the children are told, and he taught them how to read. Thus once again the pupils learn that good Mexicans show compassion for Indians. Although there is no lesson on Mexico's prehispanic indigenous

---

10. By "American" the poem means all the inhabitants of North and South America.

heritage in this book, the children are given a hint about the special status this history has in Mexico by an illustration in which a pennant on the wall of a classroom says "Club Cuauhtémoc"; the accompanying reading selection deals with how good it is to organize and participate in a school club.

The second-grade text elaborates on the theme of how dutiful Mestizos help the Indians assimilate and how worthy Indians take advantage of the opportunities given to them. In the beginning of the reader pupils are introduced to Pedro, his sister Carmela and their parents. The family lives in Mexico City in a middle-class home with a maid and a pet dog. Pedro's father is a doctor who works in public health. One day, while *Papá* is reading the newspaper, he learns that a cyclone has severely battered the states of Oaxaca and Veracruz. Since Pedro's grandparents live in the region that has been hit very badly, *Papá* decides to visit the area to make sure that they are all right.

When Pedro's father returns he reports that the grandparents are fine, but that he has found a young boy who has no father and whose mother has been killed by the storm. Consequently, *Papá* has adopted the boy and brought him back to Mexico City. The child's name is Martín, and Pedro and Carmela welcome the newcomer warmly. In contrast to the Mexico City children, Martín is wearing colored *calzones*, sandals and a hat.

For several pages the reading selections only suggest that Martín is an Indian by describing his clothes, his dark complexion, his poverty and the fact that he has no father, that is, that he is an illegitimate child. Then when Martín goes to school with Pedro the *maestra* explicitly associates the boy with the Indians. The school teacher asks Martín to tell the class where he is from. Embarrassed that he comes from so far away, the boy shyly replies that he is from Oaxaca. In an attempt to reassure Martín, the *maestra* says that they are all delighted to welcome a Oaxaca boy because they know another Oaxaqueño—"an intelligent and brave little Indian who managed to become president of the Republic." In the following lesson the students learn about Benito Juarez, who against all odds overcame his Indian-ness and became a great national hero. The message is clear enough:

Martín and other Indian children are different from the idealized Mestizo pupils; however, if they try or, better yet, are adopted by middle-class non-Indians the way Martín and Benito Juarez were, they too can rise above their humble Indian origins and make great contributions to Mexico.

In the second-grade reader the children learn about the history of Tenochtitlán and the Spanish Conquest. There is no reference at this time, however, to the fact that the Aztecs are the ancestors of modern Mexicans. The children also read about the War of Independence and about Benito Juarez in more detail. Then in the workbook the second graders are introduced to the educator Justo Sierra, who is described as having said that the Indians must progress in order to assure the social development of the country.

In the third grade the emphasis shifts. Instead of discussing the Mestizos' need to help the humble contemporary Indians, the text presents the student with the glories of Mexico's prehispanic past, with explicit reference to the fact that these Indians are the Mestizos' noble ancestors. Beginning with the big-game hunters who crossed the Bering Strait and finally settled in Mexico, the reading selections go through all the major pre-Columbian cultural periods and ethnic groups: the Olmecs, Mayas, Teotihuacanos, Toltecs, Chichimecs, postclassic Mayas, the Nahua tribes, Tarascans, Mixtecs, Zapotecs and Aztecs. The story then switches to Mexico's other heritage, that of the Spanish conquerors. The new section is introduced by the following text:

> In the first pages of this book we said that we are Mexicans and that we must love and serve our country.
>
> Now we are familiar with the interesting history of the first inhabitants of our country whom we call indigenous since their ancestors came here in remote times.
>
> In the following pages we shall see what part another people took in the formation of Mexico today.

Given the government's interest in creating an image of Mexico that dramatizes the dynamic synthesis of two races and cultures, it is not surprising that the history presented minimizes the

atrocities committed by Cortés and the conquerors and empha-
sizes instead those aspects of the Conquest in which there were
mutual aid and compassion. Thus Malinche, the Tlaxcalans and
the Cholulans[11] are sympathetically drawn as invaluable and
noble assistants to the Spaniards in the conquest of the Aztecs.
In the same conciliatory spirit, more space is devoted to the missionary priests and their work of "teaching the Indians good
customs" than to the cruel *encomenderos*. After a description of
the gentle priests, the third-grade text ends with a brief summary of the Mexican Revolution. As for the long and complicated
history of colonial Mexico and the first hundred years of the
nation's independence, this is saved for the fourth grade.

In sum, most of the third-grade reader is devoted to the telling of the story of the Indians, the Spaniards and how these two
peoples met. Although the two groups are described as having
contributed to the development of contemporary Mexico, the
text makes it clear that neither alone represents the modern
Mexican. The fourth-grade reader turns away from talking about
racial and cultural origins and presents the complete history of
the hybrid Mexican of today. The story of the Mestizo begins in
the colonial period, and as the fourth-grade text introduces the
chapter on the subject, it underlines the significance of this
history as follows:

> During those three centuries [1521-1821] two races and two
> cultures, the indigenous and the Spanish were mixed. [And from
> this mixture] was formed the present-day Mexican people, [the
> people] to whom you belong.

The Hueyapeño children, however, have just finished learning
about how little they do belong. They do not bathe daily or brush
their teeth or live in pretty well-furnished homes with gas ranges
and refrigerators. Instead they are much more like the Indian boy
in the first-grade reader and Martín in the second-grade book.
And their parents resemble the smiling people dressed in Indian

11. Malinche is the Indian woman who became Cortés' mistress. She
learned Spanish and helped the conqueror by serving as an interpreter. The Tlaxcalans and Cholulans fought with the Spaniards against the Aztecs.

clothes who are frequently depicted in the margins of the pages watching the happy Mestizo school children at play. Thus, since the Hueyapeños are different from the Mestizos, it follows that their history must be different; for if the Indians and the Mestizos have the same history, why are there still two groups today?

The students learn that after the heroic death of Cuauhtémoc the Indians were converted to Catholicism by kindly priests and were cruelly exploited by *encomenderos*. From then on, however, the only mention of the Indians is in connection with the poor Mestizos: both groups are badly mistreated by Mexico's enemies (usually the landlords) and bravely defended by the nation's heroes (frequently priests). As to what criteria were used throughout history to differentiate between the Indians and the Mestizos, the students learn virtually nothing. All they see is that by the time we reach modern-day Mexico there are still Indians in the country who are supposed to be different from the idealized Mestizos.

In the fifth and sixth grades, history books no longer treat national affairs but consider Mexico in the context of the history of North and South America. Discussion of local national themes is left to reading selections in the national language texts. Although the Indian is not mentioned at all in the sixth-grade reader, in the fifth-grade book the concept of Mexico's indigenous people reaches its most acceptable form for contemporary Mestizo-oriented Mexico. The student reads about the adventures of a class of pupils in Mexico City who go on several excursions around the country. On two of the trips the children visit archeological ruins in the Yucatán and Chiapas. Their guide tells them that there are eighty-one distinct archeological zones in Mexico and 12,000 registered ruins. The students also visit the Tarahumara Indians and learn about their difficult working conditions, their indigenous customs and the fact that they are slowly improving themselves by sending their children to school.

National Holidays and School-Run Assemblies

In Hueyapan school teachers sponsor a series of patriotic programs which repeat the lesson the children have been learning in school: in Mestizo-oriented Mexico the villagers are still Indians. Through these ceremonies the school teachers are continuing the process of incorporating the villagers ideologically and ritualistically into the post-Revolutionary national cultural system, while preventing them from identifying with the heritage of the venerated Mestizo. Thus, after convincing the villagers that it is desirable to be Mestizo, the *maestros* point out —through these patriotic assemblies—that Hueyapeños do not yet belong to this group.

As I have been suggesting, the government has managed to integrate yet segregate the villagers by employing techniques first introduced by Catholic missionaries. In the case of these national ceremonies, the influence of Catholic ideological and ritual motifs is strong. The government has not only transformed so-called indigenous customs and then incorporated them into a new hispanic context the way the Catholics did, but it has also borrowed the entire structure of the Catholic fiesta system for its secular ceremonies. Consequently, major national holidays follow in the Catholic tradition, with processions that feature national and state *santos* (decorated portraits of Hidalgo, Morelos and Zapata), with "religious" ceremonies led by members of the government "clergy" (school teachers and Cultural Missions workers) and with customary *mole* meals served in the homes of *presidentes de fiestas patrias* (fiesta sponsors). On primary-school graduation day the parents even select special *padrinos* (godparents) for the occasion and dress their graduating children in Confirmation clothing. Furthermore, just as every *barrio* is obligated to celebrate the anniversary of the saint whose name it bears, so is it held responsible for the fiesta commemorating the particular national event for which its school, plaza and/or streets have been named. For example, since the school in San Felipe is called 20 de Noviembre, it is expected to organize the celebration for the Mexican Revolution on every November 20; and since the San Bartolo plaza and one of the *barrio*'s streets have been named after Emiliano Zapata and another street bears the name 10 de Abril, the date on which the Morelos hero was killed, San Bartolo is in charge of running the Zapata fiesta every April 10. Whenever possible the national processions are routed along the streets that have the appropriate names, just as in Hueyapan the Good Friday procession during Holy Week always goes along Calvary Street.

For purposes of this discussion, I describe only two patriotic programs; however during the year 1969-1970 the school sponsored about twenty-five patriotic assemblies, of which eight were major pueblo celebrations. I look first at the anniversary celebration of Emiliano Zapata's death and then at an official ceremony organized to welcome Felipe Rivera Crespo, the candidate for governor, and his campaign party. Specifically I contrast the way the school teachers treat the question of being Indian in a ceremony for Hueyapeños alone with the way they treat the question in a ceremony for hispanic dignitaries. I also elaborate on how national celebrations resemble Catholic rituals, suggesting that by using the Catholic fiesta system model, the government has borrowed more than just structure and has in fact adopted hispanic Catholic attitudes about salvation and the value of Indian culture for a non-Indian Mexico.

The Zapata Fiesta   The anniversary of Zapata's death receives little official recognition in Mexico except in the hero's native state of Morelos, where April 10 has become one of the most important holidays. Hueyapeños actually began the 1970 festivities at 8:00 on the evening of April 9. At this time the school presented a short program in an open-air theater constructed in the San Bartolo plaza for the occasion. Brief speeches were delivered by teachers, and patriotic recitations, a comedy skit and folk dances representing various regions of Mexico were performed by the children. Not until the following morning did the program turn to the more serious aspect of the holiday—the commemoration of the death of Zapata.

At 5:00 A.M. Maestro Demetrio, the director of the San Miguel school, turned on the record player and amplifying system, waking up the villagers with blaring *ranchero* music. Between songs the Maestro announced that all school children were expected to be in the plaza by 6:00 to participate in the flag-raising exercises. One by one, sleepy children, wrapped up in wool *rebozos* and *serapes*, wandered into the plaza. Finally by about 7:00 there were enough pupils to begin. The flag was hoisted up the flagpole, the children sang the national anthem and then the teachers dismissed the students so they could eat breakfast, wash and dress for the procession and morning assembly program.

By a little after 10:00 over 1000 people had gathered in San Bartolo Barrio and the school teachers began to organize the procession. First in line were the major officers of the community, who were responsible for carrying the portraits of Zapata, Hidalgo and Morelos, in that order. The national *santos* were decorated with striped streamers in Mexico's colors: green, white and red. After the village dignitaries came the band that was hired from another village for the occasion, then the school children and finally the public at large. The procession started on Calle Emiliano Zapata, turned onto Calle Popo—named after the volcano Popocatepetl that can be seen from almost every part of Morelos—and then onto Calle 10 de Abril.

Once the procession returned to the plaza benches were arranged and the "religious service" began. The assembly started with a request that the public observe one minute of silence in honor of Zapata. After this private devotion the band played the national anthem. Next the director of the San Bartolo school, Maestro Octavio, gave the official speech, describing in eloquent prose how Emiliano Zapata gave his life so that Mexico's peasants would have "Land and Liberty." As the Maestro recounted the heroic deeds and martyred death of Zapata, the image of Christ came to mind, for the Maestro had taken this "deep myth of culture"[12] as his model and was creating the "Passion of Zapata." The school teacher ended his speech in the following way:

> Don Emiliano Zapata never wanted power; his sword was ready to fight against ambition and treason. Zapata called out the name of the fields and made the land his candidate. He sought freedom with great dignity . . . for that reason, Mexican peasants, do not forget Emiliano Zapata who gave us land for our use, for our sustenance,

---

12. This term is borrowed from Victor Turner, *Dramas, Fields and Metaphors* (Ithaca, N.Y., 1974), pp. 122ff.

for our future. And by congregating here on this occasion and in this act we have come in order to praise him publicly and express our gratitude, our affection, our respect for that individual who died for the land. With his motto "Land and Liberty," the call was heard throughout the country.

Citizen General Don Emiliano Zapata, we swear to you that we shall always remain alert before all danger in order that farming land will always be free and we shall repeat as often as necessary [your saying] "the land must belong to those who cultivate it with their own hands."

The present agrarian reform has its advantages. It brings social justice, improved crops; it organizes the peasants, thereby ending their suffering; it teaches how to use agricultural machinery; it introduces new ways of farming; it opens up unused fertile lands; it builds roads and schools. Article 27 of our Magna Carta presents the flag of the Plan de Ayala for the benefit of and the better future for the Mexican people.

Ladies and Gentlemen, Zapata died for the land.

Thank you.

The program continued with several recitations, speeches and one song dedicated to Zapata. There were also several more recitations in honor of other national heroes and patriotic themes. A number of folk dances were performed, as well as another comedy routine. The assembly then ended with the singing of the national anthem.

What was singularly missing from all the patriotic fanfare was the integration of the villagers' local history into what was supposed to be a Morelos state holiday. For example, although there were a few veterans from the Mexican Revolution still alive in the pueblo in 1970, these people did not receive any recognition in the ceremony. Furthermore, the few old men who still remembered ballads from the Revolution were not invited to sing these songs for the community. Finally, not one speech delivered about Zapata and the Revolution mentioned the fact that two villagers reputedly signed the Plan de Ayala or that the Hueyapeños themselves personally participated in the suffering during the long struggle for "Land and Liberty." Instead of glorifying the part played by villagers in the fight for freedom and prosperity, the teachers assigned the Hueyapeños an entirely

Children dressed in colonial Spanish costumes dance at the fiesta commemorating the death of Zapata. Zapata's photograph, decorated with streamers of Mexico's national colors, holds the place of honor, much like an image of a Catholic saint.

passive role in the process, instructing them only to express their gratitude for the sacrifices *others* made for *them*. From Christ to Zapata, therefore, the villagers have been taught to feel indebted to outsiders for almost every "improvement" they have acquired throughout their history, be it religion, land or what is referred to in general as "culture."

The insignificance of the villagers' local tradition was further reinforced by the fact that the region was not represented in any of the fiesta dances or costumes. No dance from the state of Morelos was performed, and the children's outfits, which were specially sewn for the occasion, depicted the styles of the North, South and West of Mexico, but not that of Hueyapan or the state of Morelos. For instance, one of the school teachers introduced the dancers for one number in the following way: "And now some *charros* (dudes) from Jalisco and women from the state of Puebla are arriving and they tell us that they are going to perform a beautiful typical dance entitled 'Jarabe Tapatío.' "

Mention of the Indian per se occurred twice during the course of the school program. First a young girl recited a poem about the national hero Cuauhtémoc, and then two teenagers performed a comedy skit that poked fun at the uncultured, irresponsible behavior of a present-day Indian woman. These two presentations clearly illustrate the double image of the Indian that Hueyapeños have come to accept. There is the noble Indian of the past who has been incorporated into the sacred history of the elite, and then there is the humble Indian of the present who has little to recommend him. The poem about Cuauhtémoc told the story of how the last Aztec emperor was tortured by the Spaniards but would not reveal where the Indians had buried their treasures. The skit about the contemporary Indian, entitled "The Confession of the Indita," was about a young woman who goes to confession to tell the *padre* all about her mischievous deeds that have angered her husband: she has flirted with another man, has stolen money out of her husband's trousers, etc. After describing one silly incident after another, the woman gives the lame excuse that she did not really mean to do any of these things. The paternalistic priest reprimands the woman severely, but in the end absolves her for her sins. To add to the deprecating, childish impersonation of the Indian, the *indita* speaks Spanish in the stylized, grammatically incorrect dialect associated with Indian speech throughout Central Mexico.

After the school assembly, Padre Diego, at the request of members of San Bartolo Barrio, performed a Mass on a hill in the *barrio*. Then there was a *mole* meal and a dance. The major expenses for the festivities were paid by the *presidente de fiestas patrias*, i.e., the secular *mayordomo*. Furthermore, all villagers who owned *ejido* lands were expected to contribute some corn, acknowledging in this way their gratitude to Zapata for the *ejido* land reform.

The Welcoming Ceremony for Lic. Felipe Rivera Crespo, the Candidate for Governor of the State of Morelos

Now that we have looked at one fiesta that was organized for the benefit of the Hueyapeños, let us turn to a program that was presented in honor of an important outside government dignitary. In February 1970 the national party candidate for governor of Morelos came to Hueyapan on a campaign tour. Since his election was guaranteed, the official purpose of his visit—aside from the publicity—was to give the Hueyapeños the opportunity to present the incoming governor with petitions. Anticipating this important event, school teachers met with village officers and parents to plan the welcoming ceremony.

Whereas the teachers rarely, if ever, encouraged the villagers to use customs associated with their Indian-ness in programs presented for Hueyapeños alone, they used all of their influence—even overriding an objecting faction—to convince the villagers that they should put on an ethnic show for the candidate. In other words, although school teachers usually ignored or denigrated the image of the contemporary Indian in the classroom and on the stage, now that Rivera Crespo was coming to town they were promoting the villagers' Indian-ness as though it were an asset. As a result the teachers were instructing Hueyapeños to entertain Rivera Crespo with a little presentation that glamorized the very identity that previously the *maestros* had been teaching the villagers to want to lose. Given the object of the future governor's visit, such a performance seemed particularly inappropriate, for the villagers were supposed to ask Rivera Crespo to help them overcome their Indian-ness.

Since the Hueyapeños had very few customs that could be used for the "ethnic" show, the teachers combined the products of their own imaginations with what little "raw material" existed in the village and fabricated a ceremony that was as alien to the Hueyapeños as were many of the practices teachers had been introducing over the years. Nevertheless, the program served its purpose: Hueyapeños were used to pay tribute to the Mestizo's indigenous heritage, and the candidate for governor left the village delighted to see that Mexico's Indian culture was being preserved.

The performance itself was a simple affair and illustrates clearly how government workers have integrated vestiges of the villagers' so-called indigenous traditions into a new cultural context, changing the customs, but not the Hueyapeños' Indian identity, in the process. Four teenage girls were dressed in the costume associated with old women in Hueyapan today: *xincueites*, embroidered cotton blouses, wool shawls and agave-fiber sandals. Carrying a wreath of fresh flowers, the girls went to the entrance of the pueblo to greet Rivera Crespo and his campaign party. When the candidate arrived at the bridge the girls presented him with the wreath and, speaking in Nahuatl—which the candidate did not understand—and in Spanish, welcomed him and his entourage to the village. Next the girls accompanied the politicians to San Miguel Plaza, where the ceremony continued.

After a series of formal exchanges between the director of the school and Rivera Crespo, a sixth-grade boy recited a poem in Nahuatl and Spanish that is popularly thought to have been written by the prehispanic poet-king Netzahualcoyotl. The poem is entitled "Nonantzin" ("My Mother") and can be found in Spanish translation in the nationally distributed second-grade workbook. From this school-book Spanish version, native teachers, with the help of a few other Hueyapeños, translated the poem into Hueyapan Nahuatl.[13]

---

13. According to Classical Nahuatl scholars, "Nonantzin" was actually composed after the Spanish Conquest and therefore could not have been written

The program then continued with the more serious matter of discussing with Rivera Crespo what the villagers hoped the politician would be able to do for them once he took office. Maestro Rafael presented one of the most important petitions. Representing the village's self-named Progressive faction, the native school teacher asked the candidate to support the Hueyapeños in their wish to secede from the municipality of Tetela. Maestro Rafael explained that the villagers wanted to form their own *municipio*, because as a satellite of Tetela Hueyapan was not progressing rapidly enough. Furthermore, Maestro Rafael maintained, it was not right that Hueyapan, which had a larger population, should be governed by the smaller Tetela. The candidate listened politely, embraced Maestro Rafael three different times and promised to do what he could. The petitions presented by other members of the community asked Rivera Crespo to do the following: improve roads between Hueyapan and Tlacotepec and Hueyapan and Tetela, install a permanent market place, provide running water, make available the necessary funds so that the school teachers' house could be renovated, and help the villagers set up a more adequate health center. In addition, almost every *barrio* asked the candidate to provide money for the construction of such public facilities as basketball courts. Finally, the village's local musical ensemble, Los Norteños, asked the candidate to provide the members of the group with special *charro* costumes.

The candidate thanked and embraced every petitioner and pledged to do everything in his power to help the Hueyapeños. He then excused himself, and he and his entourage moved on to Tetela. After directing the villagers to plaster the walls with Rivera Crespo posters, some of the school teachers joined the candidate's party as it moved on to the municipal seat.

Although many Hueyapeños remained enthusiastic and op-

---

by Netzahualcoyotl, who died nearly one hundred years before the fall of Tenochtitlán. All the same, the nationally distributed primary-school text publicizes the poem as the work of the poet-king and school teachers throughout Morelos—and undoubtedly throughout Nahuatl-speaking Mexico—have had the poem translated into the Nahuatl dialects of the communities in which they work. For further discussion of the date of this poem see B. Leander, *La poesía náhuatl: Función y carácter* (Göteborg, Sweden, 1971), p. 50.

Young girls dressed in indigenous Hueyapan costumes for a fiesta in honor of government dignitaries. The headdresses worn by the girls in the last row are not traditional.

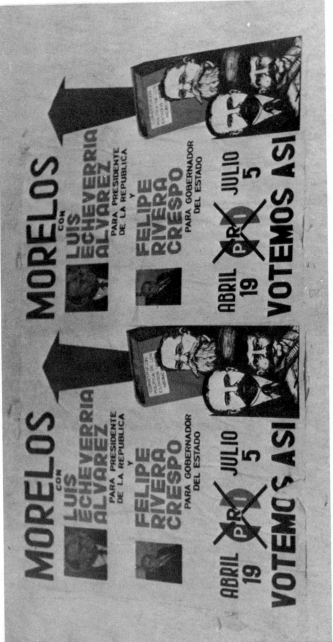

One of the posters pasted up in the plaza after Rivera Crespo's campaign visit. In addition to photographs of the national party (PRI) candidates, the poster shows the Mexican Constitution with a grouping of three revolutionary heroes—Carranza, Madero and Zapata. Although the grouping implies a harmonious political tradition, actually Madero and Carranza became enemies of Zapata and Carranza was responsible for having the Morelos hero killed.

timistic about Rivera Crespo's visit for several days, cynicism soon set in. One native school teacher said that he knew that the incoming governor would not keep his promises and that the entire campaign tour was a publicity stunt out of which nothing would come. Given this rather critical view of the matter, I asked the teacher whether he would bother to vote for Rivera Crespo in April and then for Echeverría in the presidential election that July. The Maestro seemed surprised by my question and replied that of course he would; he was Mexican, after all.

When I returned to Hueyapan nearly two years after Rivera Crespo's tour and twice since then, I found that the Maestro's pessimism had been well founded. Although there have been a number of changes in the village, as I point out in Chapter 3, few are the result of Rivera Crespo's campaign pledges. As far as the February 1970 ceremony is concerned, it accomplished primarily one thing: a hispanic dignitary was entertained with a little show that glamorized, while it reinforced, the very image of the Hueyapeños that the villagers had hoped the candidate's visit would help to eradicate.

CULTURAL EXTREMISTS

7

We are now ready to turn to the last group of non-Indians who have come to Hueyapan to teach the villagers about their Indianness. Over the last twenty-five years, members of an urban-based, primarily middle-class organization have been visiting Hueyapan and a number of other so-called indigenous communities in Central Mexico to encourage the Indians to take pride in their indigenous heritage and to preserve it. These individuals want the Indians to continue to practice their indigenous customs not simply as a tribute to Mexico's Indian past, but as a model for Mexico's "autochthonous" future. Representing what I call the cultural extremist element of post-Revolutionary Mexico, these people have been campaigning to rid Mexico of all Spanish and other foreign influences and to revive indigenous traditions, so that the country might reemerge as the great cultural and political nation it had been in prehispanic times.

Although the Mestizo-oriented government considers the views of the extremists absurd, it has not been able to ignore them. First, much to the government's consternation, its own interest in glorifying Mexico's indigenous heritage has at times been confused with the position of the extremists.[1] Furthermore, there have been moments when the extremists managed, with varying degrees of succèss, to put the government on the defensive by promoting the idea that the nation was being ruled by people who were anti-Indian and consequently anti-Mexican.

Perhaps the most celebrated controversy between the government and the extremists took place in 1949-1950. A historian by the name of Eulalia Guzmán announced to the press that she had discovered the bones of Cuauhtémoc in Ichcateopan, Guerrero.[2] When government anthropologists examined the find, however, they concluded that Guzmán had unearthed the remains of at least five different skeletons including those of women and children. Yet since the cultural extremists had already aroused considerable patriotic fervor over the Guzmán discovery, many people were unwilling to accept the official report. Hostile feelings against the anthropologists were so pronounced, in fact, that a few newspapers even suggested that these men be shot in the back like traitors.[3]

Even during my field stay in Mexico, twenty years after the Guzmán incident, government representatives were concerned enough about the cultural extremists to feel compelled to defend the official view against them. Early in his campaign for the presidency Luís Echeverría condemned the idea that Mexicans should reject their Spanish heritage and reasserted the traditional post-Revolutionary position that the concept of the Mestizo, not the Indian alone, integrated Mexico's national identity. A few days after Echeverría spoke on the subject, a reporter interviewed Alfonso Caso, Director of the National Indigenist Institute (INI), to ask this government anthropologist what he thought of Echeverría's statement. The interview appeared in one of Mexico's most important newspapers, *El día*, and received a two-column spread. The headline read: "Showcase *In-*

1. G. Aguirrє Beltrán, "Indigenismo y mestizaje," *Cuadernos americanos*, Vol. 78 (July-August 1956), p. 44.

2. J. Vázquez de Knauth, *Nacionalismo y educación en México* (Mexico City, 1970), p. 219.

3. Vázquez, p. 219.

digenismo—To Reject the Spanish, One of the Two Sources of Our Nationalism, Would Be a Painful Mutilation: Caso." Agreeing with Echeverría, and calling the extremists "raving indigenists" (*indigenistas delirantes*), the anthropologist presented the situation in the following way:

> "These indigenists whom I would call raving claim, for example, that we should abandon Spanish and speak Nahuatl. Isn't that unbelievable? And why Nahuatl, I ask? Why not Maya, or one of the other sixty or so languages that still exist in our country? These—let us call them for the time being—raving indigenists, do not understand that Spanish is the national language, that is to say, a means of communication among all Mexicans.
>
> "Look, I have dedicated my life—as you know—to the study of ancient Mexican cultures and what we modern Mexican anthropologists have shown the world has succeeded in gaining admiration for the products of the ancient indigenous cultures. On the other hand, we must not forget that Spain brought to Mexico European culture, which is the descendant of the Mediterranean culture that flourished from Egypt and Chaldea, passing through Palestine, Greece and Rome and which culminated with the great thinkers and artists of the Renaissance. Thus as inheritors of both cultures, we must affirm our personality and continue drinking at their fountains in order to conserve our own style, in order to be each time even more ourselves."[4]

Defending the indigenous policy of the Mestizo-oriented government, Caso explained that Mexicans had two obligations vis-à-vis the Indians: to admire the Indian of the past and to help raise the standard of living of the Indian of the present. In order to meet both of these responsibilities, he continued, the government organized "two distinct but intimately related institutions: the Institute of Anthropology and History . . . which is concerned with the study of the Indian of the past and present and the National Indigenist Institute which is concerned with . . . taking the improvements of modern civilization to the Indians."[5]

---

4. A. Caso quoted in S. Moiron A., "Indigenismo de escaparate," *El día* (Mexico City), December 2, 1969, p. 9.

5. Moiron, p. 9.

Committed as they are to the idea that the Indians are racially and culturally superior to non-Indians, the extremists rejected the national acculturation program. Also, they take issue with the concept of a Mestizo Mexico, because as far as they are concerned, there never has been a blending of cultures at any level of society and there never will be. The Spaniards, as well as other Europeans, simply imposed their ways on the indigenous peoples, the extremists maintain, and thereby interfered with the "natural evolution" of the true Mexicans. Conceding that there are mixed-bloods in the country, the extremists explain that the hybrids are the descendants of raped Indian women, that they have been robbed of their indigenous cultural heritage and that they consequently have no choice but to imitate the traditions of the White man. Given the fact that the Spaniards and other foreign influences have been oppressing the Indians and depriving the mixed-bloods of their superior race and culture, there is only one solution: expel the foreigners and educate the Mexicans in their own culture so that they might return the nation to its former grandeur.

Despite the heated disputes and the ostensibly different points of view, the Mestizo-oriented government and the cultural extremists actually have a good deal in common. First, the members of both groups belong primarily to the middle and upper classes and come from urban environments. Second, both groups consider a certain segment of the rural poor to be culturally distinct, and they identify these lower-class people as the descendants of the original inhabitants of Mexico. Third, the government and the cultural extremists are both eager to demonstrate their own pride in Mexico's indigenous heritage, and in their efforts to pay tribute, both groups—in varying degrees—have called upon the contemporary Indians to participate in these acts of veneration by glamorizing their Indianness. Finally, both groups claim to want to save the present-day Indians, the government by making Mestizos out of the Indians and the extremists by making Indians out of the Mestizos.

I am particularly interested in the ideas and programs of the cultural extremists because their "raving" campaign offers an intriguing sequel to the long history of non-Indian attempts to define and resolve Mexico's Indian problem. Since the early colonial period, when Catholic priests and Spanish landowners first began to fit the Indians into the European cultural system, hispanic political factions have been creating the image of the Indian to meet the social, economic and ideological interests of non-Indians. First the Spaniards arrived with very definite ideas about civilization—ideas that they imposed on the Indians. Indigenous ways were denigrated, and the Indians were taught new traditions so that they could be integrated into the non-Indian society. Then, throughout the colonial period and the first one hundred years of independence, champions of the Indian cause emerged from time to time among disputing hispanic factions. Usually these non-Indians were concerned about defending the Indians from the exploitation of other non-Indians rather than about fighting to revive indigenous traditions. And even on the few occasions when non-Indians fought to restore indigenous customs, this almost always meant to reinstitute practices taught to the Indians by representatives of the sympathetic factions.[6] After the Mexican Revolution the new hispanic elite claimed to be the protector of the Indians and the admirer of indigenous cultures. However, as we have already seen, the government has shown itself to be interested primarily in glorifying Mexico's indigenous past, while continuing the program, first introduced in colonial times, of integrating the so-called Indians into a non-Indian Mexico. Finally, disagreements among members of the post-Revolutionary elite have given rise to another champion of the Indian cause—a group of people who do not merely want to pay tribute to Mexico's indigenous past, but who aspire to recreate this past in the present. Yet the group's vision of an Indian Mexico has been distorted by the beliefs and values of the dominant hispanic cultural system. Cultural extremists are so dependent on European cultural standards that in order to justify their plan for turning Mexico back to the Indians, some of them have even felt compelled to show the world that European culture is just a bastardization of Indian culture, that the cradle of Western Civilization is actually in Mexico. Thus we have come full circle: first the Spaniards destroyed in-

---

6. A good example is the Caste War of the Yucatán.

digenous traditions in the name of giving the Indians "culture," and now a hispanic group wants to make the Indians the founders of the very civilization that scorned them.

Since Hueyapan is a Nahuatl-speaking community, the villagers have encountered only those cultural extremists interested in reconstructing the prehispanic culture of Nahuatl-speaking Indians. Elsewhere in Mexico, however, where other indigenous languages are still spoken, extremists have based their ideology on the restoration of other prehispanic traditions. Groups of this sort have been particularly active in the Yucatán, where Mayan is spoken.[7] As Caso's statement indicates, the Nahuatl cultural extremists have received the greatest publicity and have caused the greatest trouble for the national government.

As I mentioned in the Introduction to this book, I had the opportunity to work in Mexico City with the Movimiento (The Confederated Movement for the Restoration of Anauak), one of the most important organizations in Nahuatl cultural extremist circles today. For about three months I participated in the Movimiento's weekend reunions and in their very occasional midweek activities. However, as I became increasingly disillusioned with the Movimiento and more involved with my research in Hueyapan, I stopped attending the group's meetings.

Although my decision to go to Hueyapan was made independently of the Movimiento, upon my arrival in the village several Hueyapeños assumed that I either was from the Movimiento or would at least be interested in the group's activities. The fact that I was an anthropologist who wanted to learn Nahuatl suggested to many villagers that I too was a cultural extremist. Thus, without my even asking them about it, a number of Hueyapeños volunteered information about the Movimiento's influence in the pueblo. Before looking in detail at the villagers' experiences with cultural extremists, however, let us acquaint ourselves briefly with the history, ideology and program of the Movimiento.

7. F. Tannenbaum, "Agrarismo, indianismo y nacionalismo," *Hispanic American Historical Review*, Vol. 23 (1943), pp. 420-421.

The Movimiento in Mexico City

Rodolfo F. Nieva, a lawyer living in Mexico City, founded the Movimiento in the late 1950s. Previously Nieva and other members of his group had belonged to the Indigenous Confederation of Mexico that was under the direction of the self-styled linguist Juan Luna Cárdenas.[8] According to a Hueyapeño farmer who had been quite active in the Indigenous Confederation, this earlier group had been in existence since the 1930s.

Since Movimiento members in Mexico City were unwilling to talk about conflicts they had had with other cultural extremists, I am not entirely clear on the issues that caused the Indigenous Confederation to split. One explanation which seems plausible, however, was suggested to me by the Hueyapeño Don Juan Maya. Having participated in the activities of both groups, Don Juan says that Juan Luna and Rodolfo Nieva wanted to emphasize different things; the former was interested in practicing the Aztec religion, while the latter was devoted only to the study of prehispanic history. Although members of the Movimiento in Mexico City told me that they too had adopted the Aztec religion, the ceremonies I had the opportunity to witness bear out Don Juan's observations, for they were never dedicated to specific prehispanic deities, but to Aztec military heroes and generalized "cosmological" concepts. Such rites were quite different from the ones Juan Luna's group had previously organized to pay tribute to Huitzilopochtli, Texcatlipocatl and a number of other gods. I never saw any ceremonies sponsored by the Indigenous Confederation, for that group had disbanded before I came to Mexico. What I know about it I learned from Don Juan and another Hueyapeño whose name is Don Eliseo Cortés.

Under Nieva's direction the Movimiento organized a political party (El Partido de la Mexicanidad), a newspaper (*Izkalotl*), a school for teaching Nahuatl (Mexikatlahtolkall), as well as innumerable political, cultural and commemorative gatherings. The Movimiento was so successful, in fact, that it

---

8. He is no relation to Lázaro Cárdenas, Mexico's president in the 1930s.

managed to add to its list of members such illustrious figures as the controversial Eulalia Guzmán and the former president of Mexico, Miguel Alemán.[9] Furthermore, by 1964 the group's campaign to promote Nahuatl had been effective enough to prompt a major American newspaper to publish an article entitled "Nahuatl Language Gaining in Mexico." Although the report did not identify the Movimiento by name, it told about the First Congress of the Nahuatl Language that the group sponsored and it mentioned the authors of the Nahuatl grammar *Izkalotl*,[10] one of whom happens to be María del Carmen Nieva, Rodolfo's sister. According to the article, this book was being used in the schools of an "Indian community" located on the outskirts of Mexico City.

In September 1968 Rodolfo Nieva died and the Movimiento went into a decline almost immediately thereafter. Clearly the problem was one of having no adequate successor for the charismatic founder. The leadership was left to Rodolfo's brother Jorge, also a lawyer, and to his sister María del Carmen, who until recently had been an inspector in the federal school system. Jorge has shown little interest in the Movimiento and has left María del Carmen almost exclusively in charge. Since the latter feels that she has no aptitude for political matters and since she has always been responsible for the Movimiento's cultural activities, María del Carmen has continued to carry out her original duties and has allowed the political aspects of the group's program to disintegrate.

Thus by the time I met the group in July 1969 all that was left of the organization's activities were occasional group outings,

---

9. In the book *Mexikayotl* (Mexico City, 1969), published by María del Carmen Nieva, Rodolfo's sister, there is a photograph of the founder with Eulalia Guzmán and another of him with Miguel Alemán. In the first photograph we see Guzmán, who is described as the "notable investigator of anthropology," congratulating Nieva on his work. In the second we see Miguel Alemán, who is identified as Mexico's former president, receiving a plaque engraved with the symbol of the Movimiento. Alemán, we learn, has just been made an honorary member of the Movimiento.

10. The book was published early in the year 1964. The name *Izkalotl* is also the name of the Movimiento's newspaper.

a few cultural ceremonies and regular Saturday afternoon Nahuatl classes at María del Carmen's home.

Despite their lack of organization, a number of Movimiento members did try to keep Rodolfo Nieva's political campaign alive. Speeches made at cultural gatherings continued to use Nieva's rhetoric. Also, although the newspaper *Izkalotl* was no longer published monthly, when it did appear the articles reflected the militant tone associated with Nieva. Finally, the founder's philosophy and style have been preserved in the book *Mexikayotl*, which his sister, María del Carmen, wrote after he died.

In 1969 I was told that the Movimiento had between 400 and 800 members in Mexico City and thousands in the countryside. Perhaps such had been the case when Rodolfo was alive and organizing congresses; however, things had changed. During my brief contact with the group I never attended a gathering where there were more than twenty-five members, and many of these were children. With the exception of one young girl who was the daughter of María del Carmen's maid, all the youngsters came from middle- or upper-class homes.

Among the thirteen or fourteen regular adult members, over half of them were teenagers or in their early twenties. These young people also came from middle- and upper-class homes. The president of the student group, for example, who was supposed to have been communicating with preparatory schools throughout the city, was the son of a wealthy agrarian engineer. This young man, whose name was Cuauhtémoc,[11] had just finished preparatory school and was about to enter the National School of Agriculture in Chapingo, State of Mexico. Then there were several young women who made up the dancing group. Two were still in preparatory school and one was teaching primary

---

11. In addition to a Cuauhtémoc, the group counts among its members one Tlacaelel, one Tetlazohtlani, one Kuamatzin and one Xochitl. Xochitl is the daughter of María del Carmen's maid. The others are adult men: Tlacaelel owns a factory; Tetlazohtlani writes for the newspaper and I do not know what he does outside of that; and Kuamatzin is a school teacher.

school. The other two or three teenagers who attended were
friends and/or relatives of the above-mentioned young people.

Of the members who were over thirty, three were school
teachers (including María del Carmen), one was María del
Carmen's maid, two owned factories, one was an engineer and
one rented fields to farmers. This last gentleman, Señor Castillo,
was the most picturesque member—the "pet Indian" in the
group. He had grown up in a Nahuatl-speaking community in
the State of Mexico and spoke a bit of the language himself.
Much to everybody's approval, Señor Castillo used to come to
every meeting dressed in *charro*.[12] Finally, with very few excep-
tions, the members were all light complected; María del Carmen
even dyed her hair a flaming red color.

The Movimiento calls upon history to justify its campaign
for the restoration of "Nahuatl culture" in Mexico. According to
the group's creation myth,[13] the inhabitants of North, Central
and South America originated in these lands and did not come
over from other continents, as the Europeans would have us
believe. The Western Hemisphere was called Ixachilan (Immen-
sidad, or Vastness), and those who lived in it belonged to the Ixa-
chilankatl race.[14] One of the subgroups of this race was the
Nahuatl people, and their domain, known as Anauak, included
all of North America, extending as far south as Nicaragua.[15]

The history of the Nahuatl people, the myth tells us, is
divided into a number of epochs: Olmekatl, Maya, Teotiuakatl,
Toltekatl and Mexikatl. The most important of these various
stages is the Mayan period, for it was during that time that the
Nahuatl people traveled around the world and profoundly influenced the subsequent cultural evolution of Western Civiliza-

---

12. This costume is associated with the *mariache* players in contemporary
Mexico. Originally the dress of the colonial landowners, it consists of tight black
pants with silver studs up the sides, a tight-fitting black shirt, a little ribbon tie
and a wide *sombrero*.

13. My information comes from Mexico City informants and María del
Carmen Nieva's book.

14. Nieva, pp. 35-36.

15. I was told that Nahuatl place names still exist outside of Mexico:
Nicaragua means "near the water"; Michigan means "where there are fish."

Naughty history

tion. Although no other dates were given, we learn that about 2500 years ago the Mayas already recognized the fact that the world was round and explorers set out from the Atlantic coast to circle it. Passing through the Strait of Gibraltar, the Mayan explorers arrived in Egypt, built pyramids and taught the Egyptians the essence of the Nahuatl religion: the concept of Teotl.[16]

From Egypt the Nahuatl people, who were known as Atlantes,[17] moved on to Greece, influencing Solon and later Plato. The writings of Plato in particular capture the spirit of Nahautl culture, Nieva claims, and in the *Republic* the Greek philosopher introduced the Kalpull—the Anauak kinship and land-tenure traditions—to the people of the Mediterranean.[18] After Greece, Nahuatl culture was passed on to Rome and finally formed the basis of Christian theology, albeit in an adulterated form. The Christians, we learn, took from Roman culture the ideas of the Nahuah, which they then "dressed over with all the religiosity and mysticism of the Jewish people." Specifically, the Christians adopted the concept of Teotl—creation. That the Christian god evolved through the Nahuah and not through the Jews is indicated by the fact that the Christians used the Latinized version of Teotl—Deus—instead of the Hebrew one— Jehovah.[19]

As the Roman Empire dissolved and distinct European countries emerged, the name "Deus" underwent the following phonetic transformations in the languages of the various nations: "Dieu" in French, "Dìo" in Italian and "Dios" in Spanish,

> which is the way it [Teotl] returned to us, suffering in this fashion the fate of all the raw materials which we have produced and continue producing and which we export so that the foreigner might embellish and return it to us at a higher price. And what a price we

---

16. Teotl means God in Nahuatl. For further discussion of this epoch of Nahuatl history, see Nieva, pp. 37-38.

17. The Egyptians asked the Nahuah (plural for Nahuatl) where the latter came from, and since the people of Anahuac responded "Atlantike," which means by the sea, i.e. Atlantic, the Egyptians called them Atlantes.

18. Nieva, p. 148.

19. Nieva, p. 70.

Mexicans have paid for the concept of Teotl transformed into the Dios of the Christians! That price consists in having almost lost the instinctive Mexican nature, in having suffered the great crimes that the dominators of our country committed against our ancestors in order to force on them the Catholic religion.[20]

According to Nieva, on August 12, 1521, one day before Cortés conquered Tenochtitlán, the Ueyi Tlahtohkan,[21] ruler of the Great Confederation of Anauak (a higher official than Moctezuma), ordered the Nahuatl people to preserve their culture secretly, passing it down by word of mouth from one generation to the next until such a time as Mexico might be freed from foreign domination.[22] This decree was obeyed, the Movimiento maintains, and now the group would like to prepare the Mexican people so that they will be able to rise up, expel the foreigners and reinstate the nation's legitimate culture. As to how and when the Revolution will occur, the group says nothing; nor does it explain—except in the vaguest terms—what the political, social and cultural organization of the country will be.

All that I was able to determine about the future state is that Mexico's national language will be Nahuatl and that the political organization will be based on the "Nahuatl family," the Kalpull. Inspired by the generative and creative force of Teotl, the Movimiento members describe themselves as "cosmological socialists," and they criticize Marx for having limited himself to a philosophy of material socialism. María del Carmen, incidentally, points out in her book that Marx's theory is a poor imitation of the original doctrine of the Nahuah: the German philosopher, she says, learned about the Kalpull from Plato.[23]

Thus, while the group awaits the expulsion of the foreigners, it has been trying to develop a following by educating the Mexican people emotionally, politically and culturally. In the newspaper *Izkalotl* (*resurgimiento*, reappearance), slogans like the following are printed in bold type: "The superior Anauak

---

20. Nieva, p. 71.
21. According to our ethnohistoric information there was no such person.
22. Nieva, pp. 22-23.
23. Nieva, pp. 148-149.

world of our ancestors"; "Spanish colonization, Mother of all our troubles and miseries"; "The Nahuatl language will unite the Mexicans"; "It is the duty of every Mexican to learn his Mexican language"; and "We must insist that they teach us our true history."[24] The articles themselves report on Movimiento cultural activities and on archeological finds; Aztec calendar stones are particularly popular. There are also Nahuatl language lessons and Nahuatl crossword puzzles.

Featured in each issue of *Izkalotl* are several articles dealing with the interpretation of history. Most of these pieces criticize the way Mexicans have been taught about their own past. The dramatization of the atrocities committed by the Spaniards during colonial and postcolonial times is a popular subject. Another favorite theme of these articles is the unfortunate consequence of Columbus' error of thinking that he was in India: for centuries the people of Mexico have been forced to bear the name "Indian" even though they are not from India. Righting this wrong, the newspaper refers to the indigenous people of Mexico as the Mexicanos, Mexikah, Nahuah or Autóctonos. As for the Spaniards, the Movimiento calls them Gachupines;[25] and those Mexicans who collaborate with foreigners are derogatorily associated with Cortés' indigenous mistress Malinche and are called Malinchistas.

In an effort to encourage the Mexican people to pay tribute to the great moments in their "autochthonous" history, the Movimiento organized a ceremony on July 6, 1969, in commemoration of the night Moctezuma's brother Cuitláhuac defeated the Spaniards in Tenochtitlán (Mexico City). Known in the Spanish chronicles as the Sad Night, the occasion was renamed the Victorious Night by the Movimiento. The ceremony took place, appropriately, at the impressive monument erected by the Mexican government in Cuitláhuac's honor, located on the busy Mexico City Avenida de la Reforma. Since the emperor

---

24. The information I have about *Izkalotl* comes from three issues of the paper: December 1968, March 1969 and December 1969.

25. The term Gachupin comes from the Nahuatl *catzopin; cac* means shoe and *tzopin* means, in this context, kicking. The Spaniards were so named because they used to kick the Indians.

Moctezuma II had already been made a prisoner of the
Spaniards, it was Cuitláhuac who led the Aztecs into battle on
July 6, 1519. Not until two years later were the Spaniards able to
reconquer the city.

Although it was reported in *Izkalotl* that a large crowd had
gathered to participate in the 1969 ceremony,[26] actually the turn-
out was poor. At most twenty people were there. Despite the
small group, the members maintained their good spirits and the
ritual was performed as planned. First a floral arrangement in
the shape of the Movimiento's symbol (Figure 3) was placed at
the foot of the statue of Cuitláhuac, high above the people who
were standing at the base of the statue's pyramidal platform.
Next a young man climbed up to where the flowers were and blew
a conch shell, while at the base of the monument another young
boy beat a Plains Indian tom-tom and a young girl solemnly
walked back and forth before the monument waving copal incense. Afterwards several Movimiento members made short

FIGURE 3
Naui Olli, the Insignia of the Movimiento
(After Nieva, p. 225)

26. *Izkalotl,* December 1969, pp. 1 and 5.

speeches calling to all Mexicans to recognize their true heritage, and with that the ceremony came to a close. The entire program did not take more than thirty minutes.

Since the Movimiento is not only interested in venerating the past, it also participates in presentations concerned with promoting the indigenous present and future. On October 21, 1969, for example, I had the opportunity to attend a performance sponsored jointly by the Movimiento and an organization of hair stylists known as the Mexican Beauty Group. The theme of the evening was how to be "chic" and "autochthonous" too. The program took place in the fashionable Teatro del Bosque, which is located in Mexico City's Chapultepec Park. First the Movimiento performed a "Nahuatl ceremony." María del Carmen, listed in the program as Maestra Izchalotzin of the Institute of Mexican Culture, gave a little talk about the significance of the "ceremony." Dressed in a floor-length Spanish lace gown, the woman explained that we would see "an act of veneration to our race." Then, describing briefly the cosmological concepts of the Movimiento—its ideas about the creative forces of the "Natural" Mexican—she told us that the dance to be performed would be a "philosophy without words."

First a maiden of the Anauakxochitl (Flower of Anauak) dance group appeared on stage. She blew a conch shell and then lit some copal incense. Next the entire corps of eleven dancers, all women and young girls, came out and performed the "Autochthonous Dance of Happiness." María del Carmen accompanied the dancers on a drum, and the women moved around in a circle doing a slow hopping step. Several days later I asked one of the dancers about the choreography, and she told me that María del Carmen had made it up and that the Maestra claimed that every step had a meaning.

The dancers wore two-piece off-white linen costumes. Their blouses were decorated with large colorful representations of the Movimiento's symbol, and the skirts, which were mid-calf length, had colorful stripes on the bottom halves. In addition, the maidens wore wreaths of red flowers in their hair, and dried bunches of the *coyoli* fruit were tied around their ankles, creating rattling sounds as they danced.

After the Movimiento finished performing—they were on stage for about twenty minutes—ten female models came on. One woman was dressed in what was supposed to be a traditional costume of the Yalalteca Indians of Oaxaca and her hair was combed in the rather distinct Yalalteca style. The other nine models were dressed in modern clothes, and each one was wearing a variation of the Yalalteca hairdo (Figure 4). For those in the audience who were interested in trying the basic modern variation of the Yalalteca style, the theater program offered diagrams that illustrated how to set the hair correctly. Furthermore, there were photographs of several of the models showing some of the alternatives to the basic set.

The private gatherings at María del Carmen's home are much more informal than the public ceremonies. The ritual blowing of the conch shell and the lighting of the incense are not observed; nor does the Maestra often discuss the underlying philosophy of the Movimiento. These get-togethers are primarily social affairs which might touch casually on Movimiento themes. However, on December 22, 1969, the Nahuatl New Year, there was more of an attempt to keep the spirit of the Movimiento's philosophy and concerns alive. The dancers put on a little performance, and the guests were invited to play a game similar to bingo, using symbols of the Aztec calendar.[27] The evening ended with a slide show of calendar stones and other archeological finds that members of the Movimiento had recently come across during their travels around the country.

Finally, on Saturday afternoons young children and teenage members of the group are expected to attend a Nahuatl class at María del Carmen's home. These lessons are based on the Maestra's published grammar *Izkalotl*. María del Carmen's teaching method consists of giving her students a list of vocabulary words to learn. Since the Movimiento is particularly interested in etymological studies, María del Carmen concentrates on presenting her students with the derivation of such words as "Mexico" and "Tenochtitlan." She also teaches the

---

27. This is a variation of the game called *loteria* in Mexico.

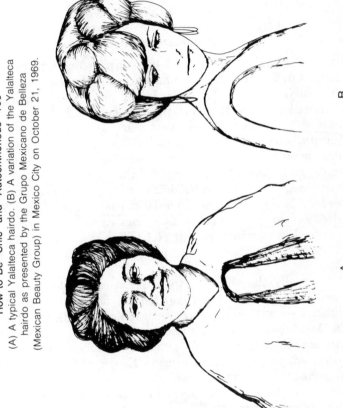

FIGURE 4

How to Be "Chic" and "Autochthonous" Too

(A) A typical Yalalteca hairdo. (B) A variation of the Yalalteca
hairdo as presented by the Grupo Mexicano de Belleza
(Mexican Beauty Group) in Mexico City on October 21, 1969.

pupils the Nahuatl words for such modern devices as the automobile and the train. No attempt is made to teach the group grammar, even at the most elementary level, and the pupils are never even asked to try to make sentences.

Cultural Extremists and Hueyapeños

For the villagers, the cultural extremists represent one more group of urban Mexicans who have come to the pueblo to teach the Hueyapeños about their Indian-ness. Once again the villagers have been told that they are culturally deprived, but that with the help of outsiders they will soon acquire the "culture" that they presently lack. What they are missing this time, however, is their own so-called original culture. In other words, no matter what the criteria, the villagers never seem to meet the standards set by outsiders and are always told that they need the latter's assistance in order to change accordingly. First religious and government missionaries came to the pueblo to save the Hueyapeños from being too Indian, and now the cultural extremists have appeared to save them from not being Indian enough.

Actually, the cultural extremists have succeeded in converting only a handful of Hueyapeños to their movement. Most villagers are more eager to lose their indigenous identity through the Mestizo-oriented government acculturation program than they are to emphasize it. Nevertheless, the extremists cannot be dismissed, primarily because many Hueyapeños have associated—some might say confused—the work of the cultural extremists with what the villagers see to be a general trend among middle- and upper-class Mexicans. Whenever a group of well-dressed outsiders drives up in a private car, the villagers assume that the visitors are looking for Indian culture and will be disappointed if they do not find what they expect. Thus, tourists, anthropologists and government workers—when the latter are performing acts of veneration to Mexico's indigenous past—are all classified with the cultural extremists. As far as the

Hueyapeños are concerned, all these people want the villagers to conform to the outsiders' glamorous image of the Indian.

Accustomed as they are to accommodating the wishes of the elite, the villagers usually comply, as we have seen, and "play" Indian for their honored guests. Still, most Hueyapeños remain much more interested in exchanging this Indian identity for a Mestizo one. As Indians the villagers might provide a bit of regional charm, but as Mestizos they will enjoy the socio-economic advantages of a higher status.

The person in the village who has had the longest and most intimate contact with the cultural extremists is Don Eliseo Cortés. In 1939 he attended a Nahuatl congress in Milpa Alta. Then in 1945 he met Juan Luna Cárdenas, and the two men became good friends. The circumstances surrounding this encounter are rather significant, for they suggest that cultural extremists and government representatives are frequently the same people. Not only did María del Carmen serve as a school inspector and do several Movimiento members have teaching positions, but Juan Luna himself had been head of the linguistics division of the Department of Indigenous Affairs, and it was in this capacity that the linguist introduced Don Eliseo to cultural extremism.

It seems that a school teacher in Hueyapan had suggested to Don Eliseo that he go to the Department of Indigenous Affairs in Mexico City to see whether the government office might provide one of Eliseo's sons with a scholarship to continue his education. At the Department, Don Eliseo met Juan Luna. Although the Hueyapeño did not succeed in securing the money for his son, Don Eliseo returned to the village with several Nahuatl grammars that had been given to him by Juan Luna and by another member of the Department.

Several years later, in the early 1950s, Don Eliseo, Don Juan and two other villagers went to Mexico City to study Classical Nahuatl at Juan Luna's school, In Uey Tlatekpanaliztli (The Great Society of Aztec Fellows). Regular Nahuatl classes were conducted by Juan Luna's brother and another gentleman, Juan Chavez Orozco, gave a course on calendar stones. Chavez was a painter associated with the Bellas Artes in Mexico City, and had studied with Diego Rivera, Don Juan told me.

Don Juan said that Juan Chavez often took students to see calendar stones on Calle Moneda in Mexico City and interpreted extensively from them. These calendar stones explained world history in such detail, the teacher claimed, that even the story of the founding of Hueyapan was included. Thus Don Juan learned that the Xochimilcas were not the first settlers of Hueyapan, as the villagers were told in school; instead a group of people known as the Metzintin were the original inhabitants. Not until the age of Petl, after the First Flood, did the Xochimilcas finally arrive.

Since the cultural extremists did not provide the Hueyapeños with lodging and food, the villagers finally had to give up their studies with the group. Of the four, only Don Eliseo had been invited to teach Nahuatl at the school, and even he was offered such a low salary that it was financially impossible for him to remain. As Don Juan described things, the other students were lawyers, engineers and school teachers who lived in Mexico City and had high-paying jobs. The Hueyapeños, however, were poor and their only means of making a living was on the land. Thus after a few months the villagers returned home, but the initial contact had been made and Don Eliseo in particular came back with great aspirations to revive Nahuatl culture in Hueyapan.

In 1956, with the help of Juan Luna, Don Eliseo opened a school in the village to teach "pure" Nahuatl, uncorrupted by Spanish interference. During that year the Mexico City linguist visited Hueyapan quite frequently, giving classes in the school and organizing meetings in Don Eliseo's home to practice the Aztec religion. Furthermore, Juan Luna offered Hueyapeños the free services of his group to arbitrate local land disputes.

While Juan Luna was working in the school about fifty villagers sent their children to classes. However, once he left the school soon folded. Today only a handful of villagers continue to take an informal interest in studying "pure" Nahuatl.

Another villager who had been active with Juan Luna and then later with Rodolfo Nieva was Lino Balderas, a former singer at the Bellas Artes. This Hueyapeño was among the first group of

villagers who studied Nahuatl in Mexico City, and afterwards he
entered the world of music. In addition to singing in the Ballet
Folklórico chorus, Lino Balderas made a recording of a Nahuatl
translation of the traditional Mexican birthday song, "Las Mañanitas."

Although I met this famous Hueyapeño, I was unable to interview him, since a few years before I arrived in the village he
had been in a terrible car accident and had suffered severe brain
damage and crippling. What I know about the man I learned
from other villagers. Apparently the singer never made very
much money either at the Bellas Artes or from his record, and
consequently left Mexico City a very bitter man, complaining
that he had been taken advantage of.

Lino Balderas was also responsible for making a Spanish
translation of a Nahuatl poem that the Mexico City teacher Juan
Chavez had taken from the *ozomatl* (tiger) glyph of the calendar
stone. The villager wrote a Nahuatl song himself about a man
wooing a beautiful maiden with blond hair, and he served as a
Nahuatl informant for the well-known scholar of ancient Mexico
Miguel León-Portilla.

Accepting the fanciful account of the Hueyapeño cultural
extremist, León-Portilla actually published a prayer that the
singer claimed his "old mother" used to recite to the prehispanic
rain god Tlaloc.[28] Unlike the prayers published by Miguel
Barrios, this one is written in "pure Nahuatl," so "pure," in fact,
that when Elvira Hernandez went over the text with me she
pointed out several expressions which Hueyapeños probably
never used. Furthermore, aside from Don Eliseo, Lino Balderas
and a few other cultural extremists, nobody in Hueyapan prayed
to prehispanic deities. Even the pueblo's mushroom-eating rainmakers called on the Christian god and the saints in their rituals.

That the Hueyapeño singer was able to make a name for
himself in Mexico City by capitalizing on his Indian-ness has impressed a number of villagers. But the fact that he returned to

28. M. León-Portilla, "El canto de Oztocohcoyohco," *Tlalocan*, Vol. 4, No.
1 (1962), p. 62.

the pueblo a dejected and penniless man has affected them even more. The story of this singer represents for many villagers the classic case of what happens to a poor, ignorant Indian who tries to get ahead and stay Indian at the same time.

Another Hueyapeño's experience with cultural extremists is the story of Don Adelaido Amarro. In 1965 Don Adelaido was selling fruit in the Manzanares market in Mexico City and there he met an acquaintance of his who was from the lowland community of Jumiltepec. The friend told Don Adelaido about the Movimiento and took the Hueyapeño to a meeting held at Nieva's office. Don Adelaido told me that Nieva received him warmly, and was delighted to have somebody with whom he could speak Nahuatl. The two men chatted in Nahuatl for a while—Nieva spoke very poorly, Don Adelaido recalled—and the lawyer invited the villager to join the group. Nieva also wanted Don Adelaido to represent the Movimiento in Hueyapan and to see that Nahuatl was taught in school there. Don Adelaido asked the lawyer to send him a formal document authorizing the Hueyapeño to act in the name of the Movimiento, for otherwise the villagers would assume that Don Adelaido had made the whole matter up while wandering about the streets of Mexico City drunk.

Rodolfo Nieva complied with Don Adelaido's wish and sent a formal letter to Hueyapan announcing that Don Adelaido was authorized to act in the name of the Movimiento. Don Adelaido informed Maestro Rafael, who was at this time the director of the village primary school, of the Movimiento's wishes. Although Maestro Rafael expressed an interest in the project, nothing was ever done about initiating classes in Nahuatl.

In 1966 Nieva sent Don Adelaido an announcement inviting him to attend a Movimiento congress that was going to be held in Morelos. However, by the time the notice arrived the congress had already taken place. Greatly disappointed, Don Adelaido, with the help of Maestro Rafael, wrote a letter to Nieva asking the lawyer to send any information available about how the Hueyapeños might participate in later congresses. The letter also told Nieva that Maestro Rafael was now in charge of organizing the Nahuatl school. This letter was the last communication between Hueyapan and the Movimiento. A year and a half later Rodolfo Nieva died.

Don Adelaido was intrigued by, but never committed to, the Movimiento. He told me that the people he met at the Mexico City meetings were all rich professionals. They had time to indulge themselves. He, however, had a large family to care for and could not remain in Mexico City with a group that did not even offer him a meal, let alone a job or a place to stay. Nevertheless, the idea that his Indian-ness was attractive to the wealthy did make a deep impression on him, and he has put it to some use at home.

Capitalizing on his wife's exceptional weaving skills, Don Adelaido has cultivated an acquaintance with the head of the Cuernavaca branch of the Burlington Textile Mills, who is a fancier of indigenous textiles. Known in the pueblo as the Ingeniero (engineer), Juan Dubernard has been employing Hueyapeño men to work in his factory since 1953 and has been visiting Hueyapan to purchase woven goods since 1960.

The combination of his wife's talents and his own promotion campaign has paid off for Don Adelaido, for as far as Dubernard is concerned, Doña Epifania is the best weaver in the village[29] and the Ingeniero does almost all his business with her. Thus whenever Doña Epifania has a couple of extra pieces of cloth Don Adelaido takes his wife into Cuernavaca to see the Ingeniero, and on these special occasions he always insists that she wear her *xincueite*—although she almost never wears the traditional skirt at home—for the Hueyapeño has learned that he and Doña Epifania are received more enthusiastically when his wife arrives at the factory dressed like an Indian.

A bit of a cultural extremist himself, Dubernard told me that he was distressed to learn that the Cultural Missions were trying to modernize the indigenous weaving technology. As he put it, "they are ruining things." In Hueyapan Dubernard has even tried to make the weaving more authentic than he found it

---

29. Thanks to Dubernard, some of Doña Epifania's weaving is presently being exhibited in the new museum in Cortés' Palace, Cuernavaca.

originally by teaching Doña Epifania about prehispanic dyes. As far back as Doña Epifania can remember—she was about 45 in 1969—Hueyapeños have always used commercial dyes. Doña Zeferina, who is twenty years older than Doña Epifania, also cannot remember a time before commercial dyes.

CONCLUSION: THE ANTHROPOLOGIST AND THE INDIANS

8

Although I was the first anthropologist to live in Hueyapan for an extended period of time, I was neither the first representative of the discipline nor the first American to visit the pueblo. In the mid-1960s several Mexican anthropology students from the Museo Nacional de Antropología spent a few months, on and off, in Hueyapan. They were doing field work in partial fulfillment of their undergraduate degrees. Then a North American linguist came to the pueblo in 1966 to find a Nahuatl speaker to take back to the United States for a year. Thus, I was hardly a new phenomenon for the villagers; they had already had experience with other members of my trade. Moreover, as far as the Hueyapeños were concerned, we anthropologists were just another breed of cultural extremists.

When I arrived in Hueyapan and announced that I wanted to learn Nahuatl, the villagers had me pegged. Those who knew how immediately offered to sing Nahuatl songs, recite the schoolbook poem "Nonantzin" and teach me such exotic words as "train" and "airplane" in Nahuatl. Others volunteered to show me how to spin and weave. Villagers who were unfamiliar with fabricated "indigenous" customs or could not weave simply spoke to me in Nahuatl and laughed as I tried to reply.

Frankly I was insulted that the Hueyapeños had so quickly lumped me and my kind with the cultural extremists. After all, I had just left Mexico City because the Movimiento had disappointed me. I hardly wanted the "real" Indians to confuse me with people I considered to be fakes. Yet by the time I left Hueyapan, a year later, I was grateful to the villagers for their insight, for the fact that they had forced me to confront the similarities that existed between me and the cultural extremists. In the end I saw that by embarrassing me the villagers had actually helped me to understand a basic contradiction that had been interfering with my original research plans and with my life. Since I have returned to the United States the issues have become even clearer to me, and I see all the more how much I am indebted to the villagers.

When I first went to Mexico to work with the Movimiento I expected to find a grass-roots political organization with a large indigenous constituency. Instead I found a group of light-skinned middle-class businessmen, professionals and youths who were masquerading as representatives of Mexico's indigenous peoples. Next I went to Hueyapan, hoping to find "real" Indians with a sense of pride in their indigenous culture and heritage. I discovered, instead, a community of people who had been forced to give up virtually all their indigenous culture hundreds of years ago, but who were still being discriminated against for being Indian. Far from proud, these villagers were embarrassed to be Indian and many saw that they had but one option: to lose their Indian-ness, a task made difficult for them by government representatives and cultural extremists who have been trying to entice the villagers to "play" Indian for the sake of glorifying Mexico's indigenous heritage.

Once I was back in the United States I saw variations of the Hueyapeños' doubly binding conflict everywhere. Despite the fact that the American government was not interested in glorifying the heritage of the Blacks, these people were encouraged by members of the White middle class to preserve their so-called direct, natural, uncomplicated souls. Similarly, women were told how lucky they were that they could be mothers, for bearing children was such a satisfying experience that they did not have to succeed in other areas to be fulfilled. How convenient such reasoning was for societies trying to dissemble discriminatory practices. How obvious it seemed all of a sudden that attributes associated with "making it" in the western world were the antithesis of the romanticized, quaint, natural ways of the oppressed. Finally, how disturbing it was to discover that as an anthropologist I was actually contributing to the villagers' confusion and oppression by asking the Hueyapeños to be Indian for me.

Although some may feel that I am being unnecessarily hard on both myself and my profession, there is little question that anthropologists working in Mexico have played an important role in promoting the idea of the Indian. More than simply joining other non-Indians in the search for the Indian in Mexico, anthropologists have led the campaign, giving scholarly justification for the popular belief that Indians belong to different cultures. Although most post-Revolutionary Mexican anthropologists have been concerned with determining how best to assimilate rather than preserve indigenous peoples—an issue that did not concern most American and European anthropologists conducting research in Mexico—still they began by assuming that Mexico had an "Indian," not simply a socioeconomic, problem on its hands. Anthropologists felt that before they could help solve this "Indian" problem, they had to determine *who* the Indians were. Thus for years anthropologists and other social scientists have studied and argued among themselves about how they should define what it means to be Indian.

There is no need here to review the literature on how anthropologists have defined the Indian, since excellent summaries on the subject abound elsewhere.[1] Let me point out, however, that despite the increasingly sophisticated theoretical treatments that have been made over the last forty years,

---

1. See, for example, A. Marino Flores, "Indian Population and Its Identification," *Handbook of Middle American Indians*, Vol. VI (Austin, 1967), pp. 12-25.

somehow anthropologists continue to talk about Indians as if they differ culturally in significant ways from other Mexicans. Although Wolf[2] and Stavenhagen,[3] for example, have minimized the cultural differences between Indians and non-Indians and have emphasized the fact that indigenous communities should be discussed in terms of their structural relationship to the larger society, still the designation "Indian" remains. And although Foster[4] and Gibson[5] have written extensively on the subject of how the Spaniards imposed Iberian culture on the Indians during colonial times, we still talk about indigenous traditions when we really mean colonial Spanish introductions and/or transformations. Finally, in defense of his analysis of Tarascan folk religion, Pedro Carrasco notes that "Tarascans will pass their Christianity test with honors if we compare their religion with the folk religion of Catholic southern Europe,"[6] yet still we distinguish indigenous folk religion from that of the culture of the dominant elite.

Although I agree that there are visible differences between traditions found in so-called indigenous communities like Hueyapan and those encountered in Mexico City, I maintain that the distinctions reflect the same social and cultural systems. Since many other anthropologists have been making the same point, why have we been holding on to a term that suggests that a certain group in Mexico continues to have a unique racial, cultural and historical identity? The concept of the Indian in all its various guises was created by the Spaniards, and by adopting the Iberian terminology, we anthropologists have also incor-

2. E. Wolf, "Virgin of Guadalupe: A Mexican National Symbol," *Journal of American Folklore*, Vol. 71 (1958), pp. 34-39.

3. R. Stavenhagen, *Clases, colonialismo y aculturación*, Cuadernos del Seminario de Integración Social Guatemalteca, No. 19 (Guatemala City, 1968). See also the articles by A. Warman and G. Bonfil in Warman *et al.*, *De eso que llaman Antropología Mexicana* (Mexico City, 1970).

4. G. Foster, *Culture and Conquest: America's Spanish Heritage*, Viking Fund Publication in Anthropology No. 27 (New York, 1960).

5. C. Gibson, *The Aztecs under Spanish Rule* (Stanford, Calif., 1964).

6. P. Carrasco, "Tarascan Folk Religion, Christian or Pagan?" *The Social Anthropology of Latin America: Essays in Honor of Ralph Beals*, edited by W. Goldschmidt and H. Hoijer (Los Angeles, 1970), p. 6.

porated into our thinking the hispanic perception of the problem. Thus, even though we have modified the definitions, we have helped to preserve the "Indian" category, together with its long hispanic cultural tradition and negative connotation.

The strong feelings I express here reflect my growing concern about the political implications of anthropological research. Throughout the United States and Mexico an increasing number of anthropologists have begun to question their motives for doing field work among exotic peoples in far-off places and among the poor of their own countries. Who benefits from our research and who might get hurt by it? Although most of us went into anthropology out of a sincere interest to learn about people different from ourselves, many of us have come to realize that our innocent enthusiasm needs to be reevaluated. Furthermore, much to our horror, we have discovered that we count among our ranks individuals who openly participate in government-sponsored counter-insurgency activities.

In the late 1960s, a period of general political unrest in the United States, Mexico and Europe, some anthropology students and faculty met and formed an organization called Anthropologists for Radical Political Action. Also, a number of minority and ethnic groups within the anthropological association started to caucus. In particular, Native Americans and women organized themselves to discuss what action might be taken to correct the White male bias prevalent in anthropological literature and in the classroom.

Today many young anthropologists feel that our research must grow out of our political commitments; the two cannot be separated. Since many of us have come to believe that our political obligations and problems are at home, among our own people, the new trend has been to encourage middle-class people to study middle-class people, women to study women, Blacks to study Blacks, Indians to study Indians and Jews to study Jews. Thus, although my experience in Hueyapan was an important political education for me at the time, given my position today, it is unlikely that I would choose to do the same kind of research again.

To return to the relationship between the anthropologist and the Indian in Mexico, we should keep in mind that in this country the anthropologist has been particularly influential. Since the post-Revolutionary government has had a special ideological interest in glorifying Mexico's indigenous heritage, it has enthusiastically sponsored anthropological research and publicized the findings in a spectacular manner. Consequently, although some might say that anthropologists have been obscure or erudite in their discussions of the significance of the Indian in Mexico, nobody would dispute the fact that anthropologists have generously provided the public with ethnographic and historical information about the Indians. As we have already seen, everybody in Mexico knows about the Indians; one learns about them in school, in the museums, on weekend excursions and even from the monuments on the streets. Yet by making anthropological data available to the nonspecialist without appropriate and readily accessible analyses, anthropologists have merely added to the general confusion and fostered discriminatory attitudes.

When Doña Zeferina was in Mexico City she once met a man who owned an *ixcuintle* (Mexican hairless), the now very rare and expensive breed of dog said to be a descendant of the Aztec dogs that were fattened up for food. Never having seen one before, Doña Zeferina told the gentleman that she thought the dog was very ugly—it happens to be squat and completely hairless except for a few coarse bristles on its stomach and back and tufts of soft fur on its head and tail. The owner of the *ixcuintle* was quite surprised by Doña Zeferina's reaction and told her that this was a real Aztec dog, domesticated by *her* ancestors; she should be proud of it. Doña Zeferina replied that first of all she was *not* Aztec and secondly the dog was *still* ugly!

BIBLIOGRAPHY

Aguirre Beltrán, G. "Indigenismo y mestizaje." *Cuadernos americanos,* Vol. 78 (July-August 1956), pp. 35-51.

Alba, V. *Las ideas sociales contemporaneas en México.* Mexico City, 1960.

"Alcoy." *Blanco y negro* (Madrid), December 27, 1969, pp. 39-54.

Barrios, M. "Textos de Hueyapan, Morelos." *Tlalocan,* Vol. 3, No. 1 (1949), pp. 53-75.

Beals, R. *The Contemporary Culture of the Cahita Indians.* Bureau of American Ethnography, Bulletin No. 142. Washington, D.C., 1945.

Bede, The Venerable. *History of the English Church and People.* Translated by Shirley Price. London, 1968.

Bennett, W., and J. Bird. *Andean Culture History.* American Museum of Natural History Handbook Series No. 15. New York, 1960.

Boban, E. *Documents pour servir à l'histoire du Mexique.* Vol. I. Paris, 1891. Pp. 381-382 and Plate No. 25.

Borah, W. *New Spain's Century of Depression.* Ibero-Americana, No. 35. Berkeley, 1951.

———, and S. F. Cook. *The Aboriginal Population of Central Mexico on the Eve of the Spanish Conquest.* Ibero-Americana, No. 45. Berkeley, 1963.

Campos, R. *El folklore y la música mexicana.* Mexico City, 1928.

Cantares de la Revolución. HNOS Zaizar. Series 1000, No. 1014. Peerless Recordings, Mexico City.

Carrasco, P. "Tarascan Folk Religion, Christian or Pagan?" *The Social Anthropology of Latin America: Essays in Honor of Ralph Beals.* Edited by W. Goldschmidt and H. Hoijer. Los Angeles, 1970. Pp. 3-14.

Caso, A. *Métodos y resultados de la política indigenista en México.* Instituto Nacional Indigenista, Mem. 6. Mexico City, 1954.

Castellanos, P. *Horizontes de la música precortesiana.* Mexico City, 1970.

Coe, M. *Mexico.* New York, 1962.

Cumberland, C. *Mexico: The Struggle for Modernity.* New York, 1968.

Díaz, B. *The Bernal Díaz Chronicles.* Translated and edited by A. Idell. Garden City, N.Y., 1956.

Dozier, E. "Two Examples of Linguistic Acculturation." *Language,* Vol. 32 (1956), pp. 146-157.

Durán, Fray Diego. *Historia de los indios de Nueva España y Islas de Tierra Firme.* 2 volumes. Prepared by A. Garibay. Mexico City, 1967.

Echanove Trujillo, C. *Sociología mexicana.* Mexico City, 1948.

Engels, F. "Socialism: Utopian and Scientific." *Marx and Engels' Basic Writings on Politics and Philosophy.* Edited by L. Feuer. New York, 1959. Pp. 68-111.

Foster, G. *Culture and Conquest: America's Spanish Heritage.* Viking Fund Publication in Anthropology No. 27. New York, 1960.

Friedrich, P. *Agrarian Revolt in a Mexican Village.* Englewood Cliffs, N.J., 1970.

————. "Revolutionary Politics and Communal Ritual." *Political Anthropology.* Edited by M. Swartz, V. Turner and T. Tuden. Chicago, 1966. Pp. 191-220.

Fuentes, C. "Viva Zapata." *The New York Review of Books,* Vol. 12, No. 5 (March 13, 1969), pp. 5-12.

Gamio, M. "Static and Dynamic Values in the Indigenous Past of America." *Hispanic American Historical Review,* Vol. 23 (1943), pp. 386-393.

Gerhard, P. "El señorío de Ocuituco." *Tlalocan,* Vol. 6, No. 2 (1970), pp. 97-114.

Gibson, C. *The Aztecs under Spanish Rule.* Stanford, Calif., 1964.

————. *Spain in America.* New York, 1966.

————. "The Transformation of the Indian Community in New Spain, 1500-1810." *Journal of World History,* Vol. 2 (1954-1955), pp. 581-607.

Helguera R., L., S. López M. and R. Ramírez M. *Los campesinos de la tierra de Zapata, I: Adaptación, cambio y rebelión.* Mexico City, 1974.

Horcacitas, F. *De Porfirio Díaz a Zapata.* Mexico City, 1968.

Izkalotl (Newspaper of El Movimiento Confederado Restaurador de Anauak), December 1968, March 1969, December 1969.

Leander, B. *La poesía náhuatl: Función y carácter.* Göteborg, Sweden, 1971.

León-Portilla, M. *Aztec Thought and Culture: A Study of the Ancient Nahuatl Mind.* Translated by J. Davis. Civilization of the American Indian Series, No. 67. Norman, Okla., 1963.

——. *Broken Spears.* Translated by L. Kemp. Boston, 1962.

——. "El canto de Oztocohcoyohco." *Tlalocan,* Vol. 4, No. 1 (1962), pp. 62-63.

Lewis, O. *Life in a Mexican Village: Tepoztlán Restudied.* Urbana, Ill., 1963.

Malcolm X. *The Autobiography of Malcolm X.* Written with the assistance of Alex Haley. New York, 1966.

Marino Flores, A. "Indian Population and Its Identification." *Handbook of Middle American Indians.* Vol. VI. General Editor, R. Wauchope; Volume Editor, M. Nash. Austin, 1967. Pp. 12-25.

Martínez-Marín, C. *Tetela del Volcán.* Mexico City, 1968.

Mendieta y Nuñez, L. "El tratamiento del indio." *América indígena,* Vol. 4 (1944), pp. 113-122.

Moiron A., S. "Indigenismo de escaparate." *El día* (Mexico City), December 2, 1969, p. 9.

Molina, A. de. *Vocabulario náhuatl-castellano castellano-náhuatl.* Mexico City, 1966.

Nash, M. "Introduction." *Handbook of Middle American Indians.* Vol. VI. General Editor, R. Wauchope; Volume Editor, M. Nash. Austin, 1967. Pp. 4-11.

Nieva, M. *Izkalotl: Texto nahuatl-español-inglés.* Mexico City, 1972.

——. *Mexikayotl.* Mexico City, 1969.

——, and P. F. Garcia. *Izkalotl: Texto para el aprendizaje del idioma mexicano según las reglas de la Mexikatlahtolkalli.* Mexico City, 1964.

Paredes, A. (editor and translator). *Folktales of Mexico.* Chicago, 1970.

Paso y Troncoso, F. del. "Relación de Tetela y Ueyapan." *Papeles de Nueva España.* Vol. VI. Madrid, 1905. Pp. 283-290.

Perez Moreno, C. "Memoria de práctica profesional y servicio que presenta el alumno: Cecilio Perez Moreno en su examen profesional para obtener el título de Profesor de Educación Primaria." Unpublished. Hueyapan, Morelos, Mexico, 1962-1963.

Reed, N. *The Caste War of Yucatán.* Stanford, Calif., 1964.

Rendón, E. "La historia del Emperador Carlo Magno que se dominan los Dos Paises de Francia." Unpublished. San Juan Amecac, Puebla, Mexico, 1845.

Ricard, R. *La "conquête spirituelle" du Mexique.* Paris, 1933.

Riley, C., and J. Hobgood. "A Recent Nativistic Movement among the Southern Tepehuan Indians." *Southwestern Journal of Anthropology,* Vol. 15 (1959), pp. 355-360.

Schneider, D. *American Kinship.* Princeton, N.J., 1968.

Schoembs, J. *Aztekische Schriftsprache.* Heidelberg, 1949.

Siméon, R. *Dictionnaire de la langue nahuatl.* Graz, Austria, 1963.

Soustelle, J. *The Daily Life of the Aztecs.* Translated by J. O'Brian. New York, 1962.

Stavenhagen, R. *Clases, colonialismo y aculturación.* Cuadernos del Seminario de Integración Social Guatemalteca, No. 19. Guatemala City, 1968.

Strickton, A. "Hacienda and Plantation in Yucatan: An Ecological Consideration of the Folk-Urban Continuum in Yucatan." *América indígena,* Vol. 25 (1965), pp. 35-64.

Swadesh, M., and M. Sancho. *Los mil elementos del mexicano clásico.* Mexico City, 1966.

Tannenbaum, F. "Agrarismo, indianismo y nacionalismo." *Hispanic American Historical Review,* Vol. 23 (1943), pp. 394-423.

Turner, V. *Dramas, Fields and Metaphors.* Ithaca, N.Y., 1974.

Van Zantwijk, R. "Supervivencias intelectuales de la cultura nahuatl en el municipio de Milpa Alta, D.F." *América indígena,* Vol. 18 (1958), pp. 119-129.

Vázquez de Knauth, J. *Nacionalismo y educación en México.* Mexico City, 1970.

Villa Rojas, A. "La civilización y el indio." *América indígena,* Vol. 5 (1945), pp. 67-72.

Villoro, L. *Los grandes momentos del indigenismo en México.* Mexico City, 1950.

Warman, A., *et al. De eso que llaman Antropología Mexicana.* Mexico City, 1970.

Wolf, E. *Sons of the Shaking Earth.* Chicago, 1959.

———. "Virgin of Guadalupe: A Mexican National Symbol." *Journal of American Folklore,* Vol. 71 (1958), pp. 34-39.

Womack, J. *Zapata and the Mexican Revolution.* New York, 1970.

INDEX

Abogón, Don, 115
Acculturation program: cultural
    extremists' rejection of, 168;
    resembling colonial policies, 67-68,
    79, 128, 130. *See also* Cultural
    Missions, Department of
Adobe steam bath, 24n-25n
Agriculture. *See* Economy
Aguirre Beltrán, G., 166n
Alcoholism, 143
Alemán, Miguel, 172
Amarro, Don Adelaido, 9, 61, 186-87
Anauakxochitl dance group, 179
Angel (Quico; child of Doña Juana and
    Maestro Rafael), 5, 6; daily life of, 8,
    10, 17, 19, 23, 26; sleeping quarters
    for, 7n
Angelina, Maestra (daughter of Doña
    Zeferina), 5, 41, 49, 50; daily life of,
    8, 10, 12, 17-19, 22-24; languages
    spoken by, 85; sleeping quarters for,
    7n; and Virgin of Guadalupe fiesta,
    115
"Angelitos Negros" (soap opera), 78-79
Ansures, Don Zenaido, 115, 116, 119-20
Anthropologists, 189-94
Anthropologists for Radical Political
    Action, 193

Apaches, 76
Arturo (son of Maestro Rafael), 4;
    daily life of, 8-12, 19; sleeping
    quarters for, 7n
Augustinian missionaries, 56, 101
"Autochthonous Dance of Happiness,"
    179
Ayala, Plan de, 61, 156
Ayaquica, Fortina, 60
Aztec dog, 194
Aztec religion, 171
Aztecs, xiii, xiv, 88, 113n, 123, 150;
    language of the, 86n *(see also*
    Nahuatl)*;* Victorious Night of the,
    177-78

Backstrap looms, 86-89; preferred over
    mechanical looms, 134
Balderas, Lino, 136, 184-86
Ballet Folklórico, 185
Barreto, Don Lucio, 31
Barreto, Doña Zeferina. *See* Zeferina,
    Doña
Barrios, Miguel, 100, 123, 142, 143, 185
Bathing, 23-24; chamber for, 24n-25n
Bautista, Don Francisco, 34-35
Bede, The Venerable, 103n
Bellas Artes, 184, 185

199

Benjamín, Don, 35, 38-40
Bennett, W., 92
Bird, J., 88n, 92
Black Power, xv
Blacks, 190, 193
Boban, E., 102n
Bonfil, G., 192
Bridges, 133
Bronchitis, recipe for curing, 99
Burlington Textile Mills, 187
Buses, 19, 64

"Canto Bienvenido" (song), 125-27
"Canto Cualle Micaqueh" (song), 125-27
Cárdenas, Lázaro, 145, 146, 171n
Carranza, Venustiano, 163
Carrasco, Pedro, 192
Casares, Augustín, 57n
Cash crop industry, 64
Caso, Alfonso, 166, 167, 170
Castellanos, P., 137n
Castillo, Señor, 174
Catholic fiesta system, 114-15; in
    national holidays, 153; in Zapata
    fiesta, 153-59
Catholicism, 28, 56, 68; as bond with
    outsiders, 101; conversion to, 101-3,
    152; cultural extremists and, 176;
    and healing prayers, 99; indigenous
    religious traditions and, 99-100;
    Nahuatl and, 123-24; Protestant
    missionaries and, 122-23
Cecilio, Maestro, 143-44, 146
Central Campesino Independiente
    (CCI), 81-83
Charro costume, 174
Chavez Orozco, Juan, 183-85
Chemical fertilizers, 61-64, 70, 133
Chichimecas, 76
Chichimecs, 150
Christianity. See Catholicism;
    Protestantism
Clothing, 28, 92-96, 174, 188
Colds, healing of, 14, 19, 21-22
Colonial period, xiii, xiv, 68;
    acculturation resembling, 67-68, 79,
    128, 130; clothing in, 92-93;
    conversions to Catholicism in, 101-
    3; cultural extremists and, 168, 176,
    177; Cultural Missions and, 132;
    definition of Indian-ness in, 168-69;
    fiestas conforming to traditions
    established in, 114-15 (see also
    Catholic fiesta system); Hueyapan
    changes status in, 54-55; indigenous
    traditions in, xv; present-day

Indian-ness and, 83-100; ridding
    Mexico of influences of, 165-67; in
    school, 150-51; white characteristics
    in, 77
Columbus, Christopher, 177
Commerce, 12-16, 65-67
Commercialization of indigenous
    culture, 129
Confederated Movement for the
    Restoration of Anauak, see
    Movimiento
"Confession of the Indita, The" (skit),
    158-59
Conservatives, 79-83
Constitution of 1917, 61
Consumer-oriented economy, effects
    of, 63
Cooking technology, 96-98
Corn grinders, women as, 62-63, 67
Corn mills, 63, 67
Corregimiento, 54-56
Cortés, Don Eliseo, 171, 183-85
Cortés, Hernán, xiv, 53-54, 68, 150-51,
    176, 177
Cosmological socialists, 176
Council of the Indies, 54
Creation myth, 174
Crisantos, Rafael, 28, 36
Cuauhtémoc (Aztec hero), xiv, 152,
    158, 166
Cuauhtémoc (young man), 173
Cuitláhuac, 177-78
Cultural extremists, 165-88;
    anthropologists taken for, 189-91.
    See also Movimiento
Cultural Missions, Department of, 67,
    130-44; changes brought into village
    life by, 133-35; as civilizing, 73;
    goals of, 130-31; organization of,
    131-32; program mistaken for
    religious project, 133; promoting
    indigenous identity, 135-36
Cultural system, defined, xvn
Cultural training, 67-68
Culture: deep myth of, 155; defined,
    xvn; development of national, xiii
    (see also Nationalism); Indian-ness
    and lack of, 75. See also Indian-ness;
    Indigenous tradition
Customs, Indian, xv, 83-100

Dark Virgin, see Virgin of Guadalupe
David (grandson of Don Zenaido
    Ansures), 115
Deep myth of culture, 155
"Deer Game," 142
Delfino, Don, 112-14, 123

Demetrio, Maestro, 146, 154
Díaz, Bernal, 53*n*
Díaz, Porfirio, 144*n*
Diego, Padre (Padre Diego Sanchez), 109, 159
Discrimination, xvii
Dominican missionaries, 56, 102
Dress (clothing), 28, 92-96, 174, 188
Dubernard, Juan, 187-88
Durán, Fray Diego, 53, 54
Dyes, clothing, 94, 188

Echeverría, Luís, 164, 166, 167
Eckholm, G., 88*n*
Economic and Cultural Action, committees of, 132
Economy: chemical fertilizers, 61-64, 70, 133; commerce, 12-16, 65-67; corn grinders, 63, 67; electrification, 26, 65, 81-82; fruit, 64-65, 134; land, *see* Land; looms, backstrap, 86-89, 134; looms, mechanical, 134; reorganizing rural, 132; standard of living, 68; transportation, 19, 64-65, 133; weaving, 86-92, 134; work force, *see* Work force
Education, free and compulsory, 144. *See also* School; Teachers
Ejido lands, 61
El día (newspaper), 166-67
El Partido de la Mexicanidad, 171
Electrification, 26, 65, 81-82
Eligio, Maestro, 32, 145, 146
Eliseo, Don (Don Eliseo Cortés), 171, 183-85
Encomienda, 54, 68
Epidemic during Revolution, 58-59
Epifania, Doña, 9, 74, 89, 187-88
Ermena Hilda, Doña, 78
Ernestino (son of Doña Zeferina), 3*n*, 5, 40, 41, 50
Escandón, Pablo, 30
Escobar, Don Pedro, 35
Estrada, María de, 53-54
Estrella Roja bus line, 19, 64

Facundo, Don, 56-58, 61
Falconériz, Don, 35, 38-40
Fatalism, 75
Federales (soldiers), 57, 59
Fertilizers, chemical, 61-64, 70, 133
"Flor Delgada" (song), 140-41
Flores, Don José. *See* José, Don
Food, 96-98; Indians and ordinary, 73-74; scarcity of, during Revolution, 58
Foster, G., 88*n*, 192

Fruits, 64-65, 134
Furniture, 134

Games, 142-43
Gas stoves, 115*n*
Geertz, C., xv*n*
Gerhard, P., 54
Gibson, C., 102*n*, 192
Government: confused with cultural extremists, 165-66; honoring visitors from, with show of Indian-ness, 159-61, 164; promotes Indian-ness, 129-31
Government agencies, 128-64; aims of, 128-31. *See also* Cultural Missions, Department of
Great Society of Aztec Fellows, The (In Uey Tlatekpanaliztli), 183
Gregoria, Doña, 73, 133
Grupo Mexicano de Belleza (Mexican Beauty Group), 179, 181
"Güilotl Istac" (song), 136, 138-39
Guzmán, Eulalia, 166, 172

Hacienda, 55-56
Hallucinogenic mushrooms, 100
Headaches, healing of, 18, 22
Healing, 98-99; bronchitis recipe, 99; of colds, 14, 19, 21-22; of headaches, 18, 22; requirements for, 42, 43; sick call, 19, 21-22
Héctor (child of Doña Juana and Maestro Rafael), 4-5; daily life of, 8-12, 23; sleeping quarters for, 7*n*
Helguera R., L., 70*n*
Hernandez, Don Pedro, 49
Hernandez, Don Timoteo, 10, 58
Hernandez, Elvira, 74, 122, 185
Hernandez, Rómulo F., 145
Hidalgo y Costilla, Miguel, 153, 155
History of Charlemagne and the Admiral Balán, The (play), 109-14
Housing, 134
Huerta, Victoriano, 58
Hueyapan: background to study of, xv-xvii; *barrios* of, 13*n*; changes status under Spaniards, 54-55; geographical distribution of political factions in, 80-81, 83; history of, 53-70; land returned to villagers of, 56, 61; population of, 63; school system in, 56 (*see also* School; Teachers); "secularized," 56; Spanish conquer, 53 (*see also* Colonial period); streets of, 29*n*, 69
Huitzilopochtli (god), 171

Icacingo version of play, 107
"In Tamalera" (song), 137-38
In Uey Tlatekpanaliztli (The Great
    Society of Aztec Fellows), 183
"Indian Boy" (poem), 148
Indian language. *See* Nahuatl
Indian-ness, 72-100; ahistorical view
    of, 71-72; anthropologists and, 189-
    94; colonial period and present-day,
    83-100; Cultural Missions
    promoting, 135-36; customs
    identified with, xv, 83-100; defined,
    xiv-xv, xvii, 71; government
    promoting, 128-31; honoring
    government visitors with show of,
    159-61, 164; Indian as "bad" person,
    73; Indian as ignorant, 73, 74; *indio*
    as insulting word, 72, 76; inferiority
    feeling basic to, 72-74; internalized
    hispanic elite view of, 72; in national
    holidays, 158-59; as negative, 71, 74-
    76; political factions and, 79-83;
    politics and attempts to define, 168-
    70; primary-school textbooks and,
    147; school teachers' attitudes and,
    143 (*see also* School; Teachers);
    trying to lose, 76; villagers
    embarrassed by, 72. *See also*
    Indigenous tradition
Indigenous Affairs, Department of, 183
Indigenous Confederation of Mexico,
    171
Indigenous tradition, xiii, xiv; daily
    life of peasant and traces of, xviii;
    destroyed, 72; incorporated into a
    new cultural context, 160; in
    religion, 103; reviving, xvi;
    structural relationship of hispanic
    culture to, 71; teachers and, 135-36,
    142-43. *See also* Indian-ness
Innocence, 75
Institute of Anthropology and History,
    167
Institute of Mexican Culture, 179
Instituto Federal de Capacitación
    Maesterios, 5
Izchalotzin, Maestra, 179. *See also*
    Nieva, María del Carmen
Izkalotl (grammar), 172, 180
Izkalotl (newspaper), 171, 173, 176,
    178

Jacoba, Doña (mother of Doña
    Zeferina), 27, 28, 31-38, 43, 49
"Jarabe Tapatío" (dance), 158
Jehovah's Witnesses, 122
"Jesus Christ" (game), 142-43

Jews, 143n, 175, 193
José, Don (Don José Flores; husband
    of Doña Zeferina), 50-52;
    characteristics of, 3; daily life of, 8,
    9, 11, 12, 18, 19, 23; death of, 52;
    language spoken to, 85; sleeping
    quarters for, 7n
Juan, Don (Don Juan Maya), 2, 18,
    107, 171, 183, 184
Juan Diego, 104-6, 116
Juana, Doña (second wife of Maestro
    Rafael): characteristics of, 4; daily
    life of, 7-8, 10-12, 17-19, 22-24, 26; on
    Indians, 73; language spoken to, 85;
    sleeping quarters for, 7n; and Virgin
    of Guadalupe fiesta, 115
Juarez, Benito, 144, 149, 150
Julia ("adopted" child of Doña
    Zeferina), 50
Justo Sierra, 144, 150

Kalpull (kinship and land-tenure
    traditions), 175, 176
Kuamatzin, 173n

Land, 1; and Kalpull, 175, 176;
    returned to villagers, after
    Revolution, 55-56, 61; villagers'
    working of, 61-63
Languages. *See* Nahuatl; Spanish
"Las Mañanitas" (song), 185
Lauro, Don, 12
Lavana, Doña Modesta, 135
Leander, B., 161
León-Portilla, Miguel, 185
Lilia (daughter of Maestra Angelina),
    5-7; daily life of, 9, 10, 22-23
"Little Black Angels" (soap opera),
    78-79
López M., S., 70n
Lotería (game), 180n
Luna Cárdenas, Juan, 171, 183, 184

Madero, Francisco, 58n, 163
Malinche, 151, 177
Manners, 73, 74
María, Doña, 29-31
Maribel, (Maruca; daughter of Doña
    Juana and Maestro Rafael), 5, 6;
    daily life of, 8, 10, 19, 21-23; sleeping
    quarters for, 7n
Marino Flores, A., 191n
Market place, 12-16, 65-67
Martín Partidor, Alonso, 54
Martínez-Marín, C., 54, 56, 101n
Marx, Karl, 176
Maya, Don Estebán, 34-35

Maya, Don Juan, 2, 18, 107, 171, 183, 184
Maya, Don Reyes, 2, 7
Mayas, 150, 174-75
Mechanical looms, 134
Medicine and Cultural Missions, 134-35. *See also* Healing
Memorization, 32
Merchants, wandering, 65, 67
Mestizos: cultural extremists and, 168; history of, 151-52; as ideal Mexicans, 77, 153; identification with, as national goal, 129-30; integration of national identity and, 166; monument to honor, xiii-xiv; in political factions, 79-81; in primary-school textbooks, 147-50. *See also* Nationalism
Methodists, 122
Metzintin (people), 184
Mexican, defined, xiii-xiv. *See also* Mestizos
Mexican Beauty Group (Grupo Mexicano de Belleza), 179, 181
Mexican hairless dog, 194
Mexican Revolution (1910-1920), xiii, 32; celebrating, 153; guerrilla actions following (1930s), 43-49; Hueyapan during, 56-60; incidents in, 33-35; land returned to villagers after, 56, 61; school during, 144-45; in school textbooks, 151; Yaquis in, 76; Zapata fiesta and, 153-59
Mexikayotl (book), 173
Miguel, Don, 35
Mills, corn, 63, 67
Mixtecs, 150
Moctezuma II (Aztec emperor), 176-78
Moiron A., S., 167*n*
Montúfar, Bishop, 104
Moors and Christians (in play), 105-14, 117, 119, 120
Morelos y Pavón, José María, 153, 155
Mortality rate during Revolution, 58
Mountain, magical, 29
Movimiento (Confederated Movement for the Restoration of Anauak), xv-xvii, 170-87, 190; history, ideology and program of, 170-82; and villagers, 170, 182-88
Museo Nacional de Antropologia, 189
"My Mother" ("Nonantzin," poem), 160, 189

Nahua tribes, 150
Nahuatl (language), xvi, 28, 84-87; anthropologists and, 189-90; cooking

terms in, 96; Cultural Missions' use of, 136, 137; promoting, 172; Protestants and, 123-24; religious hymns in, 123; school for teaching, 171; Spanish compared with, 85-87; spinning and weaving terms in, 90; teaching, 180, 182, 184-87; terms for clothing in, 95; terms for parts of backstrap loom in, 91-92
Nahuatl music, 141. *See also* Songs
Nahuatl people, and Movimiento's creation myth, 174-76
Nahuatl renaissance culture movement, 123
Nasia, Doña, 115-19
National Commission of Free Textbooks, 147
National holidays, 152-64
National Indigenist Institute (INI), 166, 167
Nationalism: Catholic symbol and ritual incorporated into, 128, 129, 131; development of, xiii; educating villagers in, 68; promoted by Cultural Missions, 132. *See also* Mestizos
Netzahualcoyotl (king), 160, 161*n*
Nieva, Jorge, 172
Nieva, María del Carmen, 172-74, 176, 179-83
Nieva, Rodolfo F., 171-73, 176, 184, 186
Noceda, Don Rosalio, 40
"Nonantzin" (poem), 160, 189
Nursing program, 134-35. *See also* Healing

Obregón, Alvaro, 145
Ocampo, Don José, 27-28, 31
Octavio, Maestro, 146, 155-56
Olmecs, 150

Paco, Don, 116, 120
"Paloma Blanca" (song), 136, 138-39
Parsons, Talcott, xv*n*
Paso y Troncoso, F. del, 102*n*
Patrilocal residence pattern, 27
Pentecostals, 122
Perez, Francisca, 28
Plato, 175, 176
Plays in folk religious tradition, 105-14
Prayers: in healing, 98-99; memorizing, 32; to Virgin of Guadalupe, 22-23
Private space, Spanish architectural ideas about, 1
Progressives, 79-83, 123

Protestantism, 113*n*, 122-27; Cultural Missions confounded with, 133
Public Education, Secretary of, 131

Quetzalcoatl (god), 106

Race, 76-79
Rafael, Maestro (Rafael Vargas), 41, 161; birth of, 36; characteristics of, 3-4; daily life of, 8, 10-12, 16, 18, 19, 23-26; defends his mother, 35; as director of primary school, 81-83; helps mother in trade, 40, 42; languages spoken by, 85; Movimiento and, 186-87; sleeping quarters for, 7*n*; as sponsor for Virgin of Guadalupe fiesta, 115; transition of, from Indian to Mestizo, 76
Ramírez M., R., 70*n*
Raúl (son of Doña Juana and Maestro Rafael), 4; daily life of, 8-12, 22; sleeping quarters for, 7*n*
Raúl (son of Doña Zeferina and Don Felipe Vargas), 36, 42; death of, 41, 49, 50
Reading, 32
Red Power, xv-xvi
Regino, Maestro, 18-19, 21
Reina (daughter of Doña Juana and Maestro Rafael), 5; daily life of, 8-11, 23; sleeping quarters for, 7*n*
Religion, 99-127, 133. *See also* Catholicism; Prayers; Protestantism
Rendón, Don Estanislao, 106-7, 109
Republic (Plato), 175
Ricard, R., 103*n*, 106*n*
"Rich Man and the Poor Man, The" (tale), 142
Rivera, Diego, 184
Rivera Crespo, Felipe, 154, 159-61, 163, 164
Roads, building of, 64-65
Rodriguez, Enrique (Tallarín), 44-46
Roman Empire, 175
Rosa (daughter of Doña Juana and Maestro Rafael), 4, 121; daily life of, 8-12, 19, 26; sleeping quarters for, 7*n*
Rosalía (daughter of Doña Zeferina and Don Felipe Vargas), 36

Sad Night, 177-78
San Juan Amecac version of play, 107, 109-14
Sanchez, Padre Diego, 109, 159
Sanchez Farfán, Pedro, 54

Sancho, M., 90, 95
Sardinias, Don Dionisio, 29-31
Sardinias, Don Manuel, 29
Schneider, D., xv*n*
School, 81-83, 144-64; cleanliness inspectors for, 135; goals of, 130, 131; integrated into national school system, 145; and patriotic programs, 152-64; primary-school textbooks, 147-52; Protestants as godfathers in graduation ceremonies, 122*n*. *See also* Teachers
School-run assemblies, 152-64
Seventh-Day Adventists, 122
Shadows, as cause of illness, 99*n*
Sick call, 19, 21-22
Siméon, R., 90
"Slender Flower" (song), 136-38, 140-41
Soap operas, 78
Solon, 175
Songs, 136-42; Cultural Missions' use of, 136; European features in, 136-38
Soustelle, J., 88, 92, 93*n*
Spanish (language): cooking terms in, 96; Indians' supposed inability to speak, 74; Nahuatl compared with, 85-87; spinning and weaving terms in, 90; terms for clothing in, 95
Spanish heritage, 129-30, 150-51. *See also* Colonial period
Spanish influenza, 58-59
Spinning, 87-92
Spiritualists (Protestants), 122
Standard of living, improving, 68
Stavenhagen, R., 192
Stories, 142
Stoves, 115*n*, 134
Swadesh, M., 90, 95

Tallarín (Enrique Rodriguez), 44-46
Tannenbaum, F., 170*n*
Tarahumaras, 152
Tarascans, 150
Teachers: conflict (1930s) between townspeople and, 146; conflicting attitudes toward Indian-ness among, 143-44; Cultural Missions and, 131; fostering Indian-ness, 159-60; indigenous culture and, 135-36, 142-43; patriotic programs sponsored by, 152-64. *See also* School
Television, 78, 115
Teotihuacanos, 150
Teotl, 175-76
Tetlazohtlani, 173*n*

Texcatlipocatl (god), 171
Three Cultures, Plaza of (Tlatelolco), xiii-xv
Timoteo, Don (Don Timoteo Hernandez), 10, 58
Tlacaelel, 173n
Tlaloc (god), 106, 185
Tlalocan (journal), 143
Tlatelolco (Plaza of Three Cultures), xiii-xv
Tlaxcalans, 151
Toltecs, 150
Tonantzin (goddess), 104
Transportation, 19, 64-65, 133
Trucks, 64
Turner, Victor, 155

Ueyi Tlahtohkan, 176
Universalists (Protestants), 122
Urbanization, 63-64

Vargas, Don Felipe, 35-36
Vargas, Rafael, see Rafael, Maestro
Vázquez de Knauth, J., 144n, 145n, 166n
Victorious Night of the Aztecs, 177-78
Villa, Pancho, 58
Virgin of Guadalupe (Dark Virgin), 103; fiesta of, 104-9; praying to, 22-23

Wages, peons', 62
Warman, A., 192
Water, introduction of running, 67
Weaving, 86-92; and Cultural Missions, 134
"Welcome Song, The," 125-27
Western civilization, 174-75
"White Dove" (song), 136, 138-39
Wolf, E., 192
Womack, John, 57n, 58, 59, 60n
Work force: in commerce, 65, 67; migrating, 61-63; urbanization of, 63-64

"Xipatlani Ompa" (song), 136
Xochimilcas, 53, 76, 184
"Xochipitzauac" (song), 136-38, 140-41
Xochitl, 173n

Yalalteca hairdo, 180, 181
Yaquis, 76

Zapata, Emiliano, 33, 57n, 59-61, 76, 163; fiesta of, 153-59
Zapatistas, 57
Zapotecs, 150
Zeferina, Doña (Doña Zeferina Barreto), 1-52, 83, 106, 137; on Apaches, 76; and Aztec dog, 194; characteristics of, xviii, 3; and clothing, 94, 96; and commercial dyes, 188; and Cultural Missions, 133; daily life of, xvii, 8-26; in days of Tallarín, 43-49; education of, 32; escapes from San Juan Ahuehueyo, 38-40; father of, 27-28; first marriage of, 35-36; grandparents and great grandparents of, 27-31; as healer, 42-43 (see also Healing); hiding poverty, 75; history of, 27-52; "Jesus Christ" game explained by, 142-43; living away from home, 32-33; as maid, 36-38; in market place, 12-16; mother of, 27, 28, 31-38, 43, 49; in nursing program, 134-35; possessions of, 1-2; and race, 77; and Revolution, 33-35, 58; schooling of, during Revolution, 60; sleeping quarters of, 7n; use of language by, 85, 87; and Virgin of Guadalupe fiesta, 115; as wandering merchant, 40, 42; working the land, 62
Zeferino (son of Don Felipe Vargas and Doña Zeferina), 36
Zumárraga, Bishop, 104, 116